A NEW TEACHER's
Guide to Best Practices

YVONNE S. GENTZLER

Skyhorse Publishing

First Published in 2005 by Corwin Press

First Skyhorse Publishing edition 2015

Skyhorse Publishing books may be purchased in bulk at special discounts for sales promotion, corporate gifts, fund-raising, or educational purposes. Special editions can also be created to specifications. For details, contact the Special Sales Department, Skyhorse Publishing, 307 West 36th Street, 11th Floor, New York, NY 10018 or info@ skyhorsepublishing.com.

Skyhorse® and Skyhorse Publishing® are registered trademarks of Skyhorse Publishing, Inc.®, a Delaware corporation.

Visit our website at www.skyhorsepublishing.com.

10 9 8 7 6 5 4 3 2 1

Library of Congress Cataloging-in-Publication Data is available on file.

Print ISBN: 978-1-63450-307-5
Ebook ISBN: 978-1-5107-0104-5

Printed in the United States of America

Contents

Introducing the Quest

"We teach to change the world."

—STEPHEN D. BROOKFIELD (1995, p.1)

Congratulations, and welcome to the professional rank of being an educator! This is the beginning of your own professional development quest. Until now, most of your preparation as an educator fit within someone else's framework of what you needed to know to be a practitioner. By this point, you may feel as if you are on your own. What now? The purpose of this book is to help you meander through the daily experiences of teaching; to help you think about what happens in your day, your weeks, and the semester; and to help you set a course of action to improve your effectiveness as an educator. *A New Teacher's Guide to Best Practices* is designed to be a self-reflection manual that will help you navigate your beginning years of teaching and serve as a guide on your personal quest toward best practice.

Book Overview

This book is divided into 10 sections, called challenges, that represent 10 months of the academic calendar. The challenges deal with planning and preparation, curriculum, classroom climate, classroom management, instruction, professional roles, collegiality, assessment, professional development, and administrators, parents, and the community. Each challenge provides you with an opportunity to write about what you presently observe or think about the topic and poses questions intended to stretch your thinking so that you may consider new ideas about the topic. Quotes from a variety of sources present you with even more thoughts to ponder. Questions that are often raised by beginning teachers are highlighted with several possible solutions. You will also encounter numerous new and innovative ideas for managing the classroom, which can be altered to fit your particular needs. After exploring a topic from various angles, you are encouraged to revisit your original ideas at the end of the year so that you may reflect on what you have learned about the topic. Ultimately, the content of this book will assist you in establishing a professional development plan to guide your own growth as a teacher. It will help you to identify successes that you could include in your teaching portfolio.

Even though the book is systematically organized, you need not read the challenges in a particular order. Each challenge is self-contained so that you may tackle each at your own pace, deciding which one to focus on depending on your own professional development needs. Each challenge is interrelated and integrated so that you may select among them according to your needs.

A master teacher or mentor within your school system can also use the book to guide you or a group of teachers. The book can be used as a springboard for discussion with a group of peers who are working through it together. If this book is used as part of a mentoring relationship, there are a few strategies for implementing a successful mentoring relationship a professional development coordinator can consider. These strategies are outlined below:

- **Before school begins, introduce the mentor and mentee so that a relationship can be established. Plan a schedule for meetings and time for working on the challengeS.**

- **Identify additional resources/teachers/mentors who might be helpful to the development of the new or beginning teacher.**

- **Establish a professional development plan that spans a three-year period. Identify those activities that could be beneficial for the beginning teacher's development.**

- **Structure study groups of new teachers and mentors.**

- **Establish periodic meetings with the principal and administrator for the mentor and mentee to share the success of the new teacher.**

- **Create a structure for peer evaluation of teaching. New teachers should observe master teachers and master teachers should observe beginning teachers.**

- **Set up a buddy plan for attending and debriefing inservice training.**

- **Establish a recording method for beginning teachers to document success.**

- **Create an evaluation at periodic times throughout the first few years with constructive feedback.**

A professional development coordinator may choose to consider the guidelines for mentors and mentees shown in Figure 1.1. This information can also be used as a framework for a course or series of workshops with a group of beginning teachers. See Figure 1.2 for professional development plans that a group of beginning teachers might use in conjunction with this book.

The Journey Begins

As an educator, you provide a tremendous service to society. The future of any civilization relies on the knowledge, skills, and application of that knowledge and those skills to improving the human condition. Education is central to life and to our survival as a civilization.

Wisdom and knowledge have been passed on through the generations by various methods. In some cultures, teaching was and still is accomplished through storytelling. In others, master craftsmen taught children by passing along skills and knowledge through practical experience. And in yet other cultures, people were taught to read and were educated through the written word. Regardless of the method by which one is educated, few would argue that most every encounter, experience, and waking moment reveals opportunities for learning. Consequently, all of life is about learning.

EXPECTATIONS FOR THE MENTEE AND THE MENTOR

The following list provides ideas and examples of what a mentee should bring to the interaction with a mentor and the responsibility the mentor has to the mentee. The use of these strategies should help to ensure successful implementation of the activities in this book in a mentor/mentee relationship.

MENTOR	MENTEE
1. Communicate his or her expectations and objectives for the relationship.	1. Understand that the relationship is designed to support the mentee.
2. Encourage the mentee to develop his or her own teaching style; invite the mentee to observe his or her teaching.	2. Be willing to experiment with new ideas and suggestions and observe mentor's professional practice. Develop new lesson plans that reflect varying formats.
3. Provide new ideas, research, and resources as they become available	3. Identify new ideas to try.
4 Arrange for introduction to other staff members, administrators, and school personnel. Share information regarding extracurricular opportunities.	4. Assume responsibility for getting to know the facilities, personnel, environment, and political structure of the school.
5. Share classroom management plans, a variety of assessment strategies, curriculum guides, etc.	5. Develop a classroom management plan and a variety of assessment strategies.
6. Identify his or her own learning style and discuss with the mentee how this sytle impacts his or her teaching.	6. Identify personal learning style and explore how that style impacts teaching.
7. Encourage and arrange observations in other classes, levels of ability, and grade levels.	7. Observe other teachers from a variety of subject areas.
8. Communicate with the mentee daily.	8. Communicate with the mentor teacher daily.
9. Model teaching strategies, language, interactions, and curriculum decisions that reflect the multicultural identities of students.	9. Address the various learning styles and multicultural identities of students.
10. Serve as an advocate when issues become problematic and as a promoter when mentee accomplishes goals.	10. Share problematic situations and triumphs with the mentor.
11. Share curriculum materials.	11. Ask for help and materials.
12. Observe the mentee and offer noncritical suggestions in the areas of curriculum design, assessment, classroom management, etc.	12. Allow the mentor to observe teaching on a regular basis.
13. Maintain confidentiality and discuss career paths, goals for the future, legal issues, state requirements, etc.	13. Trust the mentor with confidences.

Figure 1.1

PROFESSIONAL DEVELOPMENT PLANS

One-Year Professional Development Plan

This plan is based on a rigorous yearlong program in which you would read the introduction before school begins and then spend a month on each challenge. You can select any challenge for the month because they are self-contained modules.

Introducing the Quest
- Planning and Preparation
- Determining the Curriculum
- Classroom Space and Establishing the Climate
- Classroom Management and Organizational Strategies
- Instruction
- Professional Roles and Responsibilities
- Collegiality
- Assessment, Evaluation, and Grades
- Professional Development
- Administrators, Parents, and the Community

Two-Year Professional Development Plan

This plan is based on dividing your professional development into a two-year program in which you would focus on the issues inside the classroom in your first year and those outside the classroom in your second. Each challenge is self-contained so you can select them in the order that they are most appropriate and timely for your individual needs.

Inside
Introducing the Quest
- Classroom Space and Establishing the Climate
- Classroom Management and Organizational Strategies
- Instruction
- Assessment, Evaluation, and Grades

Outside
Planning and Preparation
- Determining the Curriculum
- Professional Roles and Responsibilities
- Collegiality
- Professional Development
- Administrators, Parents, and the Community

Three-Year Professional Development Plan

This plan outlines in sequential order what most beginning teachers claim to be the most pertinent areas of need when they enter the classroom. It assumes you will take a longer period of time to focus on each of the areas outlined in the challenges. It is a good model to use for a self-directed program. You can record what you learn in your professional portfolio.

Year 1
Introducing the Quest
- Planning and Preparation
- Classroom Space and Establishing the Climate
- Classroom Management and Organizational Strategies

Year 2
Determining the Curriculum
- Instruction
- Assessment, Evaluation, and Grades

(continued on next page)

Figure 1.2

PROFESSIONAL DEVELOPMENT PLANS (continued)

Year 3
Administrators, Parents, and the Community
- Collegiality
- Professional Roles and Responsibilities
- Professional Development

Figure 1.2 continued

Your caregivers had a tremendous impact on you as an infant. As you grew, you learned through the influence of those around you. What you learned was manifested in your creativity, your actions, and your behaviors. Before long, you could see that what you knew, coupled with what you could learn, had the potential to create new ideas and actions.

Education, therefore, is the cornerstone of our existence. Becoming an educator is an exciting challenge and one worthy of serious respect. A teacher has a remarkable ability to shape the future. Your college degree is a testament to the knowledge and skills necessary to enter the professional ranks of education. No doubt you have brought along a wealth of experiences that make your teaching style unique. Your university degree program established a certain set of requirements for you to become a teacher. However, no one would expect any other professional to rely solely on what he or she had learned in college as sufficient for professional practice. The choices you make today as an individual will determine how effective you will be as an educator. Now you have the potential and responsibility of determining those activities and experiences necessary for your own growth as an educator.

You will find that your college preparation, in some cases, equipped you for what you will experience in the classroom. In other situations, you might find you need additional skills and knowledge to meet the challenges you will face. Whatever the case, it now becomes your role to build a repertoire of creative ideas, skills, and abilities for your success.

What makes a good teacher? Researchers claim it's a variety of abilities. But abilities without the wisdom to know when, where, and how to enact those abilities can lead to frustration. Wisdom in teaching comes through experience and reflection—it requires commitment, practice, and a plan. Familiarity and practice will assist you as you embark on this exciting journey.

One of the most difficult tasks of being a teacher is realizing that the sincerest desire will not assure perfect practice. The complexity of teaching and learning complicated by human relationships challenges teachers to continually reflect on their practice. As is true with people in all walks of life, teachers are sometimes unaware of why they respond the way they do in a given situation. Students, colleagues, mentors, administrators, and the public you serve will no doubt occasionally have different interpretations of your responses, your intents, and your behaviors. It is important not to blame yourself for how others perceive your actions. Developing an ability to *critically reflect* on your practice, to understand and interpret its meaning for you and your learners, will help you define your purpose and clarify your role as an educator.

Many questions set the stage for using this book—for beginning your quest toward best practice. What assumptions do you have about teaching and learning? What assumptions do you presently have about your role as an educator? Do you see yourself as a person willing to reflect on your actions and to modify them appropriately to enhance student learning? Without the ability to reflect on your practice, you run the risk of repeating questionable judgments.

Prescribing a set of rules, standards, guidelines, or activities in some ways contradicts the notion of being a reflective practitioner. To do so suggests that if you follow those rules or guidelines, you will be effective. This, however, is not the case. What you think is good for your learners may result in a negative outcome. For example, if you place the names of students on the desks so that when they arrive to your class the first day they will know where to sit, some students may perceive this as being controlling and manipulative. They may be turned off immediately because they were not given the opportunity to choose where to sit. Others may like that the seating decision was made for them and desire to get on with the work in the class. Either way, you may have intended only to save the time it would take to verbally assign seats. Assuming a student who did not like your decision to assign seats makes his or her opinion known to you, you cannot then presume all students feel the same way and judge yourself negatively for your decision to assign seats. As you reflect on your action, you may find out more about yourself as an educator. What assumptions did you make regarding the amount of time it would take to make the name cards versus the amount of time it would have taken to say each student's name to verbally assign seats or have them sit wherever they desired? Or were you trying to establish a climate of being organized? Whatever your motivation, as you reflect, you will want to challenge the assumptions you have that drive your decisions and actions as a teacher.

Critical Reflection

Becoming a reflective practitioner demands more than simple thinking about practice. Smyth (1992), Zeichner (1994), and Brookfield (1995) point out that the reflection becomes insignificant if teachers use it *only to justify the practice that they prefer*. Zeichner (1994) claims, "It has come to the point now where the whole range of beliefs about teaching, learning, schooling, and the social order have become incorporated into the discourse about reflective practice. Everyone, no matter what his or her ideological orientation, has jumped on the bandwagon at this point, and has committed his or her energies to furthering some version of reflective teaching practice" (p. 9). Brookfield (1995) clarifies the difference between reflection and critical reflection. He claims that just because a teacher reflects on his or her practice, the process of reflection may not be critical. All reflection is important to growth and (ultimately) change, but critical reflection is central to revealing that which is necessary for substantive change. Brookfield delineated between reflection and critical reflection when he suggested that "reflection becomes critical when it has two distinctive purposes. The first is to understand how considerations of power undergird, frame, and distort educational processes and interactions. The second is to question assumptions and practices that seem to make our teaching easier but actually work against our own best long-term interests" (p. 8).

Being a critically reflective practitioner suggests that you cannot expect to find all the answers to your questions about being an educator neatly packaged in a book, on the Web, or in a workshop. These resources will certainly provide knowledge for your reflection but alone will prove insufficient for true transformation. This type of thinking suggests that someone or something "out there" will provide the answers needed to solve problems. Brookfield (1995) contends that the difficult problems faced by educators do not have standardized solutions. Instead, he suggests that the educator recognize that resources must be integrated with knowledge of local conditions and adapted to personal circumstances. This requires active participation in the process of questioning the values inherent in our practice as educators.

Brookfield (1995) also outlines six reasons why assuming a critical reflective stance is pertinent to sound professional practice. First, he claims that it helps teachers to act from an *informed position* rather than an *unexamined perspective.* If someone challenges your action as an educator, it is beneficial to know why you do what you do based on your assumptions about teaching and learning. We expect our learners and colleagues to understand our actions. Being able to rationally critique and justifiably articulate our practice will help to ensure understanding and support among everybody who is involved in the educational practice. The second reason Brookfield supports critical reflection as central to sound professional practice is that it helps the educator to "know why we believe what we believe" (p. 23). It is important for us as professionals to have the *ability to articulate* why we make the choices we do. We often do this through examined critique by wrestling with the ideas that form our beliefs about teaching, discipline, knowledge, and practice. Without this grounding, teachers are subject to political or pedagogical whims. Equally important to this process is Brookfield's third objective for being critically reflective, which is to *avoid blaming self* for students' inability or unwillingness to learn. Sometimes teachers become frustrated and blame themselves for the hostility or anger that their students express. Brookfield suggests that student resistance instead may be socially or politically sculpted. The reflective teacher will find appropriate ways to turn resistance into enthusiasm for learning. Being *emotionally grounded* is Brookfield's fourth purpose for teachers to critically reflect. Without this ability, teachers' morale could easily suffer. For example, success or failure related to teaching has the potential to send a teacher on a roller coaster of emotions. Consequently, actions are subject to the perceived effects of daily experiences. This has the potential to frighten new professionals who do not know how to reflect critically on their practice. Without this ability, they may select to leave the classroom.

Brookfield is the fifth reason to use critical reflection is that it enlivens the classroom. Students watch and observe teachers. If a student sees a teacher who shares his or her passion for critical reflection within the context of the content and the course, that student is more apt to trust the teacher. Teachers who are willing to share their ideas with students invite students to engage in the critical reflective process. This whole practice has the potential to provide an important indicator of teacher effectiveness. Finally, Brookfield recognizes that what teachers do makes a difference in the world. Students learn to trust one another within a democratic society through how they are treated as persons within the learning process. How the teacher responds to any given situation is a learning experience for the student and provides a model for teaching critical reflection.

The ability to critically reflect on practice as an educator is perhaps the most important quality a teacher can develop. This book is designed to assist you in assuming a critical posture in the situations outlined below, to help you focus on certain components of teaching and dig beneath the surface to critically analyze the values and beliefs that manifest themselves in your practice. Consider what it means to be a critical reflective practitioner in these situations:

- Planning and preparing for teaching
- Selecting the curriculum
- Organizing your classroom space and establishing the climate for your learners
- Managing your classroom and carrying out organizational strategies
- Preparing for instruction
- Accomplishing your professional roles and responsibilities
- Developing relationships with colleagues
- Assessing, evaluating, and grading learners
- Determining your personal plan for professional development
- Interacting with administrators, parents, and the community

Darling-Hammond and Sclan (1996) agree with Brookfield (1995) that teachers need to be able to challenge the obstacles they face related to quality teaching and learning. To do so is one way to engage teachers in the process of educational reform. All teachers should be engaged in personal and professional development that involves critical reflection of one's teaching experience, including beliefs and practices. Engaging teachers in assessing, observing, and reflecting can assist them in perceiving themselves as learners and teachers (Darling-Hammond & McLaughlin, 1995). This type of professional development requires reflective practices.

This book is designed to help you, the beginning teacher, to reflect on those things you believe, experience, and practice. By working through a series of self-reflective exercises, you will become more comfortable in the role of reflective practitioner. This book's strategies rely on practice and reflection. Consequently, anyone involved in the process of assisting you will be engaged in the critical process of reflection to improve education. Reflection can be viewed from several different perspectives. Smyth (1989) suggests that it can "vary from a concern with the micro aspects of the teaching/learning process and subject matter knowledge, to macro concerns about political/ethical principles underlying teaching and the relationship of schooling to the wider institutions and hierarchies of society" (p. 4).

Regardless of the angle from which one views reflection, most researchers agree that the process is a complex study. According to Sparks-Langer and Colton (1991), three elements of teacher reflection have been the focus of study: the ability to process information and make decisions; the understanding of what drives thinking, such as the experiences, personal goals, values, and social implications; and teachers' narrative expressions of events that occur within their lives. This book will help you to experience each of these three areas of focus as you think about your practice, draw connections to your reasons for acting based on your values and ways of viewing your practice, and interpret these two components within the context of your life experience as an educator.

Dewey (1938) believed that an interactive connection exists between education and personal experience. He suggested that individuals learn by connecting their former experiences with new knowledge. He warned, however, that this practice needs to be guided so as to avoid simply reinforcing an "automatic skill in a particular direction," which could result in perpetuating a rut (p. 26). He also believed that positive learning occurs when individuals engage in guided learning by interacting with others. Using his theory, this text can help you to find meaning in your experience by reflecting on your personal practice. One needs to know, however, that knowledge and self-reflection are socially and culturally constructed. There is no single truth about teaching or education. The learning process is unpredictable.

Being an educator is a rewarding and challenging professional position. Using this book as a guide for your professional development will yield many exciting opportunities for your growth. The strategies outlined in the challenges are designed to encourage mindful thinking and positive change and to support you in your quest toward best practice.

The Challenges

Each challenge contains a mix of tools designed to help you reflect on and explore the topic at hand. These tools are designed to help you develop a plan of action for tackling the challenge. The tools in each challenge are explained in more depth below.

Assessment and Reflections Log

Each challenge begins with an **Assessment and Reflections Log**. Use the log to document your *current beliefs* about the content within the challenge. After you record your present beliefs, outline your aspirations. The log is designed to walk you through the process of documenting your present beliefs, spelling out your goals, and setting a course of action to accomplish your objectives. This cognitive process is important, but it will not result in action unless you put your thoughts to use. The remainder of the challenge, and the activities within each section, are designed to assist you in that process. At the end of each section you should have acquired more experience, entered into dialogue with colleagues, and taken steps to do something designed to encourage growth toward your goals. Each challenge contains quotes sprinkled throughout that relate to the challenge content.

Practical Problem

Also included in each challenge is a question framed as a **Practical Problem**. Practical problems are the situations all teachers encounter daily that require thought and action, such as *what to do about something* they are facing in their roles as educators. Through self-reflection and dialogue with colleagues and mentors, teachers can envision a better way to handle situations, which can, in turn, begin to reshape the way we all look at educational issues. Therefore, practical problems are asked in the form of a question, such as, "What ought to be done about planning and preparation for teaching?" Framing challenge content in this way helps the educator to see the issue from a perspective that requires thoughtful consideration. The questions do not call for a specific answer; rather, they help set the stage for critical reflection and deliberate action.

Valued Ends

Practical problems are followed by **Valued Ends**, which are examples of a possible end result of the original question(s). When determining *what ought to be done* in any given situation, it becomes clear that there are no specific answers. However, if one considers the best possible scenario, a valued end is reached. Valued ends are the ultimate goals or objectives when considering all possibilities of the original question(s) or practical problem(s). Eventually, it would be ideal if all educators could reach the valued end. Teachers are accustomed to working to accomplish goals and objectives; however, a valued end is designed to be a *quality* worth attaining. A valued end is only one example of what could be achieved.

"I am wondering . . .?"

When determining how one might get to the valued ends, teachers ask a lot of questions. Examples of questions teachers have asked in each challenge are listed in the section titled **"I am wondering . . .?"**. Such questions set the stage for beginning teachers to understand the concepts central to problem-based education and practical reasoning. You are encouraged to write your own questions in the space provided in this section.

Focus on the Issue

The challenge issue is explored in the section called **Focus on the Issue**. This section contains an up-to-date overview of relevant scholarship in each challenge. Before long, you will be engaging in active teacher research, and this section will be helpful to you in that process.

Students Speak Out

Students Speak Out comprises a series of responses to open-ended sentence stems related to the challenge topic. Students at the middle, junior, and high school levels throughout the country have responded to the sentence stems. These student voices will assist the beginning teacher to "hear," through the voice of a learner, those things that teachers do—or don't do—that students find helpful or troublesome. Keep in mind that an idea or conclusion does not demand change. It simply encourages thoughtful reflection and consideration.

The Teachers' Lounge

The Teachers' Lounge comes after the student voices. Beginning teachers often feel disconnected or isolated in their new environments as they begin to tackle their roles as educators. Teachers' lounges may suffer from a negative stereotype in some situations, but they also provide a valuable resource opportunity for teachers to share ideas with one another. Teachers who have responded in this section are seasoned and in many cases have served as cooperating or mentor teachers for university programs nationwide.

Teacher Tips

Teacher Tips includes additional tips that may not have been mentioned by a mentor or an experienced teacher in the preceding section.

A Mentor Moment

Each challenge includes a section for the teacher and his or her mentor called **A Mentor Moment**. You are encouraged to record additional questions you have for your mentor. Recording these questions will help you to see how far you have come when you review this book and your thoughts in your second and third years of teaching.

Shared Strategies

Shared Strategies focuses solely on specific examples of how to use the content related to each challenge.

Each challenge contains **An Amusing Story** written by a teacher or student about the challenge content. These stories are real accounts of situations that beginning teachers have encountered.

Personal Reflection Journal

Each challenge provides ample space for you to keep a **Personal Reflection Journal**. You can document and examine what you are learning about your existing practice and reflect on your personal growth and change.

Standards

Although schools differ in their acceptance of teaching standards, it is generally agreed that educators need to possess a certain level of competence to be successful. Because of their generic nature, the Interstate New Teacher Assessment and Support Consortium (INTASC) standards have been used as a framework for thinking about best practice. Relevant standards for each of the challenges have been identified in the **Standards** section. Beginning teachers are encouraged to think about the merit of each standard in relation to the challenge content and his or her personal goals for success. Additionally, in the appendix, there is ample space to incorporate specific content and national, state, or school standards as well. The INTASC standards are listed in the appendix.

Reflections Log

Each challenge includes a **Reflection Log** that you can use to reflect on your learning.

Congratulations, You Made It!

Each challenge also includes space for documenting personal success, called **Congratulations, You Made It!** These sections can be combined and included in your teaching portfolio.

Wrap-Up

The **Wrap-Up** at the end of the book provides some forms that can be used to document what you accomplish in your beginning years of teaching. The documentation, which provides insight into accomplishments and successes, can be used for teacher evaluations.

The **appendix** contains both the complete INTASC standards to augment the specific INTASC standards represented in each chapter, as well as the National Education Association (NEA) Code of Conduct. This Code of Conduct is a reminder of a teacher's commitment to the teaching profession and all that it entails.

Goals

A New Teacher's Guide to Best Practices is intended to assist you in supporting students in their learning process. At the same time, it provides guidance for you to reflect on your teaching practice and consider alternative strategies for improving your practice. It also affords ample opportunities for you to interact with colleagues, peers, and mentors as you seek to identify and interpret your role as an educator.

The purpose of this book is not to continue the process of teaching you *about* teaching but to assist you in the process of *becoming* a teacher through self-reflection. The book is designed to assist you in reflecting about your practice to produce new insights and actions based on personal professional development. The book provides the "voices" of teachers, mentors, and students for you to consider as you think about and explore the process of teaching.

And now the process begins! Look through the book and decide which challenge you plan to tackle first. Teaching is an incredible career. This is your professional calling. You hold the future in your hands! You owe it to yourself to set the stage for your own professional growth. Set aside time in your daily or weekly schedule to focus on what you need to do to accomplish your goals. This book is designed to be your guide, your mentor, and your quest for success. Good luck, and enjoy the process!

Completing the Quest

Being a teacher is an incredibly exciting role within any society. It is demanding and challenging. Teaching is a position that demands the ability to make decisions constantly. One needs to be continuously prepared, and at the same time constantly evaluate decisions to determine if there is a better way to handle similar situations.

A New Teacher's Guide to Best Practices uses the INTASC standards as an example of criteria for you to aspire to if your school does not have specific standards expected of beginning teachers. You may also ask your supervisor to supply a copy of the form that is used for your evaluation. Look over the instrument and decide in which areas you can realistically document growth in the coming year(s). This is a good starting point for you to establish a professional development plan. Additional forms for documenting evidence of standards are also provided in this Wrap-Up section. As you work through each challenge in this book, keep a record of the goals you can realistically accomplish and what evidence you have to document that growth. You can then assemble these items in an electronic or paper portfolio.

Your teaching portfolio will change each year you are teaching. What you learn your first year will be updated and enhanced with additional experience and knowledge. Do not destroy the examples you provide in your first year(s) of teaching. In fact, save them as reminders of how much you have grown with more experience. Make connections between where you were when you began and where you are at the end of year one, year two, year three, etc. You will appreciate seeing your growth, and your administrators will respect your time and effort toward assuming a self-directed approach to your professional development.

As Brookfield (1995, p. 1) claimed, "We teach to change the world." You are an integral part of a dynamic system established to improve the human condition. Your role is central to the lives of those you touch. Congratulations on selecting a worthy profession and continued best wishes as you move into your teaching career.

> *What sculpture is to the block of marble, education is to the soul.*
> —JOSEPH ADDISON

Standards

List the standards that your school expects you to work toward in your first year(s) of teaching. Refer to this list each time you complete a challenge to determine which standards you will include in your portfolio. You will need to provide evidence that you have met each standard. Along with the evidence develop a reflection piece that shows the growth that has taken place as a result of the experience. Include this documentation in your teaching portfolio.

1. _____

2. _____

3. _____

4. _____

5. _____

6. _____

7. _____

8. _____

9. _____

10. _____

Planning and Preparation

Assessment and Reflections Log

Record your initial beliefs and goals about planning and preparation in this log before.

My beliefs about <u>planning and preparation</u>:

My goal(s) for <u>planning and preparation</u>:

How am I going to accomplish my goal(s)?

Who and what can help me?

Challenges to accomplishing my goal(s):

The process or procedure for reaching my goal(s):

Planning and Preparation

"I can't believe school starts this soon!"
–First-Year Teacher

Planning and preparing for teaching includes everything you do to get organized for your role as a teacher. It is cyclical in nature and happens continuously. Because you are engaged in the learning process, you will constantly plan and prepare for teaching. Nothing is ever stagnant in the classroom. The learning process demands constant attention. It is never ending.

Teaching young people is a unique and rewarding experience. There is a significant experiential gap between learning about teaching and performing the art of teaching. As a teacher, you will find yourself sitting in the driver's seat of the classroom, where you were formerly a passenger along for the ride. You now have many young passengers along with you. Where will you take your passengers in this journey? How will you get there?

Like a road guide for a long journey, planning is vital. Planning and preparation become your personal road guide, helping you continue on your journey as you hit bumps in the road and make an occasional wrong turn. Take time to understand the job, people, rules, and organization. Make yourself aware of potential problems, and develop some strategies to deal with those situations. These preparations will make your teaching experience an exciting and challenging journey and will reduce the chance of any costly detours.

Planning and preparation begin the moment you accept your teaching position. As you start the planning process, strive to learn as much as possible about your students and the school environment. Prepare yourself emotionally, physically, and intellectually to meet the new faces in the school and to be a positive role model. Planning does not stop there. It continues after you meet and interact with your students. Good teachers do much

> *The best preparation for good work tomorrow is to do good work today.*
> —ELBERT HUBBARD

more than share their knowledge with students. Successful teaching stems from a plan to create a warm and respectful relationship between your students and yourself. Because personal relationships are time consuming, it is important for new teachers to prepare to inspire positive character traits in students in an organized way.

Plan for the future by seeking out strategies that will help you make reasonable and acceptable adaptations to the ever-evolving task of teaching in today's classroom. It is imperative for you as a new teacher to plan and prepare for managing various, fast-paced activities while maintaining control. Be prepared for change by planning strategies that will allow you to reflect critically and respond creatively to the changing forces in the classroom. According to Fullan and Hargreaves (1991), successful adaptations in the classroom involve "emotional planning," whereby teachers recognize what is important and meaningful to them in teaching and commit themselves to the implementation of those things.

The quest is a powerful metaphor for a new teaching career. Planning and preparation are important in this expedition. They allow you to focus on your destination and avoid dead ends. Planning and preparation help you to define your path on the quest toward a successful teaching career. Good luck as you set out on this new and exciting journey! You are now sitting in the driver's seat and will enjoy making the decisions as you drive along an entirely new road of teaching.

Practical Problem

What ought to be done about planning and preparing for teaching? Teachers are faced with this question daily as they plan for their roles as educators. The answer to this practical problem will be different for each professional. Regardless of how you answer the question, it serves as a framework for this challenge. In the space provided, note what you believe should be done about planning and preparing for teaching.

1. **Reflect on your own school experiences that involved planning and preparation. Develop a response to each question:**

   ■ **When you were a student, who do you remember as your most prepared teacher?**

   ■ **Why do you think he or she was so well prepared?**

   ■ **How did having an unprepared teacher make you feel as a student?**

   ■ **Did you feel as if you were a priority in the class where the teacher was not prepared? If not, how did you feel?**

   ■ **How did your teachers' preparation, or lack of preparation, affect your learning?**

   ■ **Did the prepared teacher influence you to be more prepared for class yourself?**

   ■ **Who do you remember as the least prepared teacher during your school experience?**

   ■ **Recall a story where a teacher was not prepared.**

Practical Problem (continued)

My reflections . . .

2. After reflecting on the preceding questions, answer the following question:

 ■ What should be done about planning and preparing for teaching? Identify the facts that relate to the practical problem such as the socioeconomic, political, historical, social, etc. factors that impact the problem. (Example: The school day does not provide adequate time for preparation.)

My ideas . . .

Valued Ends

Value ends are the desired results that should exist when the practical problem is addressed satisfactorily. Valued ends describe a desirable state of affairs.

Teachers who are successful in planning and preparation:

- **Know the subject matter and know where to find information**
- **Integrate and apply the subject matter into everyday life and experiences**
- **Incorporate new knowledge into existing knowledge**
- **Determine the amount of time necessary for learning to take place**
- **Develop plans to meet the needs of diverse students in the classroom**
- **Use policies, procedures, and routines in daily activities**
- **Are self-directed and participate in activities that encourage their own professional development**

In the space provided, identify other qualities that you believe are pertinent to successful planning and preparation. Also include any expectations or goals your administration has identified related to planning and preparation.

Qualities I believe are pertinent to successful planning and preparation: _____

_____

_____

Administration's expectations or goals related to planning and preparation: _____

_____

_____

What can I realistically achieve related to planning and preparation to be demonstrated in my teaching portfolio?

_____

_____

CHALLENGE 1

"I am wondering...?"

Even though you might feel isolated when you first begin your role as a teacher, remember that every other teacher has had similar experiences. Questions that other beginning teachers have raised when faced with planning and preparation include:

- **Where do I start?**
- **Should I plan for the whole nine weeks, a semester, or just a week at a time?**
- **My predecessor didn't leave anything for me to use. Now what?**
- **What do I do if my book is outdated?**
- **Where do I find current resources?**
- **What should I do to prepare for my teaching?**
- **What is important for my learners to know?**
- **How will I know if what I want my learners to know is worthwhile?**
- **How do I know how long to spend on a particular topic?**
- **Do I have a state coordinator or supervisor? What is that person's role?**

In the space that follows, list additional questions you may have about planning and preparation, and determine who can answer each question for your situation.

QUESTION	WHO CAN HELP?

CHALLENGE 1

Focus on the Issue
Planning and Preparation

Planning and preparing for instruction has been identified as one of the most important aspects of effective teaching (Henson, 1988; Kindsvatter, Wilen, & Ishler, 1988; Reiser & Dick, 1996). Planning, according to these researchers, is necessary when setting the stage for what and how you want your students to learn. As a professional educator, you possess a unique talent and skill in your area of expertise. Unlike a job where procedures are standardized, an educator makes hundreds of decisions each day. Most times those decisions are interrelated and have consequences that call for even more decisions. It is imperative, then, that you plan as precisely as possible to set the stage for your success. Planning can increase creative instruction, invigorate student participation and response, and stimulate the evaluation process. Costa and Garmston (1994) claim that the most important decisions teachers make involve planning because all other decisions in the classroom are directly related.

1. Imagine, if you will, how chaotic it would be to stand before your students and have no direction or focus. Think to a time when you were in a class or seminar and the instructor appeared to have no goal or purpose.

   ■ How did you feel?

   _____

   ■ What did you think?

   _____

   ■ What was your impression of the instructor?

   _____

   ■ What comments did you hear expressed by your classmates regarding the instructor's ill-conceived plan or lack of a plan?

   _____

   ■ Based on this reflection, what agreement do you want to make with yourself regarding planning and preparation?

   _____

> *Whether an individual will be an effective teacher depends upon the nature of his private world of perceptions.*
> —ARTHUR W. COMBS

 Consider including this agreement or goal in your teaching plan. See Wrap-Up at the end of the book.

Focus on the Issue (continued)

Planning and Preparation

2. **As a teacher, you will plan for such things as curriculum, classroom procedures, assessment, seating arrangements, etc. List as many thoughts as possible that you will need to consider when preparing to teach. Beside each item, identify what you will do to prepare for that task. It may help you to categorize your tasks into various sections, such as those listed below.**

CONSIDERATIONS	WHAT I PLAN TO DO
Classroom Procedures	
Introduction of self	
Introduction of course	
Course expectations	
Classroom management	
Discipline procedures	
Student expectations	
Evaluation procedures	
Introduction of textbook and other resources	
Student questions	
Icebreakers or get-acquainted activities	
Student feedback (time for students to reflect and raise questions anonymously)	

(continued on next page)

Focus on the Issue (continued)
Planning and Preparation

CONSIDERATIONS	WHAT I PLAN TO DO
Classroom Policies	
Borrowing	
Seating arrangements and desk placements	
Assignments	
Student disputes	
Seating	
Discipline infractions	
Students who get sick in class	
Classroom distractions	
Students who are absent	
Cellular phones	
Laptops	
Palm pilots	
E-mails	
Curriculum	
State and national standards	
Federal mandates	
Content standards	

(continued on next page)

Focus on the Issue (continued)
Planning and Preparation

CONSIDERATIONS	WHAT I PLAN TO DO
Learning Resources	
Sources	
Organization of materials	
Student forms	
Storage	
Procedures for accessing resources	
Supplies	
Student supplies	
Teacher supplies	
Storage	
Budget	
Labs	
Reserving the labs	
Use of technology	
Reserving multimedia carts	

Focus on the Issue (continued)
Planning and Preparation

After considering the broad issues related to planning for teaching, you can begin to focus on the specific learning goals you expect your students to achieve. Curriculum and lesson plans look different depending on school requirements. Although each may vary in structure and degree of information, most have elements central to all lessons. Those elements include:

- **The concept, generalization, skill, or reason for the lesson**
- **Objectives or end results**
- **Procedures to accomplish objectives and end results**
- **A method or strategy for determining whether students have met expectations**
- **A self-reflection assessment to determine what you have learned and how you intend to incorporate your learning into your practice**

Examples of questions that could guide your planning include:

- **Am I enthusiastic about this class? (Your excitement will be contagious.)**
- **Are the seats arranged appropriately for the activities I have planned?**
- **Is the lighting appropriate for student learning?**
- **Are my name, date, and course title on the chalkboard?**
- **Do I have an icebreaker or welcome activity planned?**
- **What procedure do I have for learning names?**
- **How do I plan to gather information about student backgrounds, interests, expectations for the course, questions, and concerns?**
- **Have I outlined how students will be evaluated?**
- **How and when will I make class announcements?**
- **How do I intend to gather student feedback?**
- **Can students access resources and supplies for class?**
- **When the class is over, will the students want to come back? Will I want to come back?**

List other questions you have related to planning:

-
-
-
-
-
-
-
-
-

Focus on the Issue (continued)
Planning and Preparation

Planning is a cyclic, continuous, and interactive process that occurs constantly as one teaches (Bellon, Bellon, & Blank, 1992). Ideally, you must create a plan, but you must also recognize that your plans may need to change instantly or frequently. The school day and calendar lend themselves to interruptions. The best advice is to be flexible within the parameters of your plans in order to handle the dynamics of the school day. Ultimately, the primary function of planning is to provide your students with the best environment you can for learning. Careful planning allows for the possibility of making adjustments depending on the needs of your students.

Because education revolves around student learning, it is imperative to include students in the process of planning and preparing. What better way to determine if students are learning and understanding than to solicit their support or help during the planning stages (Manderville & Rivers, 1991)? Consider these questions to involve students in planning:

■ **What have you planned for student learning? List several policies, procedures, or activities that you have developed.**

My plans . . .

Policies, procedures, or activities . . .

Focus on the Issue (continued)
Planning and Preparation

■ Have you invited your students to evaluate what you have planned and give you ideas about what worked or did not work? What ideas did they provide? How did you change your ideas, plans, or procedures to accompany your learners' perspectives? Use the following chart to record your responses. You might also invite students to brainstorm activities and procedures that they would like to try or that they have been involved with in other classes or groups. Try to incorporate their suggestions into your planning. The important component of this exercise is that you reflect on your planning and make appropriate changes to enhance student learning. You'll see in the process that your teaching may need to be altered to accomplish your goal. You are on your way to becoming a master teacher!

What I Planned	How My Students Responded to My Plans, Procedures, and Activities	How I Changed My Plans, Procedures, and Activities

Consider using this evidence in your teaching portfolio.

Students Speak Out

It is often said that the teacher learns as much as the students. Students can provide valuable insight in terms of helping you to determine whether you are an effective educator. Using the sentence stems outlined in bold type, the following statements about planning and preparation were solicited from students throughout the country:

> **I learned** more when my social studies teacher was prepared for class. When teachers aren't ready for class, I think kids take advantage of situations and cause more problems, because we know we can get away with it if the teacher is not prepared. (Britni G., ninth grade social studies)

> **I didn't like** being asked to find the answer to a question I raised in class. It makes me mad. It's like I'm being punished for asking a question that the teacher can't answer. Instead of telling me the answer or helping me find it, he made me do it for the next class. (John E., twelfth grade physics)

> **I like** it when my government teacher dresses up and pretends to be different people we are studying in class. She is always prepared for us and it makes me want to go to class. (Lauren G., tenth grade government)

> **I want** to be as organized as my math teacher. He knows where everything is. We get our papers back on time, too, and I like that. (Elizabeth E., tenth grade math)

> **I never want to** sit through another class where my teacher pretends she is ready for class. I hate it when my English teacher spends the first 20 minutes talking about stuff she read in the newspaper or saw on TV. I think she's wasting time. If I am supposed to turn in my homework on time, then I think she should do her preparing stuff on time too. (Roberto R., twelfth grade English)

The Teachers' Lounge

Every veteran teacher in your school will be able to shed insight into most any situation you present to them. When asked about planning and preparation, teachers throughout the country responded to the highlighted sentence stems in the following ways:

I LEARNED THAT BEING PREPARED IS DIRECTLY RELATED TO MY CLASSROOM MANAGEMENT. WHEN I HAVE STUDENTS ENGAGED IN THE LEARNING PROCESS, THEY ARE LESS LIKELY TO ACT UP IN CLASS.
(C. Norris, California)

I LIKE PLANNING AND DEVELOPING A VARIETY OF ACTIVITIES FOR STUDENTS THAT FOCUS ON SEVERAL OF THE MULTIPLE INTELLIGENCES. THAT WAY STUDENTS WILL LOOK FORWARD TO PARTICIPATING IN THE ACTIVITY, BECAUSE THEY KNOW IT WILL BE SOMETHING THEY WANT TO DO.
(J. Prusa, Minnesota)

I DON'T LIKE THE AMOUNT OF TIME I HAVE TO PLAN DURING THE YEAR. I DO LIKE THE AMOUNT OF TIME OUR DISTRICT GIVES US TO PLAN AT THE BEGINNING AND END OF THE SCHOOL YEAR. IT HELPS ME CONSIDERABLY. I WISH THE GENERAL PUBLIC WOULD KNOW THE TIME IT TAKES TO READ IN A VARIETY OF AREAS TO BE KNOWLEDGEABLE ENOUGH TO BE A GOOD TEACHER.
(D. Erceg, New Hampshire)

I REMEMBER OBSERVING A CLASSROOM WHERE THE INSTRUCTOR HAD STUDENTS ENGAGED IN A VARIETY OF DIFFERENT PROJECTS THAT HE CLAIMED MET INDIVIDUAL NEEDS AND PREFERENCES. I WAS AMAZED AT HOW EACH STUDENT WAS INVOLVED IN HIS OR HER LEARNING. NO ONE WANTED TO LEAVE WHEN THE CLASS WAS OVER. I HOPE I CAN ENGAGE STUDENTS THE SAME WAY. (F. Dietz, North Dakota)

I WANT TO GET A STUDENT AIDE TO HELP ME PUT EACH OF MY LESSONS ON A POWERPOINT PRESENTATION. THAT WAY I CAN CHANGE THEM IN THE FUTURE WITHOUT SPENDING A LOT OF TIME MAKING NEW OVERHEAD TRANS-PARENCIES AND VISUALS. IT MAKES IT EASIER TO GIVE THE NOTES TO A STUDENT WHO MISSES CLASS. (L. Rodriguez, Texas)

STUDENTS ARE USED TO BEING ENTERTAINED. IT'S SAD, BUT THEY WANT TO COME TO CLASS AND HAVE YOU KEEP THEIR ATTENTION FOR THE ENTIRE TIME. IF YOU DON'T, THEY TUNE YOU OUT. I HAVE FOUND THAT PLANNING IS CENTRAL TO MY SUCCESS AS A TEACHER. (E. Ireland, Washington)

NO ONE TOLD ME THAT SOME PUBLISHING COMPANIES HAVE TEACHER RESOURCE MATERIALS THAT ARE ALREADY DEVELOPED THAT CAN HELP ME AS I PREPARE. (L. Dunn, Maryland)

MY WORST NIGHTMARE IS PREPARING THE LESSON OF MY LIFE AND HAVING AN UNEXPECTED FIRE DRILL OR ASSEMBLY RIGHT IN THE MIDDLE OF IT!
(J. Stone, Oklahoma)

Teacher Tips

Master teachers have established a repertoire of skills that they draw upon when teaching. Some teachers shared these tips related to planning and preparation:

I usually start my semester by putting students in small groups and asking them to act like a machine. Examples would be a popcorn popper, ice machine, soda machine, etc. It gets the students talking and interacting and helps to break the ice. (C. Martin, Ohio)

Put plain paper on a bulletin board or a wall and ask all the students to write a short sentence or word graffiti to tell what they already know about the subject you are teaching. Refer to the sheet as you teach your new unit for reinforcement and to present new concepts. (T. Holmes, Washington, D.C.)

Take digital camera photographs of students holding a sheet where they have drawn their names using crayons or markers. Put the photographs on your computer and use them as a screen saver. (K. Grey, Virginia)

I keep a folder of lesson plan ideas that I know will work in the event that I am absent and the substitute teacher is not finding success with my lesson plan for that day. This way he or she has a "tried-and-true" lesson plan that will work. (C. Brooke, Idaho)

Create a welcome packet to hand out to students on the first day. This packet should contain a welcome letter from you, a student information sheet, a letter for the parents, a course syllabus (high school), and one or more handouts that outline classroom and homework procedures. Anything special that you want your students to have should also be in the packet. (Z. Thomas, Delaware)

I pass a calendar around the class at the beginning of the semester and ask everyone to record important dates and events for us to be aware of. It is a great way for me to see what students see as important, and I learn a lot about them as individuals. (E. Ray, Vermont)

I send a letter to each of my students before school begins asking what their expectations are of my class. I include a self-addressed stamped envelope for them to respond. I let them tell me who they are, but their doing so is optional. I get the responses and include their ideas into my course. Students seem to like this. (B. Baughman, Arizona)

CHALLENGE 1

A Mentor Moment

Ideally, you have been assigned a mentor to help you during your beginning years of teaching. If you have not been assigned a mentor, ask a teacher whom you respect if he or she will serve as your mentor. Mentors provide honest feedback in a nonthreatening and nonjudgmental way. Mentors also support you and offer worthwhile ideas that you might incorporate regularly. Even master teachers have mentors! Mentor teachers can help you in the area of planning and preparation by sharing their expertise and experiences, as this mentor teacher does:

> **One thing that all successful teachers have in common is good planning. This is directly related to every other aspect of your teaching and especially classroom management! I think lesson plans should be spelled out very carefully rather than loosely sketched out so that you have a good idea of what you are doing from one moment to the next. You don't want to keep your students in limbo as you are deciding what to do. This will cause students to be disruptive and they will lose interest. Trust me: no matter what anyone tells you about planning, make sure you have things spelled out as detailed as you can. You will not regret it. Good luck! (P. Gregory, Wyoming)**

Although teaching can be exceptionally rewarding, it helps to have another professional assist you with your daily questions about teaching. Following is a list of questions you might ask your mentor regarding planning and preparation, as well as a table you can use to identify questions you would like to discuss with your mentor. Document your mentor's responses and your thoughts about how to incorporate what you have learned into your practice.

Questions you might ask your mentor:

- **How do I know how long to spend on a particular topic?**
- **Do I have a state coordinator or supervisor? What is that person's role?**
- **Is there any funding for my program?**
- **Where do I get ideas for lessons that can accommodate a semester-long project?**
- **How much time should I spend on preparing for my classes?**
- **Should I plan more than a week in advance?**
- **How can I learn about the school district's policies?**
- **Should I use curriculum plans (if they are available) from the previous teacher?**
- **How can I accommodate small or large class sizes in my planning?**
- **How far in advance should I purchase supplies for my class?**

A Mentor Moment (continued)

Questions for My Mentor	Responses from My Mentor	How to Incorporate Mentor's Ideas into My Practice

A Mentor Moment (continued)

Now that you have had time to focus on your questions about planning and preparation with a mentor, think about what you have learned about yourself related to planning.

- **Think about some of the decisions you have already made related to planning. Did you overplan? Underplan?**

My decisions . . .

- **Why do you plan and prepare as you do? Develop a rationale for your planning and preparation procedures.**

My rationale . . .

A Mentor Moment (continued)

■ Return to this challenge at a later date and review your rationale (see the preceding item). How has your rationale changed? (You should see growth in your rationale and practice. Include this exercise as part of your yearly personal professional goals. It helps to see growth and development as you critically reflect on your practice.)

How my rationale has changed . . .

■ Identify a situation in which your students' reaction to something you planned or prepared for them wasn't what you thought it would be. How could you turn that situation into a positive experience for them and for you?

My ideas . . .

A Mentor Moment (continued)

- Is there any way you might communicate to your students the reflection you have done on this particular incident, practice, or policy? Can you share it with your students so that you may model the process of critical reflection? How might you present this to the students?

My reflections . . .

- Assuming you were able to share your thinking process with the students, what were their responses?

Student responses . . .

This process is central to the ability to critically reflect on teaching practice. It shows growth and development and can be used as evidence in your teaching portfolio.

Shared Strategies

Following are some activities and strategies that you might include in your daily practice. You can use these strategies as well as build upon them to create your own.

Strategies for Lesson Stages

Use the following chart to identify strategies to try during the opening, body, and closing of a lesson. Share your ideas with your colleagues or mentor. What worked for you? What didn't work? Continue to add to your list throughout the year. By the end of the year, you will be able to see how much you have learned.

My strategies . . .

Open	
Body	
Close	

Shared Strategies (continued)

Standards and Benchmarks

Central to all planning is consideration of standards and benchmarks for your subject. Think about the following questions when you are planning and preparing to teach. Use this list as a model for one of your lesson plans.

- What learning standards/benchmarks will be achieved?
- What is the specific learning standard?
- What assessment activities will enable students to demonstrate they have met the learning standard?
- What performance expectations are there for students to show the extent of learning that has occurred?
- How will students' difficulties be recognized along the way?
- What assessment materials are available and what materials need to be developed?
- How will assessment results be communicated to students and parents?

From Skowron, J., *Powerful Lesson Planning Models: The Art of 1000 Decisions* (p. 38). © 2001 by SkyLight Professional Development. Reprinted with permission.

Designing Lessons

The following questions will help you operationalize your planning. By addressing these questions, you will be better equipped to implement your ideas for crafting a successful lesson. Use this as a model for developing a lesson.

- What learning standard/benchmarks will be achieved?
- What is a motivating opening for the lesson?
- What strategies or activities will be used to teach the standards?
- What materials are needed to support and enhance learning?
- What is the appropriate use of technology?
- How will students be grouped for this activity?
- What opportunities will students have to reflect on their learning?
- How will student progress be monitored?
- What forms of additional practice may be necessary?
- How long will the lesson take?
- Are there any foreseeable pitfalls in this lesson?
- What alternatives are there if the lesson doesn't work out?

From Skowron, J., *Powerful Lesson Planning Models: The Art of 1000 Decisions* (p. 38). © 2001 by SkyLight Professional Development. Reprinted with permission.

> **An Amusing Story**
> *Our school requires students in the hometown to complete cards that provide basic information that we use to update our records. One of the questions asks the number we should call for an emergency. I knew it was going to be a long year when I read one of the responses: "Dial 911."*

Personal Reflection Journal

This challenge encouraged you to examine your practice in planning and preparing for teaching. Identify a situation related to planning and preparation that needs your attention. Follow the steps below to arrive at a desirable solution. Depending on the nature of your situation, you may use this exercise as a benchmark in your development. If so, include this piece in your professional portfolio.

My thoughts . . .

Identify the situation:

↓

Describe the situation:

↓

Whose advice did you seek in finding a creative solution to the situation?

↓   ↓   ↓

What did this person (or these persons) tell you to do?

Personal Reflection Journal (continued)

How did you deal with the situation?

Would you do the same thing if presented with a similar situation?

If yes, why?	If no, why?

What new knowledge or ideas come to mind as you incorporate what you have learned through this experience?

If you were to establish a goal to enhance your personal professional development in this area, what might that be?

How does what you learned compare to other areas of your teaching?

Personal Reflection Journal (continued)

Planning is central to all instruction. The preparation you have done for the term, semester, and year will pay off. Think about aspects of your role as an educator. In the space provided, outline how you can connect what you have learned about planning and preparation to other areas of your teaching.

Upon reflection, what have you learned that will enhance your development as an educator?

How will you integrate your new knowledge into your practice?

What does it mean to be a critical reflective practitioner when planning and preparing for teaching? Develop a clear and concise response that you can include in your professional development portfolio.

Consider including this in your professional teaching portfolio.

CHALLENGE 1

Standards

Every school differs in its acceptance of teaching standards. However, it is generally agreed that teachers need to possess a level of competence in order to find success. Because of their generic nature, the Interstate New Teacher Assessment and Support Consortium (INTASC) standards have been identified as a framework for you to use to reflect on your practice as an educator. The INTASC standards that address planning and preparation are as follows:

- **PRINCIPLE #1: The teacher understands the central concepts, tools of inquiry, and structures of the discipline(s) he or she teaches and can create learning experiences that make these aspects of subject matter meaningful for students.**

- **PRINCIPLE #2: The teacher understands how children learn and develop, and can provide learning opportunities that support their intellectual, social, and personal development.**

- **PRINCIPLE #3: The teacher understands how students differ in their approaches to learning and creates instructional opportunities that are adapted to diverse learners.**

- **PRINCIPLE #6: The teacher uses knowledge of effective verbal, nonverbal, and media communication techniques to foster active inquiry, collaboration, and supportive interaction in the classroom.**

- **PRINCIPLE #7: The teacher plans instruction based upon knowledge of subject matter, students, the community, and curriculum goals.**

- **PRINCIPLE #8: The teacher understands and uses formal and informal assessment strategies to evaluate and ensure the continuous intellectual, social, and physical development of the learner.**

- **PRINCIPLE #9: The teacher is a reflective practitioner who continually evaluates the effects of his or her choices and actions on others (students, parents, and other professionals in the learning community) and who actively seeks out opportunities to grow professionally.**

From Interstate New Teacher Assessment and Support Consortium, *Model Standards for Beginning Teacher Licensing, Assessment, and Development: A Resource for State Dialogue.* © 1992 by Council of Chief State School Officers, Washington, DC. Retrieved November 3, 2004, from http://www.ccsso.org/content/pdfs/corestrd.pdf. Used with permission.

Perhaps your school, district, or national organization has established standards pertinent to your professional development in this area. Review them, and the INTASC principles, to determine which one(s) you have met as a result of working through this challenge. It is not necessary to provide evidence for each standard in each challenge. However, by the time you complete this book, you should have evidence of how you can meet each principle or standard necessary for your portfolio. Document your evidence in the Wrap-Up section of the book.

Reflections Log

Fill out the following log to reflect on your learnings. It might be helpful to refer to the Assessment and Reflections Log at the beginning of the challenge to assess your growth.

What did I learn about planning and preparation?

Was I able to accomplish my goals?

How did I overcome the challenges in accomplishing my goals?

Congratulations, You Made It!

Identify something you are proud of relative to your classroom planning and preparation that you can incorporate in your professional portfolio. What evidence do you have to show your success? Use the following chart to record your responses.

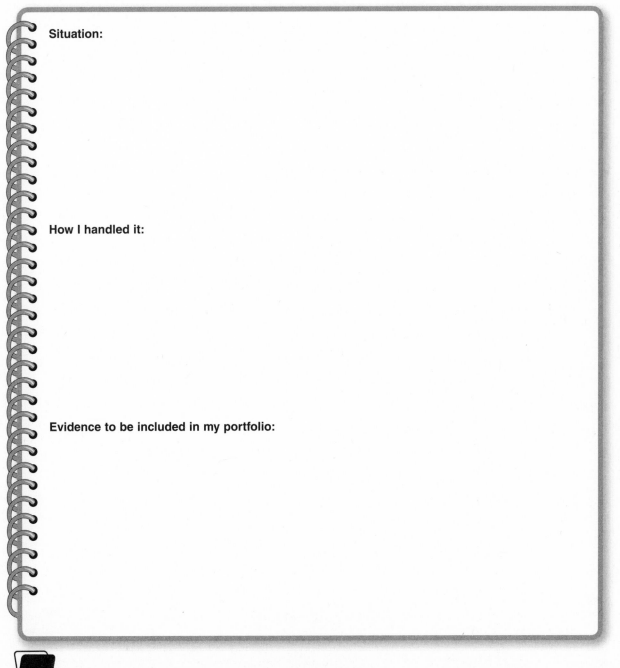

Situation:

How I handled it:

Evidence to be included in my portfolio:

Consider including this in your professional teaching portfolio.

Determining the Curriculum

Assessment and Reflections Log

Record your initial beliefs and goals about curriculum in this log.

My beliefs about <u>curriculum</u>:

My goal(s) for <u>curriculum</u>:

How am I going to accomplish my goal(s)?

Who and what can help me?

Challenges to accomplishing my goal(s):

The process or procedure for reaching my goal(s):

Determining the Curriculum

"How am I supposed to know what to teach?"

—First-Year Teacher

Curriculum refers to what you design to be taught in your classroom. Curriculum is determined by state departments of education, state boards of education, federal agendas, professional organizations, the community, and in some cases, corporate performance accountability models for learning. You, however, are the master developer of the curriculum. It is through your eyes and perspectives that curriculum for your classroom is determined. Of utmost importance in the curriculum development process is the learner. Your responsibility is to make the curriculum relevant, interesting, and meaningful to learners.

As you determine your course curriculum, decide what knowledge is most valuable. Make decisions about the core pieces of your curriculum in order to coincide with the needs and interests of your students. You make these decisions based on a set of principles you believe in and are committed to. When beginning the task of determining your curriculum, examine your personal teaching goals. Goal statements from curriculum guides and program material may help you convert your goals into precise and measurable terms. Plan carefully which materials will be most useful and at which point in the course they will be most effective. Identify which skills your students need to develop.

Working with curriculum is similar to looking at an orchestra score. As a teacher, you are the conductor of your own orchestra. You add a personal flavor to the course. You may choose to stress certain sections of the course, spend more time on one section and speed through another, or skip a topic completely. Whatever you choose to do depends largely on where you intend to go and what your learners need.

Curriculum is central to what happens in schools. This challenge is designed to encourage your critical reflective thinking about the curriculum process.

> *Expecting all children the same age to learn from the same materials is like expecting all children the same age to wear the same size clothing.*
>
> —MADELINE HUNTER

CHALLENGE 2

Practical Problem

What ought to be done about determining the curriculum? Teachers are ultimately responsible for curriculum and need to determine regularly what knowledge is most worth having. How you answer this question will be different than how other teachers answer, based on the needs of the learners. Regardless of how you answer the question, it serves as a framework for this challenge. In the space provided, note what you believe should be done about determining the curriculum.

1. **Reflect on your own experience as a student and how you viewed curriculum at that time. Develop a response to each question:**

   ■ **Did you ever ask why you had to learn some of the things your teachers taught when you were in school?**

   ■ **What class seemed totally irrelevant to you? Do you think that if the instructor had presented the content in that course from a different perspective you may have found it more interesting or relevant?**

   ■ **What did you need to know as a junior high school student? What did you care about at that time in your life?**

   ■ **What did you need to know as a high school student? What did you care about at that time in your life?**

   ■ **What course of study did you like the most in high school?**

   ■ **Describe a teacher who was passionate about his or her subject.**

   ■ **What do you remember as the course that most prepared you for life?**

Practical Problem (continued)

My reflections . . .

2. After reflecting on the preceding questions, answer the following questions:

   ■ What should be done in regards to determining the curriculum? Be sure to consider the socioeconomic, political, historical, and social impact on this question. (Example: Students should be included in the process of developing the curriculum.)

My ideas . . .

Practical Problem (continued)

■ Now that you have thought through each of these questions, what do you now believe about curriculum? You may find it useful to discuss your ideas with a mentor, colleague, or peer.

My ideas . . .

CHALLENGE 2

Valued Ends

The following list describes the skills, behaviors, and attitudes associated with teachers who are successful in determining curriculum. In the space provided, identify other qualities that you believe are pertinent to successful curriculum development. Also include any expectations or goals your administration has identified related to curriculum development.

Teachers who are successful in curriculum development:

- **Consider their learners and what is necessary to maintain a positive learning environment when determining curriculum**
- **Have extensive perceptions about their subject field and are able to find relevant information and assemble it in a manner in which students can find meaning**
- **Model and possess an insatiable thirst for knowledge**
- **Are able to discern what knowledge is most worth having by assessing the students they are teaching**

Qualities I believe are pertinent to successful curriculum development: _____

_____

_____

Administration's expectations or goals related to curriculum development: _____

_____

_____

What can I realistically achieve related to curriculum development to be demonstrated in my teaching portfolio?

_____

_____

"I am wondering...?"

Every teacher develops curriculum. The beliefs you hold about curriculum, coupled with your goals, will play a key role in your curriculum development. Each teacher makes the transition from what he or she believes to actually putting those beliefs into practice. Questions that other beginning teachers have raised when faced with determining curriculum follow. Think about each one and record your response. This will serve as a springboard for discussion with your peers or mentor.

■ **Where do I start?**

■ **Should I use the curriculum that my predecessor left me?**

■ **What do I do if my books are outdated?**

■ **How do I choose between everything that is available to me as a teacher?**

■ **How am I supposed to know what is most valuable for my students?**

■ **How should I plan my curriculum with regard to multiple intelligences?**

■ **How do I know what to teach?**

■ **Where do I get curriculum guides?**

■ **Do I have to follow any school or state guidelines?**

■ **How much detail do I have to include in my daily lesson plans?**

In the space that follows, list additional questions you may have about determining the curriculum, and determine who can answer each question for your situation. Save space to record your responses.

QUESTION	WHO CAN HELP?

Focus on the Issue

Determining the Curriculum

Originally, the word *curriculum* came from the Latin word, which meant "the course to be run." Schools developed courses to be completed to earn a degree. As a result, Eisner (1985) claimed that the "curriculum of a school, or a course, or a classroom can be conceived of as a series of planned events that are intended to have educational consequences for one or more students" (p. 45).

Many researchers agree that the two most significant features of any educational enterprise are the school curriculum and the quality of teaching (Eisner, 1985; English, 2000; Hunt, Wiseman, & Bowden, 1998; LeRiche, 1993; Solomon, 1998; Spreyer, 2002). Figuring out what to teach as a beginning teacher ranges from not knowing what to teach all the way to not knowing when to stop. Students should be encouraged to make learning a personal practice. Teachers do not need to tell students everything they need to know about any given subject. Instead, students should be encouraged by what they learn in the classroom to pursue more knowledge and experiences about the content on their own. What students experience in school has a direct impact on how they perceive the outside world. Curriculum, then, should empower students with strategies for learning that will last a lifetime. Individual success or failure could have potential lifelong effects and may well affect the quality of life within society in general.

Leinhardt (1992) and Scardamalia and Bereiter (1991) claim that students learn best when instructional tasks require them to use knowledge in meaningful ways. Your job is to determine what that knowledge is and to present it in a meaningful way. Resnick (1992) indicates that new learning should be taught based on real-life problem situations because most knowledge is constructed to fit particular contexts. One way to accomplish this is to integrate curriculum, which is one of the major trends in curriculum development. Integrated curriculum organizes content around themes designed to link content traditionally separated into different disciplines. This trend is becoming increasingly important in order for schools to accommodate learner diversity (Arredondo & Rucinski, 1998; Hough & St. Clair, 1995; Resnick, 1992).

Hough and St. Clair (1995) reveal that integrated curriculum units are effective because they not only present content from multiple subject perspectives and make connections between subjects explicit, but they also place emphasis on student use of knowledge and skills within a highly learner-centered environment. You may or may not be able to do this in your classroom, but you can consider possibilities of integrating curriculum and connecting it to real-life situations, which has the potential to add interest and enthusiasm to your teaching. Regardless of how you plan and carry out your curriculum decisions, it is equally important for you to have a philosophy of curriculum that you can revise as you critically reflect on your teaching.

Ornstein (1991), Ornstein and Hunkins (2004), and Solomon (1998) stress the importance of philosophy to be the basis for curriculum decisions, suggesting that it provides teachers with a framework for organizing schools and classrooms. Further, they agree that the individual teacher can adopt philosophies as he or she develops curriculum. The overview that follows begs the question for you to determine which educational philosophy most accurately fits your perspective.

Focus on the Issue (continued)
Determining the Curriculum

Look at each educational philosophy below. Note its philosophical base and its aim. Which ones coincide with your philosophy of education? Look at the next column: how knowledge is viewed from that philosophical orientation. Determine which one coincides with your interpretation of knowledge. Next, look at the role of the teacher. How do you view yourself as a teacher? Do you fit one of these categories, or are you a combination of several? Look, then, to the focus of curriculum and see which one most closely aligns with your view of curriculum. Finally, note the related curriculum trends to determine which best describes your perspectives. Most likely, you will not see yourself in only one category. Your educational philosophy is grounded in one or several of those listed. At this point, you should refer to any previously developed educational philosophies you have written to see if you still believe what you wrote. Your next step is to reconstruct your beliefs about education using the information in the following table as a starting point. There are other educational philosophies; explore all of them as you critically reflect on your philosophy of education.

OVERVIEW OF EDUCATIONAL PHILOSOPHY

Educational Philosophy	Philosophical Base	Aim of Education	Knowledge Focus	Role of Teacher	Curriculum Focus	Related Curriculum Trends
Perennialism	Realism	To educate the rational person; to cultivate the intellect	Focus on past and permanent studies; mastery of facts and timeless knowledge	Teacher helps students think rationally; based on Socratic method, oral exposition; explicit teaching of traditional values	Classical subjects; literary analysis; constant curriculum	Great books; Paideia proposal; returning to the liberal arts
Essentialism	Idealism, realism	To promote the intellectual growth of the individual; to educate the competent person	Essential skills and academic subjects; mastery of concepts and principles of subject matter	Teacher is authority in his or her subject field; explicit teaching of traditional values	Essential skills (three Rs) and essential subjects (English, math, science, history, and foreign language)	Back to basics; cultural literacy; excellence in education
Progressivism	Pragmatism	To promote democratic, social living	Knowledge leads to growth and development; a living-learning process; focus on active and relevant learning	Teacher is guide for problem solving and scientific inquiry	Based on student interests; involves the application of human problems and affairs; interdisciplinary subject matter; activities and projects	Relevant curriculum; humanistic education; radical school reform
Reconstructionism	Pragmatism	To improve and reconstruct society; education for change and social reform	Skills and subjects needed to identify and ameliorate problems of society; learning is active and concerned with contemporary and future society	Teacher serves as an agent of change and reform; acts as a project director and research leader; helps students become aware of problems confronting humankind	Emphasis on social sciences and social research methods; examination of social, economic, and political problems; focus on present and future trends as well as on national and international issues	International education; reconceptualism; equality of educational opportunity

From Ornstein, A. C., & Hunkins, F. P., *Curriculum: Foundations, Principles, and Issues* (p. 55). © 2004 by Allyn and Bacon. Reprinted with permission.

Focus on the Issue (continued)

Determining the Curriculum

■ Write several paragraphs that explain your philosophy of education. Focus on what you believe about curriculum as it relates to your view of knowledge and purpose of education. This should form the basis of your activities as an educator and provide a justification for your decisions regarding curriculum.

My beliefs about curriculum . . .

It is not the answer that enlightens, but the question.

—DECOUVERTES

Consider including this document in your teaching portfolio.

Focus on the Issue (continued)
Determining the Curriculum

All teachers consider their conceptions of the learner, society, knowledge, and aim of education before structuring the actual goals, activities, and assessments involved with curriculum. Brown (1979) identified three perspectives in relation to the four aforementioned elements as a basis for a curriculum framework (see chart below). Depending on your perspective and philosophy, learners can be perceived in a variety of ways. In perspective A, the learner is in command of the facts and learns by conditioning and step-by-step instruction. This perspective is in juxtaposition with perspective C, which assumes the student is innately wise and good and is capable of developing his or her own unique potential. Determine which perspective of the learner, as outlined in the following chart, best coincides with your educational philosophy. The chart provides a unique look at conceptions of the learner, knowledge, society, and the aim of education.

	Perspective A	Perspective B	Perspective C
Learner	Is in command of facts and learns by conditioning and step-by-step instruction.	Is an independent, critical, and creative thinker in search of meaning and action.	Is innately wise and good, and is capable of developing their own unique potential.
Knowledge	Accretion of specific information separated from life experience.	Consists of what is known as well as the process of knowing actively.	Knowledge is private and the individual chooses what is important.
Society	Norms should be accepted as they are.	Norms must be examined in relation to democratic principles.	Society interferes with individual development of the person.
Aim of Education	Masters subject matter.	Has the ability to use what is learned in a democratic society.	Finds meaning of one's existence.

Adapted from *A Conceptual Scheme and Decision-Rules for the Selection and Organization of Home Economics Curriculum Content* by M. Brown. © 1979 by Wisconsin Department of Public Instruction.

Focus on the Issue (continued)

Determining the Curriculum

■ Think about how you developed your perspective of the learner. Is your response a result of the way you were educated? Is it based on a rational set of beliefs about learners? Develop your philosophy of the *learner* in the space that follows. This process will help you as you develop curriculum.

■ Think now about knowledge in relation to your philosophy of education. Do you believe knowledge is the accumulation of facts that is separate from life itself? If so, your curriculum will reflect that belief. Or, do you believe that knowledge is private and the individual is responsible for selecting that which is important? If so, your lessons will indicate this belief. Think now about which perspective, or combination of perspectives, best coincide with your philosophy of *knowledge.* Write your response in the space provided.

■ How you view society is central to curriculum development. Think about your perception of the norms and values of your school, community, and society. How do your beliefs coincide with those values? Develop a rationale defending your beliefs about *societal norms* in the space provided. This will also serve as an important component of your educational philosophy and will be manifested in the curriculum you develop.

Focus on the Issue (continued)

Determining the Curriculum

■ **Finally, think about your beliefs regarding the *aim of education.* Do you believe that education should help the learner to master the subject matter? If so, you will develop curriculum very differently than if you believe that education is designed to help a person find meaning for himself or herself. Consider your beliefs about education. In the space provided, develop a statement that explains your perspective regarding the aim of education. This will shape your philosophy and will be the cornerstone of curriculum development for you.**

_____

_____

_____

_____

_____

_____

_____

_____

_____

_____

_____

Consider each of your responses from the preceding exercise. These statements shape your philosophy of education. Your philosophy drives your decisions about curriculum. As an educator, you should be able to articulate your philosophy.

■ **In the space provided, write your philosophy of education. Think about why you believe what you have written and know why you believe it. Your philosophy statement should be suitable for inclusion in your teaching portfolio.**

_____

_____

_____

_____

_____

_____

_____

_____

_____

_____

_____

Consider including this document in your teaching portfolio.

Focus on the Issue (continued)
Determining the Curriculum

■ **Think now of a situation or circumstance where your curriculum decision was challenged by a student or students. Reflect on that event and how you responded to it. Instead of blaming yourself or the student(s), identify how you could use that circumstance to improve your effectiveness and student learning.**

_____
_____
_____
_____
_____
_____
_____
_____
_____
_____
_____
_____

Reflect now on how you might use this example with a student or your class to engage others in the critical reflective process. It may be as simple as sharing why you have selected to do something differently than the way you have done it in the past. Regardless, the process should help your learners see you as a critical reflective practitioner.

■ **What does it mean for you to be a critical reflective practitioner when determining the curriculum?**

_____
_____
_____
_____
_____
_____
_____
_____
_____
_____
_____

 This critical reflection would be appropriate to include in your teaching portfolio.

Students Speak Out

Students experience hours of instruction that turn into days and weeks. As the master planner of curriculum, you have the ability to create meaningful lessons that either meet their needs or turn them into passive listeners. Using the sentence stems outlined in bold type, the following statements about how teachers present the curriculum were solicited from students throughout the country:

> **I learned** more when my history teacher would give us an outline of the lesson he was teaching. This way I have a sense of what we are doing in class and where we are going. He doesn't always follow the book, so this helped me a lot. I have been sick a lot this term, too, and it is easier for me to keep up with the class because of these outlines. (Anna C., tenth-grade history)

> **I want** to take time and go to some of the places that we talk about in my social studies class. It would be cool to see some videos or documentaries about some of those places. I would really like to have a chat pal on the Internet from Australia or Bali or Egypt. (Tanya A., tenth-grade world cultures)

> **I didn't like** having to hurry to get through the book. I don't understand why we have to cover the whole book anyway. I think we should be able to pick the chapters we want to study. Some of this stuff is not too interesting. There is too much information in the book, and making us read the whole thing and go that fast is insane. (Chuck N., eleventh-grade science)

> **I like it** when my physics teacher gives us problems to solve. To figure out the answers, we have to do a lot of research that helps me to learn what we are supposed to know. I like finding information and applying it to real life rather than reading about things and not having time in class to use what we learned. (Audrey K., twelfth-grade physics)

> **I never want** to be part of a group that puts other kids down. We read poems and letters in Lit. class from kids our age who wrote about their experiences with other kids in their schools who were hurting them. It broke my heart. I had no idea that some people could be so cruel. I am glad my teacher shared these things with us. It helped me understand life from another person's perspective. (Andrea H., eleventh-grade literature)

CHALLENGE 2

The Teachers' Lounge

Following are some quotes from teachers around the country on their various experiences and thoughts on determining the curriculum using the highlighted sentence stems:

I LEARNED THAT I DON'T HAVE AS MUCH CONTROL OVER WHAT STUDENTS LEARN AS I ORIGINALLY EXPECTED. I THOUGHT THAT I COULD DETERMINE CURRICULUM BY ESTABLISHING OBJECTIVES AND PLANNING ACTIVITIES THAT WOULD MEET THOSE OBJECTIVES. HOWEVER, WHAT I FOUND IS THAT STUDENTS TAKE FROM THE EXPERIENCES IN THE CLASSROOM THAT WHICH IS MEANINGFUL TO THEM. THIS, I HAVE FOUND, IS THE HIDDEN CURRICULUM. (M. Michaelson, Colorado)

I LIKE PAUSING AFTER CERTAIN ACTIVITIES AND ASKING MY STUDENTS TO SHARE WHAT THEY HAVE LEARNED. I AM ALWAYS AMAZED AT THE VARIETY OF DIFFERENT PERSPECTIVES THEY SEE AFTER A COMMON EXPERIENCE. EACH STUDENT SYNTHESIZES LEARNING INTO HIS OR HER OWN EXPERIENCE. (T. Calub, New York)

I DON'T LIKE WHEN STUDENTS MISS CLASSES AND I NEED TO MAKE SPECIAL ARRANGEMENTS FOR THEM TO GET THE LESSON I TAUGHT IN THAT CLASS. IT TAKES FOREVER TO KEEP TRACK OF ALL THE INFORMATION THEY MISS. (D. Williams, Idaho)

WHEN I WAS STUDENT TEACHING IN FAMILY AND CONSUMER SCIENCES, I REMEMBER MY SUPERVISING TEACHER USING HER SEWING LABORATORY AS A REAL-LIFE EXAMPLE OF A FACTORY IN A THIRD-WORLD COUNTRY. SHE TREATED THE STUDENTS EXACTLY AS IF THEY WERE WORKING. TOWARD THE END OF THE CLASS, SHE STOPPED ROLE PLAYING AND EXPLAINED WHAT SHE WAS TRYING TO SHOW THEM. THE STUDENTS REALLY SEEMED TO GAIN A BETTER APPRECIATION FOR WHAT PEOPLE WHO WORK IN OPPRESSIVE SITUATIONS MIGHT BE EXPERIENCING. (D. Krough, Florida)

I WISH WE COULD INTEGRATE OUR CURRICULUM SO THAT OUR STUDENTS AT THE SENIOR HIGH COULD FOCUS ON SOME OF THE REAL ISSUES THEY WILL FACE AS ADULTS. IF A NUMBER OF DIFFERENT DISCIPLINES WOULD FOCUS ON THEMES IN THE CURRICULUM, WE MIGHT BE ABLE TO CHALLENGE OUR STUDENTS TO BECOME PROBLEM SOLVERS AND BE MORE INTERESTED IN OUR CLASSES. (W. Goodling, Michigan)

NO ONE TOLD ME THAT PARENTS WOULD BE SO INFLUENTIAL IN DETERMINING THE CURRICULUM. I WAS BLINDSIDED BY A MOTHER WHO DIDN'T THINK I SHOULD BE DISCUSSING ANYTHING ABOUT HUMAN SEXUALITY IN MY HEALTH CLASS. (M. Allen, North Carolina)

STUDENTS LEARN MUCH MORE THAN WHAT YOU PLAN IN THE CURRICULUM. THEY VIEW EVERYTHING FROM THEIR OWN LENS. THEY FILTER WHAT IS SAID, READ, AND EXPERIENCED THROUGH THEIR UNIQUE PERSPECTIVES. IT IS SOMETIMES DIFFICULT TO KNOW EXACTLY WHAT IS LEARNED AND HOW IT IMPACTS A STUDENT. BUT I THINK THIS IS THE BEAUTY OF EDUCATION. (J. Huinker, Louisiana)

I WANT TO HELP STUDENTS LEARN TO SEEK ANSWERS FOR THEMSELVES AND TO DEVELOP INQUIRING MINDS. I BELIEVE CURRICULUM SHOULD FOCUS ON THE PROCESS OF LEARNING AS MUCH AS IT FOCUSES ON THE CONTENT. (L. Nichols, South Dakota)

Teacher Tips

Master teachers have established a repertoire of skills that they draw upon when teaching. Some teachers shared these tips related to curriculum:

I have been able to increase student participation by relating the content in my class to the students' personal lives. I want them to see the relevance of what they are learning and give them a reason for understanding my course. I divide each section of the curriculum into a section that focuses on the students and permits them an opportunity to select which activity they want to be involved with. For example, when we are discussing a particular social issue, I encourage the students to find a song or poem that focuses on the issue. We play the song or read the poem and find out a little more about the author or the artists and try to find out why they wrote that song or poem. We have had a few artists correspond with class members through e-mail. It has generated a lot of excitement for my students and has made the curriculum more relevant to their lives. (B. Raab, Canada)

One of the ways I encourage relevance to my curriculum is to have the students bring in a photograph at the beginning of each unit and explain how they think the photo relates to whatever we are studying. I have all the students put the photos in a pile and then randomly assign each student a photo. Students have five to seven minutes to determine how the photo relates to the topic. This activity generates a lot of excitement, creativity, and laughs. (E. Stroud, Massachusetts)

I want my curriculum to be meaningful. I tell students what we will be studying each semester and ask them for input. Sometimes students bring a lot of knowledge to the class. I had one student who lived in Japan who was able to provide the whole class with pen pals. She knew all the students in the class from Japan and was able to help make the connections. Another student's father was a POW and agreed to share his story with my class. (V. Perez, Indiana)

Bring in as much media to the classroom as possible, such as newspapers, magazines, videos, TV newsclips, Web sites. Incorporate everything you do into what's happening in the world. Kids need to see relevance. (D. Brennemen, New Hampshire)

I use a curriculum map or storyboard to help my students "see" the curriculum. I put felt on my bulletin board and then attach each lesson with Velcro™ strips on posterboard. Arrows connect the content on each posterboard so students can see where we've been and where we're going. It's like a big puzzle. (C. Davis, Oregon)

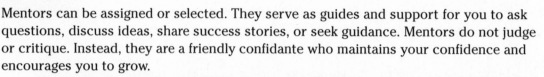

A Mentor Moment

Mentors can be assigned or selected. They serve as guides and support for you to ask questions, discuss ideas, share success stories, or seek guidance. Mentors do not judge or critique. Instead, they are a friendly confidante who maintains your confidence and encourages you to grow.

Having another professional help you with your daily questions about teaching can make your experiences as a teacher even more rewarding. Following is a list of questions you might ask your mentor regarding curriculum. On the next page is a table you can use to identify those questions you would like to discuss with your mentor. Document your mentor's responses and your thoughts about how to incorporate what you have learned into your practice.

Questions you might ask your mentor:

- How do I know what to teach?

- Where do I get curriculum guides? Who pays for them?

- Do I have to follow any school or state guidelines?

- How much detail do I have to include in my daily lesson plans?

- Is there a place in the school to help me with my curriculum development?

- What is the best way to establish relationships for collaboration?

- Should I develop my curriculum entirely by myself, or can I use a book as a guide?

- How long should a daily lesson plan be?

- How should I incorporate national standards into my daily lesson plans and my overall curriculum?

- Does the state mandate what I teach or what books I use?

A Mentor Moment (continued)

Questions for My Mentor	Responses from My Mentor	How to Incorporate Mentor's Ideas into My Practice

A Mentor Moment (continued)

At this point you have had considerable time to think about curriculum issues and discuss them with a mentor.

■ **What decisions have you made related to curriculum? Did you integrate the curriculum? How did you decide what to include and what to discard?**

My decisions . . .

■ **Write a short rationale or justification for why you believe what you do about curriculum.**

My rationale . . .

A Mentor Moment (continued)

■ Return to this challenge at a later date and review your curriculum rationale (see the preceding item). How has your rationale changed? (You should see growth in your rationale and development as you critically reflect on your practice.)

How my rationale has changed . . .

■ Identify a time in which you blamed yourself for your students', administrators', or a parents' reaction to one of your curriculum decisions. Consider how you might alter that decision or your thoughts about it so that you can grow from the experience.

My ideas . . .

A Mentor Moment (continued)

■ Now that you have had time to ask questions and to be engaged in the curriculum development and delivery stages, think about what you have learned about yourself.

My reflections . . .

■ Write a brief statement regarding how your ideas and practice have changed as a result of your critical reflection.

My ideas . . .

This process is central to the ability to critically reflect on teaching practice. It shows growth and development and can be used as evidence in your teaching portfolio.

CHALLENGE 2

Shared Strategies

Following are some activities and strategies that you might include in your daily practice. You can use these strategies as well as build upon them to create your own.

Developing Curriculum

Developing curriculum is not simply a skill. It is a process that integrates your knowledge and skill into student learning. As you develop curriculum, you will want to ask yourself the following questions, which are designed to strengthen your ability to develop curriculum. You may or may not be at a point where you can focus on that which the questions call for. At some point in your beginning years of teaching refer back to these questions. They will provide a useful assessment regarding your curriculum development.

A New Pedagogy
Identify a curriculum you have developed and used. Answer each of the questions to shed light on your ability to develop meaningful curriculum.

- How do I build on the relevant knowledge and experiences students bring to class?
- How do I take time to find out if they have accurate and sufficient background knowledge to do an academic task?
- How do I require students to consider information from a variety of sources and disciplines?
- Are my tasks complex enough and are the problems interesting to my students?
- Do I provide opportunities for students to use their strengths to create something that would benefit others?
- How do the learning experiences challenge my students to use higher-level thinking operations, such as hypothesis testing, inquiry, reasoning, interpretation, and synthesis?
- How do I give frequent and informative feedback to guide students as they plan and work through tasks?
- How do I allow students to share ideas and get feedback from others, including peers and knowledgeable "experts"?
- How can I help my students feel "safe" to take risks or experiment with varying strategies?
- How do I provide time for students to reflect and evaluate how, what, and why they learned?
- How do I help students recognize that other learning strategies might be used in the current context or that a specific strategy might be adapted for a different context?
- Do I give students opportunities to practice and develop new levels of skill and competence?
- Am I an enthusiastic expert in my content area? How do I share this with students?

Adapted from Beamon, G. W., *Teaching With Adolescent Learning in Mind* (p. 120). © 2001 by SkyLight Professional Development. Reprinted with permission.

Shared Strategies (continued)

As you develop curriculum, consider the range of verbs that you can use to encourage student learning. You will find the following words useful when planning specific lesson plans.

THE LANGUAGE OF THINKING				
Literary Meaning	**Mathematical Reasoning**	**Scientific Inquiry**	**Historical Analysis**	**Artistic Expression**
Infer	Subdivide	Speculate/Research	Investigate	Review/Scrutinize
Discern	Solve	Suggest/Suppose	Corroborate	Select
Hypothesize	Prove	Surmise/Theorize	Reflect/Establish	Re-create
Interpret/Contend	Detect/Scrutinize	Reason	Convince/Dissent	Understand
Dissent/Consider	Weigh/Conjecture	Prove	Attest	Recognize/Perceive
Conclude/Question	Dissect	Probe	Affirm	Realize/Appreciate
Ponder	Derive/Ascertain	Propose/Postulate	Explore	Muse
Predict	Calculate/Assess	Analyze/Dispute	Inquire/Suppose	Observe/Evaluate
Opine/Summarize	Comprehend	Examine/Construe	Remember/Rebut	Relate
Perceive	Deduce	Assess	Maintain/Submit	Discriminate
Critique	Demonstrate	Claim	Resolve/Recollect	Differentiate
Relate	Estimate	Confirm/Establish	Study/Restructure	Recommend
Restate	Determine	Justify	Interpret	Describe
Review	State			
Imply	Categorize			
Contrast	Rate			

From Beamon, G. W., *Teaching With Adolescent Learning in Mind.* (p. 106). © 2001 by SkyLight Professional Development. Reprinted with permission.

An Amusing Story

I have a collection of outdated textbooks that I keep in my classroom. Sometimes I refer back to them to see how much the curriculum has changed. Other times I share them with students just for fun. One of my students asked me how old one of the books was. Knowing that he was only about sixteen years old, I responded by saying that the book was older than he was. He seemed quite puzzled and replied, "That doesn't make any sense to me at all. Here they have this whole section on the Civil War and I remember when that DVD came out."

CHALLENGE 2

Personal Reflection Journal

This challenge encouraged you to critically reflect on the curriculum process. Identify a situation related to curriculum development that needs your attention. Follow the steps below to arrive at a desirable solution. Depending on the nature of your situation, you may use this exercise as a benchmark in your development. If so, include this piece in your professional portfolio.

My thoughts . . .

Identify the situation:

↓

Describe the situation:

↓

Whose advice did you seek in finding a creative solution to the situation?

↓

What did this person (or these persons) tell you to do?

Personal Reflection Journal (continued)

How did you deal with the situation?

Would you do the same thing if presented with a similar situation?

If yes, why?

If no, why?

What new knowledge or ideas come to mind as you incorporate what you have learned through this experience?

If you were to establish a goal to enhance your personal professional development in this area, what might that be?

How does what you learned compare to other areas of your teaching?

Personal Reflection Journal (continued)

Curriculum is the basis of all instruction. The curriculum planning you have done for the term, semester, and year will pay off. Think about other aspects of your role as an educator. Outline how you can connect what you have learned about curriculum to other areas of your teaching.

Upon reflection, what have you learned that will enhance your development as an educator?

How will you integrate your new knowledge into your practice?

What does it mean to be a critical reflective practitioner when determining the curriculum? Develop a clear and concise response that you can include in your professional portfolio.

Consider including this in your professional teaching portfolio.

CHALLENGE 2 Standards

Every school differs in its acceptance of teaching standards. However, it is generally agreed that teachers need to possess a level of competence in order to find success. Because of their generic nature, the Interstate New Teacher Assessment and Support Consortium (INTASC) standards have been identified as a framework for you to use to reflect on your practice as an educator. The INTASC standards that address curriculum development are as follows:

- **PRINCIPLE #2: The teacher understands how children learn and develop, and can provide learning opportunities that support their intellectual, social, and personal development.**

- **PRINCIPLE #3: The teacher understands how students differ in their approaches to learning and creates instructional opportunities that are adapted to diverse learners.**

- **PRINCIPLE #4: The teacher understands and uses a variety of instructional strategies to encourage students' development of critical thinking, problem solving, and performance skills.**

- **PRINCIPLE #5: The teacher uses an understanding of individual and group motivation and behavior to create a learning environment that encourages positive social interaction, active engagement in learning, and self-motivation.**

- **PRINCIPLE #7: The teacher plans instruction based upon knowledge of subject matter, students, the community, and curriculum goals.**

- **PRINCIPLE #9: The teacher is a reflective practitioner who continually evaluates the effects of his or her choices and actions on others (students, parents, and other professionals in the learning community) and who actively seeks out opportunities to grow professionally.**

- **PRINCIPLE #10: The teacher fosters relationships with school colleagues, parents, and agencies in the larger community to support students' learning and well-being.**

From Interstate New Teacher Assessment and Support Consortium, *Model Standards for Beginning Teacher Licensing, Assessment, and Development: A Resource for State Dialogue.* © 1992 by Council of Chief State School Officers, Washington, DC. Retrieved November 3, 2004, from http://www.ccsso.org/content/pdfs/corestrd.pdf. Used with permission.

Perhaps your school, district, or national organization has established standards pertinent to your professional development in this area. Review them, and the INTASC principles, to determine which one(s) you have met as a result of working through this challenge. It is not necessary to provide evidence for each standard in each challenge. However, by the time you complete this book, you should have evidence of how you can meet each principle or standard necessary for your portfolio. Document your evidence in the Wrap-Up section of the book.

Reflections Log

Fill out the following log to reflect on your learnings. It might be helpful to refer to the Assessment and Reflections Log at the beginning of the challenge to assess your growth.

What did I learn about <u>curriculum</u>?

Was I able to accomplish my goals?

How did I overcome the challenges in accomplishing my goals?

Congratulations, You Made It!

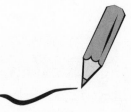

Identify something you are proud of relative to determining the curriculum that you can incorporate in your professional portfolio. What evidence do you have to show your success? Use the following chart to record your responses.

Situation:

How I handled it:

Evidence to be included in my portfolio:

📁 Consider including this in your professional teaching portfolio.

Classroom Space and Establishing the Climate

Assessment and Reflections Log

Record your initial beliefs and goals about classroom space and establishing the climate in this log.

My beliefs about <u>classroom space and establishing the climate</u>:

My goal(s) for <u>classroom space and establishing the climate</u>:

How am I going to accomplish my goal(s)?

Who and what can help me?

Challenges to accomplishing my goal(s):

The process or procedure for reaching my goal(s):

Classroom Space and Establishing the Climate

"Half of them can't remember their assigned seats."

—First-Year Teacher

Positive classroom climate is defined plainly as the environment in which effective teachers teach and students reach their individual desired goals. Classroom climate also refers to the intrinsic and extrinsic things a teacher does to set the stage for student productivity. It involves the senses, such as what a student sees, hears, feels, and touches as a result of being in the classroom. Everyone remembers when he or she had a positive experience with learning. Similarly, negative experiences are also remembered. The purpose of this challenge is to help you establish a positive learning environment where students are actively involved in a positive way with the subject matter, their classmates, and the teacher.

> *Perhaps the greatest of all pedagogical fallacies is the notion that a person learns only the particular thing he is studying at the time.*
> —JOHN DEWEY

CHALLENGE 3

Practical Problem

What should you do about establishing a positive classroom climate for student learning? The answer to this practical question will be different for each professional. It will depend on your personality, your preferences, and your philosophy of education. In the space provided, note what you believe should be done about establishing a positive classroom climate in your classroom.

1. **Reflect on the things you remember as a student that were related to classroom space and climate. Develop a response to each question:**

   ■ **Do you remember being in a classroom where you felt happy to be there as soon as you walked into the room? Record that memory.**

   ■ **Do you remember going into a classroom that made you feel uncomfortable? Describe that feeling.**

   ■ **What was unique about these classrooms?**

   ■ **What did teachers do to make you feel welcome in their classrooms?**

   ■ **How were welcoming classrooms set up?**

   ■ **Do you remember a classroom where you had a hard time focusing and learning?**

   ■ **What do you remember as distracting or hindering to your learning?**

   ■ **Describe a classroom where you felt comfortable.**

   ■ **Recall a classroom experience that was distressing.**

   ■ **Did you ever feel unsafe in a classroom? Describe that feeling.**

Practical Problem (continued)

My reflections . . .

2. After reflecting on the preceding questions, answer the following questions:

- What should be done about classroom space and establishing the climate in your classroom? (Example: I plan to welcome students into my class by standing at the door and calling them by name.)

My ideas . . .

Practical Problem (continued)

■ Now that you have thought through each of these questions, what do you now believe about classroom space and climate? Identify what you think should be done to encourage student success by paying attention to the school environment. You may find it useful to discuss your ideas with a mentor, colleague, or peer.

My ideas . . .

Valued Ends

The following list describes the personal characteristics associated with teachers who are successful in establishing a positive classroom climate. In the space provided, identify other qualities that you believe are pertinent to both setting up a classroom where students respect one another and establishing a positive classroom climate. Also include any expectations or goals your administration has identified related to these issues.

Teachers who are successful in establishing a positive classroom climate:

- **Value individual differences and exhibit characteristics of tolerance and acceptance**
- **Have a developed sense of empathy**
- **Are able to be versatile**
- **Are sensitive to people and their reaction to things**
- **View people as having worth, integrity, dependability, and importance**
- **Are sensitive to the communication patterns established by the students**

Personal and professional qualities I believe are pertinent to establishing a positive classroom climate: _____

_____

Administration's expectations or goals related to establishing a positive classroom climate: _____

_____

What can I realistically achieve related to classroom climate to be demonstrated in my teaching portfolio? _____

_____

_____

CHALLENGE 3

"I am wondering...?"

Every teacher upon walking into the classroom for the first time has a number of questions. Questions that other beginning teachers have raised about classroom space and establishing the climate include:

- How do I establish a community spirit in my classroom?
- How do I create a pleasing environment for my learners?
- How can I help all my students respect their differences?
- How do I create a safe environment for my students so that they will want to participate?
- How do I develop an equitable climate?
- How can I avoid bias in my interaction with students?
- How can I organize, allocate, and manage time, space, and activities in a way that is conducive to learning?
- How can I analyze my classroom environment and interactions and make adjustments to enhance my students' relationships with one another?
- What should I consider when placing students in groups?
- How can I motivate student learning within the confines of my classroom?

In the space that follows, list additional questions you may have about classroom space and establishing the climate, and determine who can answer each question for your situation.

QUESTION	WHO CAN HELP?

CHALLENGE 3

Focus on the Issue

Classroom Space and Establishing the Climate

It is imperative that you establish the classroom environment during the first few days of class, but novice teachers may feel awkward and may not know exactly how to go about setting up this structure (Brause, 1998; Carbone, 1993; Higgins, 1999; Kaywell & Feyton, 1992). Brause (1998) recommends that teachers should have a good understanding of the students who will be taught. What does the community look like in which they live? What are their personal aspirations? What experiences have positively and negatively impacted their lives? What are their responsibilities outside of school? What other classes do they have? Who are their role models? What are their proficiencies and interests?

Some general guidelines related to establishing a positive climate, according to Kaywell and Feyton (1992), include:

- **Establish clear classroom routines and policies and share them immediately.**
- **Pay attention to the physical arrangement of furniture.**
- **Set up a structure for organizing materials.**
- **Determine acceptable traffic patterns.**

Further, they suggest that climate is established by what you do or don't do. Additional areas to consider when thinking about your classroom climate include being prepared and planning more than you can possibly teach in each lesson. Each class has a culture and a feel to it. What students feel and sense as a result of being in your classroom is considered the climate.

What is the best way to get started? Look around your classroom and think about being a student in that environment. What would you like to see or not to see? What can you do to make your classroom more inviting? List five things you could do to make your classroom space more inviting:

- _____
- _____
- _____
- _____
- _____

Focus on the Issue (continued)

Classroom Space and Establishing the Climate

Routine practices and procedures also contribute to the climate. Think about your actions and how they will be interpreted by your students. Students' interpretations will set the stage for your classroom climate.

Following are other ways to establish a positive climate:

- **Begin class on time. Don't make students wait while you take attendance, find your papers, talk to other students or other teachers in the hall, or the like. Let the students know what you expect from them and what they can expect from you. First impressions stay with us for a long time. Make sure that the first impression your students have of you is what you want them to have.**

- **Put your class objectives on the board. Let students know what you want them to know so that they can work with you to accomplish your goals for them. Give them an opportunity to tell how they might achieve your goals.**

- **Use bulletin boards, display cases, posters, visuals, transparencies, PowerPoint presentations, and so on to show objectives, policies, procedures, and expectations. Use the media available to you to set behavioral boundaries in the class.**

- **If you teach with a team of teachers, make sure teachers use consistent discipline practices.**

- **Get to know students' names from the beginning of the semester. Students are less likely to misbehave or be disrespectful if they know you and if they have developed a positive relationship with you. Ask them what their interests are so you can use examples in your classes based on their likes and desires.**

- **Be a role model. Everything you do and say will be scrutinized by your students. Think carefully about each of your decisions and how they will be perceived by your learners.**

- **Establish a classroom crisis plan and share it with students. This way students will feel comfortable knowing you have thought through these things and will do your best to care for them should a crisis occur.**

- **End class on time. Do not try to shout over the bell or the noise that is created as a result of students passing to different classes. Make sure that assignments are given and the lesson review is completed, allowing adequate time for student questions before the end of the period.**

Establishing a community within your classroom is one of your most important tasks and responsibilities. It is your job to build a place that is welcoming and conducive to learning. The environment you create will help your students to understand their roles within the larger communities in which they interact—the school, the community, their clubs and organizations, and so on.

Students Speak Out

Getting students to talk about how they feel in a classroom is not difficult. Students can provide valuable insight that can be helpful as you reflect on your choices regarding classroom space and climate. Using the sentence stems outlined in bold type, the following statements about classroom space and climate were solicited from students throughout the country:

> **I learned** to get along with the other kids in the group I got assigned to. I like to be able to pick my own groups, but our gym teacher assigned us. I got along with this guy I really don't like. (Tia W., twelfth-grade physical education)

> **I didn't like it** when Mr. Dunlap didn't learn my name. He couldn't pronounce my last name, so he didn't even try. It didn't feel good because he knew everyone else's names. (Muhammad N., eighth-grade math)

> **I like it** when we are allowed to sit wherever we want. I have a problem with this girl in my class, and if I was made to sit by her, I would be so mad I wouldn't be able to think. (Jeslyn Z., ninth-grade biology)

> **I want** to bring in something the other kids in my class will like when I present my project. We like to eat, and food would be cool to help me talk about my project in class. (Cody M., sixth-grade speech)

> **I never want** to be treated the way that some people treat this guy in my English class. I feel sorry for him and have mentioned how he is being bullied to my teacher, but I don't think she knows what to do. It's a shame. (Meribeth H., ninth-grade language arts)

CHALLENGE 3

The Teachers' Lounge

Veteran teachers around the country weigh in on issues surrounding classroom space and establishing the climate using the highlighted sentence stems:

I DON'T LIKE THE SMELL OF MY ROOM SO I PUT SMALL AIR FRESHENERS IN THE ELECTRIC SOCKETS! I AM SURPRISED AT HOW MANY PEOPLE COMMENT ON HOW GOOD MY ROOM SMELLS. I THINK IT HELPS THE KIDS TO LEARN.
(E. Gramenez, Rhode Island)

I NEVER REALIZED THAT MY CLASSROOM IS A DIRECT REFLECTION OF MY PHILOSOPHY OF EDUCATION. TECHNOLOGY PROVIDES SO MANY OPPORTUNITIES FOR ME TO CREATE A LEARNING ENVIRONMENT THAT ENCOURAGES KIDS TO LEARN. MY TEACHING EVALUATONS HAVE IMPROVED SINCE I STRATED FOCUSING ON MAKING MY CLASSROOM A MORE INVITING PLACE.
(S. Chronister, III, Florida)

I REMEMBER HEARING THAT YOU SHOULD GIVE STUDENTS WORK THE FIRST DAY OF CLASS. IT SETS THE STANDARD OF BEING SERIOUS AND NOT WASTING TIME.
(W. Narasimham, Massachusetts)

NO ONE TOLD ME HOW MUCH STUDENTS LIKE HAVING REGULAR LAMPS IN THE CLASSROOM RATHER THAN THE FLORESCENT LIGHTS. I BELIEVE THE REASON MY STUDENTS FEEL SO COMFORTABLE IN MY ROOM IS BECAUSE IT REMINDS THEM OF HOME.
(H. J. Butler, Jr., Oregon)

I LEARNED THAT ESTABLISHING A COMPETITIVE SPIRIT BETWEEN SOME OF MY CLASSES WHO ARE WORKING ON THE SAME PROJECTS TENDS TO GET THEM MOTIVATED. I GUESS THEY LIKE COMPETING, AND IT MOTIVATES THEM TO WORK TOGETHER FOR A COMMON GOAL.
(J. Lehman, Illinois)

I WANT THE STUDENTS IN MY CLASS TO FEEL AS IF THEY ARE SAFE AND THAT ALL THEIR COMMENTS AND THOUGHTS ARE VALID. NOTHING IS WORSE THAN FEELING UNCOMFORTABLE FOR A WHOLE YEAR!
(T. Vos, West Virginia)

I LIKE TO CHANGE THE SEATING ARRANGEMENTS IN MY CLASSES ON A REGULAR BASIS. IT'S A LOT MORE WORK FOR ME, BUT IT HELPS STUDENTS GET ACQUAINTED WITH EACH OTHER AND TO EXPECT CHANGE. (D. Grove, Vermont)

MY WORST NIGHTMARE IS HAVING A ROOM WITH NO WINDOWS. I WOULD DIE IF I COULDN'T SEE OUT THE WINDOWS.
(J. Van Ercel, Iowa)

STUDENTS SHOULD BE ENCOURAGED TO PARTICIPATE IN CLASSES. DON'T LET THE SHY ONES JUST SIT.
(D. Connelly, South Carolina)

Teacher Tips

Master teachers have established a repertoire of skills that they draw upon when teaching. Some teachers shared these tips related to classroom space and establishing the climate:

Use color to establish warm centers for discussion, work, and so on. (P. Latillas, New Jersey)

Put personal items around the room to let the students get to know you. (J. Juckett, Delaware)

At the beginning of school, I ask students to write three things on 3″ × 5″ cards that are true and two things that are false. Then I put all the cards in a basket and retrieve one at a time. I read one of the statements, and the students try to figure out who it is and if the statement is true or false. It is a lot of fun, and everyone learns a lot about one another. It helps establish a sense of belonging. (D. Hunziker, Florida)

Be conscious of signs of racial or sexual harassment, whether by you, toward you, or toward members of the class. Make it clear that put-downs or derogatory comments about any group, for whatever reason, are simply not acceptable. (J. Erceg, Maine)

Encourage students to become acquainted by introducing themselves and stating something they have done that they think no one else has ever done. If someone in the class has done it, they must say something else. (L. Behler, Pennsylvania)

I always have the students write on 3″ × 5″ cards what they are feeling the first few days of school. I then ask them to turn the card over and write what they think the teachers are feeling. I record both lists on the chalkboard and compare the lists. Students see that teachers are very similar to students. (M. Blatner, Michigan)

Let students know you're a real person. Share things about yourself with them. (C. Knutson, Alabama)

Just as they say the "customer is always right," students' ideas should always be considered. (K. Hoffman, Colorado)

A Mentor Moment

Having another professional help you with your daily questions about teaching can make your experiences as a teacher even more rewarding. Following is a list of questions you might ask your mentor regarding classroom space and establishing the climate. On the next page is a table you can use to identify those questions you would like to discuss with your mentor. Document your mentor's responses and your thoughts about how to incorporate what you have learned into your practice.

Questions to consider and discuss with your mentor:

- How can I avoid bias in my interaction with students?

- How can I organize, allocate, and manage time, space, and activities in a way that is conducive to learning?

- How can I analyze my classroom environment and interactions and make adjustments to enhance my students' relationships with one another?

- What should I consider when placing students in groups?

- How can I create a comfortable, well-organized physical environment?

- How should I manage my class time, classroom space, and learning activities to ensure that my students are actively engaged in learning?

- How can I create a learning community that respects individual differences?

- How can I use a variety of strategies to increase students' desire and opportunity to learn?

- How often should I change the classroom seating chart or classroom arrangement?

- How can I tell if the students are benefiting from the setup of the classroom?

A Mentor Moment (continued)

Questions for My Mentor	Responses from My Mentor	How to Incorporate Mentor's Ideas into My Practice

A Mentor Moment (continued)

Now that you have thought about the many components of establishing a positive classroom climate, reflect on those ideas from a critical perspective.

■ **What are you learning about classroom space and establishing a positive climate in your classroom?**

My thoughts . . .

■ **Why do you set up your classroom the way you do? Why do you interact with students the way you do? Develop a rationale for each response.**

My rationale . . .

A Mentor Moment (continued)

■ Return to this challenge at a later date and review your rationale (see the preceding item). How has your rationale changed? (You should see growth in your rationale and practice. Include this as part of your early personal professional goals. It helps to see growth and development as you critically reflect on your practice.)

How my rationale has changed . . .

■ Identify an incident in which you blamed yourself for your students' reaction to something related to classroom climate or space. How might you have turned that incident into a positive experience for them and for you?

My ideas . . .

A Mentor Moment (continued)

- Is there any way you might communicate to your students the reflection that you have done regarding this particular incident, practice, or policy. Can you share it with your students so that you may model the process of critical reflection? How might you to present this to the students?

My reflections . . .

- Assuming you were able to share your thinking process with the students, what were their responses?

Student responses . . .

This process is central to the ability to critically reflect on teaching practice. It shows growth and development and can be used as evidence in your teaching portfolio.

CHALLENGE

3

Shared Strategies

Following are some activities and strategies that you might include in your daily practice. You can use these strategies as well as build upon them to create your own.

Diversity

Your attitudes, ideas, and beliefs about learners will be evident as you teach. The language you use conveys your attitudes, ideas, and beliefs, all of which contribute to the classroom climate and environment. Review the following list of words and phrases and evaluate your perspectives on each. Question your ideas and values related to each one. Circle those you want to work on in an attempt to become a better educator and help establish a positive learning environment for your learners.

I CAN'T TEACH YOU BECAUSE YOU ARE . . .

black
brown
yellow
red
white
of interracial background
a Chapter 1/Title I student
not a native English speaker
bilingual
monolingual
Limited English Proficient
a free lunch student
a reduced lunch student
a neighborhood walker
a latch-key kid
an oldest child
a youngest child
a middle child
an only child
fatherless
motherless
homeless
federally connected
a left-brain learner
a right-brain learner
without a brain
of low SES (socioeconomic status)
of high SES
from a rural area

from an urban area
from a suburban area
learning disabled
visually impaired
orthopedically challenged
speech impaired
emotionally disordered
attention deficit–hyperactivity
    disordered
autistic
hearing impaired
lesbian
gay
dyslexic
a hemophiliac
medically fragile
asthmatic
hyperactive
overactive
inactive
slow
backward
basic
a nonreader
illiterate
an underachiever
a gifted underachiever
a migrant
a transient
"at-risk"

a "jail bird"
a ward of the state
an orphan
an adoptee
a truant
the child of middle-aged parents
HIV positive
not immunized
a drop out
born after September 18
not ready for kindergarten
a Head Start recipient
a food stamp recipient
a welfare recipient (Aid to Families
    with Dependent Children —
    AFDC)
a WIC (Women, Infants, and
    Children) program participant
a public housing resident
a Section 8 resident
physically abused
sexually abused
a head trauma victim
wheelchair-bound
paralyzed
afflicted with Down's Syndrome
behaviorally disturbed
emotionally disturbed
educationally deficient
educationally handicapped

From Rodriguez, E. R., & Bellanca, J., *What Is It About Me You Can't Teach? An Instructional Guide for the Urban Educator* (p. 6). © 1996 by IRI/SkyLight Training and Publishing. Reprinted with permission.

Shared Strategies (continued)

School Environment

Many teachers believe that their classrooms are the only places where they have the authority to create the climate. However, seasoned educators know that they play a key role in the climate of the school. Students spend considerable time in the care of teachers and administrators. Following is a list of intrinsic components deemed pertinent to creating a positive school environment:

INTRINSIC COMPONENTS OF CREATING A POSITIVE SCHOOL ENVIRONMENT

Nurturing Needs for Students
Prenatal and postnatal health care
Good nutrition
Adequate housing
Sufficient sleep
Strong and healthy relationships

A Cooperative Environment in School
Cooperation and sharing
Working with others
Multiage schools
Commitment to peers, school, and community

Positive and Lasting Relationships
Connection to family or church
Positive peer relationships
Faculty and staff support
Teams of teachers working together
Long-term cooperative base groups

Monitored Out-of-School Time
Open schools (after hours, weekends, summers)
Alternative place to stay (not streets)
Alternative set of friends (not gangs)

Partnerships
Parents
Community groups
Churches
Public hearing groups
Police
Business

Long-Term Conflict Resolution/Peer Mediation Training
Long-term conflict resolution training (1–2 years)
Training integrated into school life
All students involved
All faculty and staff involved
School culture established
School grounds open to the community

Adapted from Johnson, D. W., & Johnson, R. R., *Reducing Violence Through Conflict Resolution* (pp. 9–12). © 1995 by Association for Supervision and Curriculum Development. Reprinted with permission.

An Amusing Story

One year I had a hard time getting students to realize that I was a real person and able to have a little fun. I tried telling stories and showing cartoons, but they acted as if I were trying too hard to make the class fun for them. I finally decided to walk to the window every couple of minutes and stare into the sky and say, "I know they're out there somewhere." After the third time I did this, the class broke out in hysterical laughter. I finally set the tone that I was going to have some fun while I was teaching. It broke the ice, and before long I was able to gain the students' trust. (C. Jackson, Washington, DC)

Shared Strategies (continued)

What aspects of this list might you contribute to as a beginning teacher?

My thoughts . . .

What relationships and partnerships might you establish with colleagues as you work together to create a positive learning environment for all students?

My thoughts . . .

CHALLENGE 3

Personal Reflection Journal

This challenge encouraged you to think about classroom space and establishing the climate. Identify a situation related to these issues that needs your attention. Follow the steps below to arrive at a desirable solution. Depending on the nature of your situation, you may use this exercise as a benchmark in your development. If so, include this piece in your professional portfolio.

My thoughts . . .

Identify the situation:

↓

Describe the situation:

↓

Whose advice did you seek in finding a creative solution to the situation?

↓   ↓   ↓

What did this person (or these persons) tell you to do?

Personal Reflection Journal (continued)

How did you deal with the situation?

Would you do the same thing if presented with a similar situation?

If yes, why?

If no, why?

What new knowledge or ideas come to mind as you incorporate what you have learned through this experience?

If you were to establish a goal to enhance your personal professional development in this area, what might that be?

How does what you learned compare to other areas of your teaching?

Personal Reflection Journal (continued)

Creating your classroom space and establishing a climate conducive to learning are basic to instruction. The thinking, discussion, and reading you have done will pay off. Think about other aspects of your role as an educator. Outline how you can connect what you have learned to other areas of your teaching. For example, if students cannot see one another or are positioned so that they cannot hear their classmates, it may be difficult to carry out meaningful discussions. Think of another example of how classroom space and climate relates to your instruction.

Upon reflection, what have you learned that will enhance your development as an educator?

How will you integrate your new knowledge into your practice?

How have you become a critical reflective practitioner when determining classroom space and establishing the climate? Develop a clear and concise response that you can include in your professional portfolio.

Consider including this in your professional teaching portfolio.

CHALLENGE
3

Standards

Every school differs in its acceptance of teaching standards. However, it is generally agreed that teachers need to possess a level of competence in order to find success. Because of their generic nature, the Interstate New Teacher Assessment and Support Consortium (INTASC) standards have been identified as a framework for you to use to reflect on your practice as an educator. The INTASC standards that address classroom space and establishing the climate are as follows:

- **PRINCIPLE #2: The teacher understands how children learn and develop, and can provide learning opportunities that support their intellectual, social, and personal development.**

- **PRINCIPLE #3: The teacher understands how students differ in their approaches to learning and creates instructional opportunities that are adapted to diverse learners.**

- **PRINCIPLE #4: The teacher understands and uses a variety of instructional strategies to encourage students' development of critical thinking, problem solving, and performance skills.**

- **PRINCIPLE #5: The teacher uses an understanding of individual and group motivation and behavior to create a learning environment that encourages positive social interaction, active engagement in learning, and self-motivation.**

- **PRINCIPLE #6: The teacher uses knowledge of effective verbal, nonverbal, and media communication techniques to foster active inquiry, collaboration, and supportive interaction in the classroom.**

- **PRINCIPLE #9: The teacher is a reflective practitioner who continually evaluates the effects of his or her choices and actions on others (students, parents, and other professionals in the learning community) and who actively seeks out opportunities to grow professionally.**

- **PRINCIPLE #10: The teacher fosters relationships with school colleagues, parents, and agencies in the larger community to support students' learning and well-being.**

From Interstate New Teacher Assessment and Support Consortium, *Model Standards for Beginning-Teacher Licensing, Assessment, and Development: A Resource for State Dialogue.* © 1992 by Council of Chief State School Officers, Washington, DC. Retrieved November 3, 2004, from http://www.ccsso.org/content/pdfs/corestrd.pdf. Used with permission.

Perhaps your school, district, or national organization has established standards pertinent to your professional development in this area. Review them, and the INTASC principles, to determine which one(s) you have met as a result of working through this challenge. It is not necessary to provide evidence for each standard in each challenge. However, by the time you complete this book, you should have evidence of how you can meet each principle or standard necessary for your portfolio. Document your evidence in the Wrap-Up section of the book.

Reflections Log

Fill out the following log to reflect on your learnings. It might be helpful to refer to the Assessment and Reflections Log at the beginning of the challenge to assess your growth.

What did I learn about classroom space and establishing the climate?

Was I able to accomplish my goals?

How did I overcome the challenges in accomplishing my goals?

Congratulations, You Made It!

Identify something you are proud of related to classroom space and establishing classroom climate that you can incorporate in your professional portfolio. What evidence do you have to show your success? Use the following chart to record your responses.

Situation:

How I handled it:

Evidence to be included in my portfolio:

Consider including this in your professional teaching portfolio.

Classroom Management and Organizational Strategies

CHALLENGE 4

Assessment and Reflections Log

Record your initial beliefs and goals about classroom management and organizational strategies in this log.

My beliefs about <u>classroom management and organizational</u> <u>strategies:</u>

My goal(s) for <u>classroom management and organizational</u> <u>strategies:</u>

How am I going to accomplish my goal(s)?

Who and what can help me?

Challenges to accomplishing my goal(s):

The process or procedure for reaching my goal(s):

Classroom Management and Organizational Strategies

"They didn't teach me about classroom discipline in college."
—First-Year Teacher

Classroom management includes all the daily procedures, situation analysis, leadership, and motivation you use in the classroom to enhance learning. The choices you make regarding each of these issues will determine your success. No doubt you can remember a classroom situation where the teacher successfully managed the procedures, policies, and activities. Likewise, you probably experienced an environment where the issues were handled in a less than desirable manner. Your role is to manage and organize your classroom to maximize student learning. Paying attention to these aspects of your practice is necessary to ensure a positive learning environment. This challenge addresses a variety of strategies to use in developing and maintaining a positive classroom environment.

Spreyer (2002) claims that classroom management refers to *everything,* including who you are, what you are about, what you value, and how you relate to those for whom you have responsibility. Effective classroom management begins with the pattern and procedures you establish on the first days of class. It requires continuous effort by applying appropriate teaching techniques, getting to know your students, determining what knowledge students already possess, and realizing what interest students have in your subject area.

> *Education is not a form of entertainment, but a means of empowering people to take control of their lives.*
>
> —UNKNOWN

Practical Problem

What ought to be done about classroom management and organizational strategies for the classroom? Many beginning teachers express concern about feeling ill-prepared to deal with the complex nature of managing their classrooms, organizational strategies, and the numerous situations in which they will find themselves related to student behavior. If you look into any classroom, you will note that the teacher sets the tone for the activities there by his or her attention to these important components of instruction. Dealing with all of the challenges you face as an educator will encourage you to think of new ways to organize your room, curriculum, and methods to enhance your effectiveness. The answer to this practical problem will be different for every teacher, based on the needs of the learners. Regardless of how you answer the question, it serves as a framework for this challenge. In the space provided, note what you believe should be done about classroom management and organizational strategies for the classroom.

1. **Reflect on your own school experiences related to classroom management. Develop a response to each question or statement:**

   ■ **Do you remember a teacher who rarely had to deal with discipline problems?**

   ■ **How did he or she manage the classroom?**

   ■ **What were the personal qualities of your teachers who managed their classrooms well?**

   ■ **What did your teachers do to help you want to learn and cooperate with your peers?**

   ■ **Relate a story when you got into trouble in the classroom.**

   ■ **Describe a teacher who was organized.**

   ■ **Who was the class troublemaker? Share an amusing incident involving the class troublemaker and consider how you would handle a similar situation.**

Practical Problem (continued)

My reflections . . .

Practical Problem (continued)

2. After reflecting on the preceding questions, answer the following questions:

   ■ What should you do about classroom management and organizational strategies?

My ideas . . .

   ■ Now that you have thought through each of the preceding questions, have any of your ideas changed regarding classroom management and organizational strategies? You may find it useful to discuss your ideas with a mentor, colleague, or peer.

My ideas . . .

CHALLENGE 4

Valued Ends

The following list describes the skills, behaviors, and attitudes associated with teachers who are successful in classroom management and organizational strategies. In the space provided, identify other qualities that you believe are pertinent to successful classroom management and organizational strategies. Also include any expectations or goals your administration has identified related to classroom management and organizational strategies.

Teachers who are successful in classroom management and organizational strategies:

- **Possess a unique individuality with knowledge of a variety of methods, values, and techniques**
- **Are able to facilitate, encourage, and assist in the learning process**
- **Are able to structure meaningful lessons and activities to meet student needs**
- **Establish a sense of order and fairness in dealing with all students**
- **Are able to develop and implement a variety of strategies to promote learning**

Qualities I believe are pertinent to establishing class-room management and organizational strategies: _____

_____

_____

Administration's expectations or goals related to class-room management and organizational strategies: _____

_____

_____

What can I realistically achieve related to classroom management and organizational strategies to be demon-strated in my teaching portfolio? _____

_____

_____

_____

"I am wondering...?"

Every teacher has wrestled with issues related to classroom management and organizational strategies. Questions that other beginning teachers have raised about these issues include:

- How do I manage all the aspects of teaching?
- How do I build positive relationships and manage disruptions in my classes?
- How do I keep accurate records? How do I manage all this information?
- How do I maintain control in my classroom?
- How can I manage my classroom without focusing on the negative?
- How can I understand each student's behavior so that I can be effective in the classroom?
- How can I be an equitable teacher to both boys and girls?
- What resources are available to help me teach students with special needs?
- How do I keep my students involved, listening, and on task in class?
- How do I handle a student who keeps disrupting my class?

In the space that follows, list additional questions you may have about classroom management and organizational strategies, and determine who can answer each question for your situation.

QUESTION	WHO CAN HELP?

CHALLENGE 4

Focus on the Issue

Classroom Management and Organizational Strategies

Research indicates that the most typical problem of the beginning teacher is classroom management (Bullough, 1989). Consequently, the ability to manage your classroom effectively is central to your success as an educator (Applegate et al., 1977). All too often, teachers assume that classroom management and discipline are the same.

Classroom management deals with the procedures, routines, and structure that you establish to manage the classroom. It is your responsibility to set policies and rules and to encourage students to understand and practice those policies and rules.

Discipline, however, is how the students act or behave in your classroom. For you, discipline focuses on your immediate management of a situation caused by a student or group of students. It is your responsibility to establish policies that address situations students create. As students learn procedures, they will establish routines.

When you look carefully at discipline issues you have already faced and will continue to face, you will find that students struggle with a number of issues. They may be seeking attention or power. Or they may be feeling angry or revengeful, which will create a whole different set of problems. Some might fear failure. Most, if not all, of these feelings are developed outside your classroom. They are generally a result of needs not being met in another area of the student's life. Use the mechanisms available to you to learn as much about your students as possible. Knowing their names and a hobby, talent, or special interest may be a way for you to speak to them about what their interests are. Being mindful of those who are targeted, ignored, isolated, and respected will help you understand the classroom culture. Regardless of what drives behavior, it will surely create an abundance of activity!

Students feel most comfortable when they know what is expected of them. As the teacher, you can help by establishing rules and procedures for students to follow. On the next two pages is a list of situations that students may find themselves in—and will want to know what to do. Review the list and indicate (in the right-hand column) what you want students to do in each situation.

> *The secret in education lies in respecting the student.*
> —RALPH WALDO EMERSON

Focus on the Issue (continued)

Classroom Management and Organizational Strategies

My plans . . .

WHAT STUDENTS SHOULD DO WHEN THEY . . .

Enter your classroom	
Prepare for the class (e.g., open books, gather materials, instruments, or pencils, etc.)	
Complete work early	
Have a question	
Want to get your attention	
Work in pairs or groups	
Turn in assignments	
Take tests and exams	
Complete homework assignments	
Need to make up assignments	
Miss a class or a test	

(continued on next page)

Focus on the Issue (continued)

Classroom Management and Organizational Strategies

Need to move around the classroom	
Prepare and clean up from labs	
Look for or put away classroom materials	
Need to use the restroom, visit the nurse's office, or participate in athletic events or need permission to leave the classroom for something else	
Interact in discussions	
Respond to a classroom guest	
Are tardy or have an excused absence	
Exit the classroom	

Consider inviting students to contribute to this list so that they can buy into the process and support your classroom goals.

Focus on the Issue (continued)

Classroom Management and Organizational Strategies

Orlich et al. (1980) describe the classroom as a center for dynamic interactions with numerous individual verbal and nonverbal behaviors. To effectively manage a classroom, you should be able to identify common elements that suggest a systematic way of dealing with instructional and behavioral situations in the classroom. The following table lists four types of common classroom management problems and examples of each.

SELECTED PROBLEMS ASSOCIATED WITH CLASSROOM MANAGEMENT

Problem of Motivation
1. Lack of activity for students
2. Apathetic student attitudes
3. Getting all students involved in activities
4. Uninvolved students
5. Daydreaming

Procedural Problems
1. Unclear assignments given by teacher
2. Moving the class to a different room
3. Establishing a systematic routine for procedural activities
4. Teacher did not reserve a special room or space for the activities
5. Projector or AV equipment not previously checked out
6. Films not previewed by teacher; thus, inappropriate materials presented
7. Necessary materials not available in the room

Instructional Problems
1. A need for variety of instructional techniques
2. Goals or objectives not clearly communicated to students
3. Pace too fast or too slow
4. Students who missed the orientation or prerequisite skills
5. Necessary prerequisites or entry skills not developed; thus, students fail to achieve stated objectives
6. Students who are upset over their evaluation
7. Students not following directions
8. Failure to complete all assignments

Disruptive Problems
1. Excessive talking at the beginning of class
2. Note passing
3. Cheating
4. Stealing
5. Vandalism
6. Students seeking attention
7. Students arriving late for class
8. Teacher making unenforceable threats
9. Racial tensions
10. Teacher making value judgments about students' dress, home life, or parents
11. Obscene verbal or nonverbal gestures

From Orlich, et al., *Teaching Strategies: A Guide to Better Instruction.* ©1980 by D. C. Heath and Company. Used with permission of Houghton Mifflin Company.

Consider the problems identified above and critique one of your own lessons or classes. Identify what you might do to solve the problem. Consider including your reflection and what you intend to do in your teaching portfolio. Don't forget to include how your own action was received by the students.

Focus on the Issue (continued)

Classroom Management and Organizational Strategies

MacDonald (1999) stresses the importance of competent classroom management because it reflects the teacher's ability to purposefully organize group learning activities with minimum confusion and distraction. Usually requiring a firm presence and a strong sense of purpose, the ability to effectively manage a classroom is one of the most important skills of a teacher. MacDonald and Healy can claim that, because every situation is different, it is impossible to develop a list of rules that will work to manage every classroom. However, some standards can be applied for developing and maintaining a positive and productive learning atmosphere in the classroom. Key guidelines and strategies for effective classroom management include:

1. **Anticipate what learning experiences will have meaning for your students and show a sense of confidence in your instruction.**

2. **Be mindful of your attitude when you are teaching. Certainly one who expresses confidence, enthusiasm, and purpose will be perceived differently than a teacher who is uncertain, indifferent, or lacks conviction.**

3. **Be careful not to fall into routines or ruts. If you find what you are doing is boring, so will your students, with predictable behavioral results.**

4. **Determine what is and is not acceptable behavior in your classroom. As the professional you should determine what is reasonable and acceptable group behavior and work at establishing it.**

5. **Learn to keep your finger on the pulse of the class. Move swiftly and purposefully to curb behavior that threatens to distract from the lesson. Do not get in the habit of ignoring minor behavior problems in the hope they will simply go away. In most cases they won't.**

6. **Get students in tune with you before you start teaching. Be careful not to allow slippage here. Do not attempt to talk above the competition. Use pauses, restarts, or lowering of the voice to cause students to attend to your teaching. Walk through exercises periodically with your students to keep them used to working harmoniously with you.**

7. **Learn to use silence to your advantage and learn to cultivate nonverbal communication. Your eyes and gestures are critically important.**

8. **Anticipate likely consequences of what you ask students to do. Try to avoid always being in a reactive (corrective) position with your classes. Learn to use preventive maintenance to keep yourself out of the corrective modes as much as possible.**

9. **When it becomes necessary, use corrective maintenance calmly and confidently, but make it stick. Do not interrupt the whole class to deal with one offender whenever it is possible to avoid doing so.**

10. **Do not put up with chatter in your classes.**

11. **Do not get in the habit of doing classroom management on the run. Take time and care to plan it as a key aspect of your teaching.**

From MacDonald, R. E., *A Handbook for Beginning Teachers* (2nd ed., pp. 220–221). © 1999 by Longman. Reprinted with permission.

Focus on the Issue (continued)

Classroom Management and Organizational Strategies

There is no question that the ability to effectively manage a classroom is not only desirable but indispensable for a successful career in teaching. Henson (1988) identifies motivation and discipline as key survival skills in classroom management. He believes it to be more effective when the teacher concentrates less on specific techniques and more on the general strategies for motivating students. Discipline, according to Henson, plays an essential role in classroom management because each teacher is ultimately responsible for student learning. Teaching and discipline are inseparable, as teachers have tremendous influence on the behavior of students in the classroom. Discipline needs to be a cooperative approach and focused on learning. Learning is central to an organized, well-managed classroom. When students are engaged in relevant coursework and activities, there is less time for them to focus on acting out or misbehaving. Reviewing your course content and adapting it to meet the needs of your learners is imperative to their learning and your management. Students are very similar to adults when presented with information that is irrelevant or not deemed important. They block it out. Guidelines for motivation and discipline in classrooms are listed on the following page. Consider how you might incorporate or transfer some of these ideas into your practice.

> Setting an example is not the main means of influencing another, it is the only means.
> —ALBERT EINSTEIN

Classroom management is one of the keys to your success as a teacher. Success and confidence come with practice. As much as possible, anticipate situations before they appear. Ask your colleagues and teaching mentor for suggestions. An effective classroom sets the stage for learning—one of your primary goals!

Focus on the Issue (continued)

Classroom Management and Organizational Strategies

MOTIVATION AND DISCIPLINE IN CLASSROOM MANAGEMENT

Motivation

1. It is the teacher's responsibility to convince students that the topics under study are worthwhile to the student. This requires basing motivational efforts on the students' perspectives, which may differ from the teacher's.
2. Teachers need not try to compete with the entertainment world. Teachers offer leadership, a quality that middle school and high school students need in their often unstructured lives.
3. Teachers cannot force students to become interested in a lesson. At best, the teacher can only entice student interest.
4. Application is an important avenue to motivation. Teachers should strive to show students how they can apply the content being taught to their daily lives.
5. Involving all students is a great technique, yet teachers and students seldom discuss the purpose of a lesson.
6. Positive student self-concepts are strong motivators, whereas negative concepts work against the teacher's efforts to motivate.
7. Humor holds much potential for motivation. Successful use of humor does not require the teacher to entertain students constantly. By relaxing the classroom atmosphere, the teacher can allow natural humor to develop among the students.
8. Thorough planning and a well-structured lesson will enable teachers to be less formal. A controlled degree of informality can contribute to the motivational level in the classroom.
9. Teacher enthusiasm is an indispensable element in motivation. Teachers can ensure their own excitement by planning into each lesson activities both they and the students will enjoy.
10. Class tempo is important to the motivational level. Students tend to be more highly motivated when the pace of the lesson is fast enough to challenge them but not so fast that it keeps them confused.
11. Goal clarification is essential to motivation. It is only natural that students are more interested when they know what they are doing.
12. Rewards and reinforcement should occur only following success. Therefore, teachers should assign tasks that the students can perform well.
13. Reinforcement should be spaced at varying intervals.
14. Personal teacher-student relationships add to the level of student interest.

Discipline

1. All teachers experience discipline problems.
2. Good classroom discipline is essential for maximum learning. Because the teacher is in charge of instruction, discipline is the teacher's responsibility.
3. Good discipline implies order and control. Quiet is important to the extent that it is essential for order and control and for effective communication.
4. Teachers should begin each year by being firm yet friendly. Classroom humor is desirable, but it must not lead to excessive disruptions.
5. Too many rules can cause added problems. Students should be told why each rule is necessary. Whenever feasible, it is good practice to involve students in setting classroom rules.
6. Consistency and fairness are essential to establishing and maintaining good discipline.
7. The best deterrent to discipline problems is a well-planned and well-executed lesson, with clear goals, that involves all students. Teacher enthusiasm for the lesson contributes to student motivation.
8. Effort is better spent preventing problems than trying to learn how to manage disasters. Although the latter skill may be helpful, few teachers feel they are experts in that area.
9. Teachers should avoid making threats and using sarcasm and public reprimands, because these tend to lower students' self-esteem and self-respect. Instead, teachers should look for opportunities to compliment students, thus helping build positive self-images.
10. When planned and executed correctly, private conferences can be an effective means of handling disruptive students. When private conferences fail, the teacher should arrange a joint conference with the principal, counselor, and parents or guardians.

From Henson, K. T., *Methods and Strategies for Teaching in Secondary and Middle Schools* (pp. 281–282).
© 1988 by Longman. Reprinted with permission.

CHALLENGE 4

Students Speak Out

It's no question that students will be able to offer an opinion about issues surrounding classroom management and organizational strategies. Using the sentence stems outlined in bold type, students throughout the country exclaimed the following statements about classroom management and organizational strategies:

> **I learned** parliamentary procedure from my homeroom teacher last year. She ran our homeroom just like a meeting. Each of us got to be a different part of a group by the end of the year. For two weeks I was the president, the treasurer, the secretary, the vice-president, and the parlimentarian. I have put these skills to work in my role on the student council. (Adam H., tenth-grade)

> **I didn't like** it when my history teacher lectured for thirty minutes and told us to save our questions until the end of her lecture. Sometimes I miss a point or a date or don't hear something right, and it throws me off for the rest of the period. (Callie K., tenth-grade world cultures)

> **I like it** when my teacher told the whole class what the rules are. That way we know exactly what we can get away with. Not all teachers let us do the same things. Sometimes you go to one class and do something and it's cool, and then you go to another class and the teacher gets mad. I think having rules spelled out helps us. (Joon-Wuk K., tenth-grade Spanish)

> **I want** to do well in class, but it is hard because I think my health teacher plays favorites. I feel as if he likes the popular kids in the class and ignores some of us because we aren't the jocks or the popular girls. It makes me upset. I think he grades us differently too. (Tamesha J., eighth-grade health)

> **I never want** to yell to get attention or respect. Our geometry teacher has a lot of trouble keeping some kids from talking and goofing off. She yells at them constantly. It makes it like a game. Her voice is so squeaky and sounds so lame. I don't want to scream like that when I work with people in the real world. (Ericka Z., eleventh-grade geometry)

CHALLENGE 4

The Teachers' Lounge

Veteran teachers often have valuable insight and advice about most education-related issues. When asked about classroom management and organizational strategies, teachers throughout the country responded in the following ways to the highlighted sentence stems:

Students SEEM TO LIKE MY ANSWERING MACHINE MESSAGES. I HAVE A TELEPHONE IN MY ROOM AND CHANGE THE MESSAGE DAILY. I ALWAYS INCLUDE VERY SPECIFIC INSTRUCTIONS REGARDING HOMEWORK AS WELL AS A QUOTE FOR THE DAY. OFTEN I WILL SAY THE ASSIGNMENT WITH MUSIC PLAYING IN THE BACK-GROUND—SOMETHING THAT APPEALS TO THEIR AGE GROUP. SOMETIMES I TELL A JOKE OR A FUNNY STORY. I ASK STUDENTS TO LEAVE ME MESSAGES IF THEY CALL THE ANSWERING MACHINE. I RECORD SOME OF THEIR MESSAGES, ESPE-CIALLY THE ONES WHO HAVE SPENT A LOT OF TIME BEING CREATIVE, AND PLAY THEM WHEN EVERYONE TURNS IN THEIR COMPLETED ASSIGNMENTS ON TIME OR GETS ABOVE A C ON MY TESTS. SOME CALLS COME IN DURING THE WEE HOURS OF THE MORNING! (M. Kempker, Montana)

I NEVER WANT TO MISS MY PROFESSIONAL ASSOCIATION MEETING. I GO TO IT EVERY YEAR. IT IS THE HIGHLIGHT OF MY TEACHING. I GET ALL KINDS OF NEW IDEAS ON HOW TO MANAGE MY CLASSROOM AND GET TO MEET PEOPLE WHO ARE TACKLING THE SAME THINGS I AM. (J. Hobbins, Maryland)

No ONE TOLD ME THAT STUDENTS CAN LEARN EVEN THOUGH THE CLASSROOM IS NOT TOTALLY QUIET. I HAD ALWAYS THOUGHT THAT STUDENTS WHO ARE TALKING ARE DISTRACTING, AND I WOULD ASK THEM TO STOP. WHAT I HAVE LEARNED IS THAT IN SOME CASES THEY ARE SHARING IDEAS AND THOUGHTS THAT ARE REINFORCING WHAT I WANTED THEM TO LEARN. I STOP EVERY ONCE IN A WHILE AND INVITE MY LEARNERS TO TALK OR SHARE WITH A PARTNER. STUDENTS SEEM TO LIKE THIS IDEA AND HAVE TOLD ME HOW MEANINGFUL THE STORIES ARE THAT THEY HAVE HEARD FROM THEIR CLASSMATES. (C. Iwashita, Tennessee)

I REMEMBER OBSERVING A MASTER TEACHER WHO WAS ABLE TO USE HUMOR AS A METHOD TO MAINTAIN CLASSROOM CONTROL AND AVOID CONFLICT. STUDENTS SEEMED TO RESPECT THE FACT THAT HE MEANT BUSINESS BUT WAS ABLE TO SHED LIGHT ON CERTAIN SUBJECTS BY MAKING CONNECTIONS TO SOMETHING AMUSING. (R. Schalinske, New York)

I DON'T LIKE WHEN EVERYTHING IS CLICKING IN MY CLASS, THE STUDENTS ARE HAVING A GREAT TIME, WE ARE LEARNING, AND THEN ... THE BELL RINGS. (J. Grimes, New Mexico)

I WANT TO DEVELOP A COURSE LOGO TO BE PRINTED ON NOTE CARDS AND POSTCARDS FOR CORRESPONDENCE THAT I SEND TO STUDENTS, PARENTS, AND COLLEAGUES. I WANT IT TO PROMOTE MY COURSE AND WHO I AM AS A TEACHER. THAT WAY, I CAN SEND THESE CARDS OUT A FEW WEEKS BEFORE CLASS AND WRITE A PERSONAL NOTE TO MY STUDENTS TO LET THEM KNOW SOME OF THE EXCITING THINGS I HAVE PLANNED FOR THEM DURING THE SEMESTER. (K. Myers-Hagemeister, South Dakota)

I WISH I COULD FIND A WAY TO REMEMBER ALL MY STUDENTS' NAMES EARLIER IN THE SEMESTER. I TEACH ART IN THE JUNIOR HIGH AND HAVE ALL THE STUDENTS IN MY CLASSES. I LIKED BEING CALLED BY NAME BY MY TEACHERS AND WANT TO DO THAT IN MY CLASSES. (B. Gennert, Pennsylvania)

I LEARNED NOT TO ASSIGN DETENTION BASED ON MY INITIAL OBSERVATION OF A SITUATION. SOMETIMES IT GETS FRUSTRATING HANDLING ALL OF MY RESPONSIBILITIES AND MANAGING THE CLASSROOM. HOWEVER, I FOUND THAT ASSIGNING DETENTION WITHOUT GETTING ALL THE FACTS MADE ME APPEAR UNFAIR AND SET UP A CHILLY CLASSROOM CLIMATE FOR MY STUDENTS. (R. Spencer, Ohio)

I LIKE TO BE PREPARED FOR CLASS. I THINK THAT THE MAJORITY OF DISCIPLINE PROBLEMS ARISE FROM NOT KNOWING, WITH ANY DEGREE OF CERTAINTY, WHAT I AM DOING IN CLASS. STUDENTS KNOW WHEN I AM NOT PREPARED, AND THEY TEND TO TAKE ADVANTAGE OF THE TIME. BEING PREPARED IS MY BEST DEFENSE IN MANAGING MY CLASSROOM. (B. Bortlab, Arizona)

Teacher Tips

Master teachers have established a repertoire of skills that they draw upon when teaching. Some teachers shared these tips related to classroom management and organizational strategies:

My seventh-grade geography classes have an atlas under every desk. Most days there is a geography question or two, and they must use the atlas to find the info. (B. Ellis, Indiana)

I use a nonverbal cue, such as a bell, to recapture student attention if they are working in groups. (S. Snow, Maryland)

Wooden or plastic clothespins labeled with students' names in a painted coffee can be used in a variety of ways. (A. Becker, Wyoming)

To motivate my students to submit their homework on time, I choose a secret word that I want them to know or learn. Sometimes I choose words that are difficult or that may be obscure places in the world. Every day that the entire class hands in homework, they get one letter of this word on the chalkboard. When the word is completed, the class decides how they want to celebrate. Their ideas are listed, and we decide on a celebration plan. (D. Roehr, Oregon)

When students raise their hands, I have them use a number code. One finger up means "I have to go to the restroom." Two fingers up means "I need to sharpen my pencil." Three fingers up means "I need help." You will be amazed at how much easier your day will go! (C. Pearson, New Mexico)

I develop a classroom management plan with my students. Routines are comforting to students because they know exactly what to expect. It establishes a sense of familiarity. Plan strategies and a routine for collecting and/or distributing papers, turning in assignments, and doing other record-keeping tasks. (J. Mattingly, Texas)

You can lose credibility if you send a student to the principal's office and he or she comes back without being disciplined. Be sure you know the school disciplinarian's policy on students being sent out of class. (V. Van Vorhees, Iowa)

I put the name of our mascot on the chalkboard in capital letters. If students in the class are behaving well and staying on task, I don't do anything. However, if they begin to get out of hand and unruly, I erase a letter of the mascot name. When they get back on task, I add a letter to the mascot name that I erased earlier. At the end of the week if the name is complete, I give the class a surprise. (F. Trost, Nebraska)

CHALLENGE 4

A Mentor Moment

Your mentor will no doubt be the person who can help you the most regarding classroom management and organizational strategies. A mentor teacher offers the following idea:

■ **Set the stage for an exciting classroom by positioning a clean chalkboard or dry-erase board on a stand outside your doorway. Each day, write something different on the board, such as a quote, a riddle, a joke, a "this-day-in-history" event, a mind-bender question, or just a nice thought. If the message needs an answer, write it on the board inside your classroom. Be sure to write something new each day to keep student attention. Your students will look forward to reading what you've written and will enter your classroom thinking! (V. Henry, Virginia)**

Having another professional help you with your daily questions about teaching can make your experiences as a teacher even more rewarding. Following is a list of questions you might ask your mentor regarding classroom management and organizational strategies. On the next page is a table you can use to identify those questions you would like to discuss with your mentor. Document your mentor's responses and your thoughts about how to incorporate what you have learned into your practice.

Questions you might ask your mentor to help you improve your classroom management and organizational abilities:

■ **How can I create effective communication between my students?**

■ **What rules and procedures should be developed in conjunction with teaching strategies that will help students meet their personal and academic needs?**

■ **How can I enhance student dignity and self-esteem?**

■ **What should I do to encourage students to be responsible for their behavior?**

■ **How do I find out if I have students with special needs in my classroom?**

■ **What resources are available to learn about different types of discipline?**

A Mentor Moment (continued)

Questions for My Mentor	Responses from My Mentor	How to Incorporate Mentor's Ideas into My Practice

A Mentor Moment (continued)

By taking the time to focus on the issues surrounding classroom management and organizational strategies and relating your experiences in those areas of your practice will help you to become a critical reflective practitoner.

- **Outline why you believe what you do about classroom management and organizational strategies. Be specific.**

My ideas and beliefs:

- **Develop a rationale for your actions in this area. If necessary, identify a specifc example.**

My rationale . . .

A Mentor Moment (continued)

- Return to this challenge at a later date and review your rationale (see the preceding item). How has your rationale changed? (You should see growth in your rationale and practice. Include this exercise as part of your yearly personal professional plan or teaching portfolio. It will help you to critically reflect on your practice.)

How my rationale has changed . . .

- Identify an incident in which you blamed yourself for your students' reaction to a decision you made regarding classroom management. How might you have turned that incident into a positive experience for them and for you?

My ideas . . .

A Mentor Moment (continued)

■ Is there any way you might communicate to your students the reflection that you have done regarding this particular incident, practice, or policy? Can you share it with your students so that you may model the process of critical reflection? How might you present this to the students?

My reflections . . .

■ Assuming you were able to share your thinking process with the students, what were their responses?

Student responses . . .

This process is central to the ability to critically reflect on teaching practice. It shows growth and development and can be used as evidence in your teaching portfolio.

CHALLENGE 4

Shared Strategies

Following are some activities and strategies that you might include in your daily practice. You can use these strategies as well as build upon them to create your own.

Classroom Procedures

Review the following procedures and check the ones your students will need to know and practice.

CLASSROOM PROCEDURES—DO STUDENTS KNOW WHAT IS EXPECTED OF THEM FOR ROUTINE OPERATIONS?

A. Beginning the Class

❏ How should students enter the room?

❏ What constitutes being late? (in the room, in the seat)

❏ How and when will absentee slips be handled?

❏ What type of seating arrangements will be used? (assigned seats, open seating, cooperative group seating)

❏ How will the teacher get students' attention to start class? (the tardy bell, a signal such as a raised hand, lights turned off and on)

❏ How will students behave during Public Address (PA) announcements?

❏ Others:

_____

_____

_____

_____

_____

B. Classroom Management

❏ How and when will students leave their seats?

❏ What do students need in order to leave the room? (individual passes, room pass, teacher's permission)

❏ How will students get help from the teacher? (raise hands, put name on board, ask other group members first)

❏ What are acceptable noise levels for discussion, group work, seat work?

❏ How should students work with other students or move into cooperative groups? (moving desks, changing seats, noise level, handling materials)

❏ How will students be recognized to talk? (raised hand, teacher calls on student, talk out)

❏ How do students behave during presentations by other students?

(continued on next page)

Shared Strategies (continued)

CLASSROOM PROCEDURES (continued)

❑ How do students get supplies?

❑ How and when do students sharpen pencils?

❑ How will students get materials or use special equipment?

❑ Others:

_____

_____

_____

_____

_____

C. Paperwork

❑ How will students turn in work? (put in specific tray or box, pass to the front, one student collects)

❑ How will students turn in makeup work if they were absent? (special tray, give to teacher, put in folder, give to teacher's aide)

❑ How will students distribute handouts? (first person in row, a group member gets a copy for all group members, students pick up as they enter room)

❑ How will late work be graded? (no penalty, minus points, zero, F, use lunch or recess to finish, turn in by end of day, drop so many homework grades)

❑ How and when will students make up quizzes and tests missed? (same day they return to school, within 24 hours, within the week, before school, during lunch or recess, after school)

❑ How will late projects such as research papers, portfolios, and artwork be graded? (no penalty, minus points, lowered letter grade, no late work accepted)

❑ Others:

_____

_____

_____

_____

_____

D. Dismissal from Class or School

❑ How are students dismissed for lunch?

❑ When do students leave class for the day? (when bell rings, when teacher gives the signal)

❑ Can students stay after class to finish assignments, projects, tests?

❑ Can the teacher keep one student or the whole class after class or school?

❑ What do students do during fire and disaster drills?

❑ Others:

_____

_____

_____

_____

(continued on next page)

Shared Strategies (continued)

CLASSROOM PROCEDURES (continued)

E. Syllabus or Course Outline

❑ How are students made aware of course objectives?

❑ How are students made aware of course requirements?

❑ Are students given due dates for major assignments several weeks in advance?

❑ Are students told how they will be evaluated and given the grading scale?

❑ Others:

_____

_____

_____

_____

_____

F. Other Procedures

You may need to introduce procedures related to recess, assemblies, guest speakers, substitute teachers, field trips, fire drills, teacher leaving the room, etc. List other procedures that are needed.

Recess

❑ _____

❑ _____

❑ _____

❑ _____

❑ _____

Assemblies

❑ _____

❑ _____

❑ _____

❑ _____

❑ _____

Guest Speakers

❑ _____

❑ _____

❑ _____

❑ _____

❑ _____

Substitute Teachers

❑ _____

❑ _____

❑ _____

❑ _____

❑ _____

(continued on next page)

Shared Strategies (continued)

CLASSROOM PROCEDURES (continued)

Field Trips

- ❏ _____
- ❏ _____
- ❏ _____
- ❏ _____
- ❏ _____

Fire Drills

- ❏ _____
- ❏ _____
- ❏ _____
- ❏ _____
- ❏ _____

Adapted from Burke, K. (Ed.)., *Mentoring Guidebook Level 1: Starting the Journey* (pp. 245–246). © 2002 by SkyLight Professional Development. Reprinted with permission.

An Amusing Story

I have one class on Friday afternoons where I can't seem to keep the students quiet or focused. I have tried everything to keep them on task. Week after week I developed these elaborate plans to get them involved and keep them so busy that they don't have time to chatter with one another. One day the noise was so loud that I had to shout louder than students are normally accustomed to hearing me speak. I frightened myself at how loud I was and was sure the noise would stop after I raised my voice to this degree. To my amazement, nothing happened. I was shocked. One young man in the front row continued to work on his project, but I overheard him say, "I think you're going to have to work on your yelling skills this weekend." (J. Hardy, Pennsylvania)

The Newspaper Model

Sometimes students need to be involved in classroom management and will want to contribute to creating a positive environment whereby everyone has an opportunity to learn and grow. The Newspaper Model on the next page can be used for a variety of experiences in your classroom. You might want to consider using it to help students determine what ought to be done regarding a discipline problem in which they were a part. Consider what you will do once both students have completed the form. You may want to copy the form and include it in each students' personal folder for an accurate record of a specific incident.

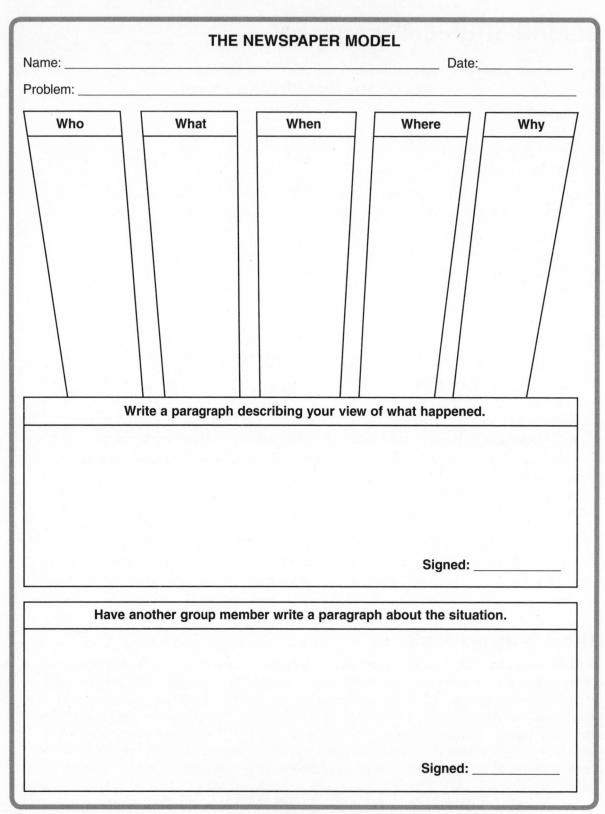

THE NEWSPAPER MODEL

Name: _____ Date:_____

Problem: _____

Who	What	When	Where	Why

Write a paragraph describing your view of what happened.

Signed: _____

Have another group member write a paragraph about the situation.

Signed: _____

From Burke, K. (Ed.)., *Mentoring Guidebook Level 1: Starting the Journey* (p. 314). © 2002 by SkyLight Professional Development. Reprinted with permission.

Personal Reflection Journal

This challenge encouraged you to think about classroom management and organizational strategies. Identify a present situation related to classroom management and organizational strategies that needs your attention. Follow the steps below to arrive at a desirable solution. Depending on the nature of your situatioin, you may use this exercise as a benchmark in your development. If so, include this piece in your professional teaching portfolio.

My thoughts . . .

Identify the situation:

↓

Describe the situation:

↓

Whose advice did you seek in finding a creative solution to the situation?

↓   ↓   ↓

What did this person (or these persons) tell you to do?

Personal Reflection Journal (continued)

How did you deal with the situation?

Would you do the same thing if presented with a similar situation?

If yes, why?

If no, why?

What new knowledge or ideas come to mind as you incorporate what you have learned through this experience?

If you were to establish a goal to enhance your personal professional development in this area, what might that be?

How does what you learned compare to other areas of your teaching?

Personal Reflection Journal (continued)

Classroom management and organizational strategies are basic to instruction. The thinking, discussion, and reading you have done will pay off. Think about other aspects of your role as an educator. Outline how you can connect what you have learned about classroom space and establishing the climate to other areas of your teaching. For example, if students cannot see one another or are positioned so that they cannot hear their classmates, it may be difficult to carry out meaningful discussions. Think of another example of how classroom management and organizational strategies relate to your instruction.

Upon reflection, what have you learned that will enhance your development as an educator?

How will you integrate your new knowledge into your practice?

How have you become a critical reflective practitioner in the area of classroom management and organizational strategies? Develop a clear and concise response that you can include in your professional portfolio.

 Consider including this in your professional teaching portfolio.

Standards

Every school differs in its acceptance of teaching standards. However, it is generally agreed that teachers need to possess a level of competence in order to find success. Because of their generic nature, the Interstate New Teacher Assessment and Support Consortium (INTASC) standards have been identified as a framework for you to use to reflect on your practice as an educator. The INTASC standards that address classroom management and organizational strategies are as follows:

- **PRINCIPLE #2: The teacher understands how children learn and develop, and can provide learning opportunities that support their intellectual, social, and personal development.**

- **PRINCIPLE #3: The teacher understands how students differ in their approaches to learning and creates instructional opportunities that are adapted to diverse learners.**

- **PRINCIPLE #4: The teacher understands and uses a variety of instructional strategies to encourage students' development of critical thinking, problem solving, and performance skills.**

- **PRINCIPLE #5: The teacher uses an understanding of individual and group motivation and behavior to create a learning environment that encourages positive social interaction, active engagement in learning, and self-motivation.**

- **PRINCIPLE #6: The teacher uses knowledge of effective verbal, nonverbal, and media communication techniques to foster active inquiry, collaboration, and supportive interaction in the classroom.**

- **PRINCIPLE #7: The teacher plans instruction based upon knowledge of subject matter, students, the community, and curriculum goals.**

- **PRINCIPLE #8: The teacher understands and uses formal and informal assessment strategies to evaluate and ensure the continuous intellectual, social, and physical development of the learner.**

- **PRINCIPLE #9: The teacher is a reflective practitioner who continually evaluates the effects of his or her choices and actions on others (students, parents, and other professionals in the learning community) and who actively seeks out opportunities to grow professionally.**

- **PRINCIPLE #10: The teacher fosters relationships with school colleagues, parents,**

From Interstate New Teacher Assessment and Support Consortium, *Model Standards for Beginning Teacher Licensing, Assessment, and Development: A Resource for State Dialogue.* © 1992 by Council of Chief State School Officers, Washington DC. Retrieved November 3, 2004, from http://www.ccsso.org/content/pdfs/corestrd.pdf. Used with permission.

Perhaps your school, district, or national organization has established standards pertinent to your professional development in this area. Review them, and the INTASC principles, to determine which one(s) you have met as a result of working through this challenge. It is not necessary to provide evidence for each standard in each challenge. However, by the time you complete this book, you should have evidence of how you can meet each principle or standard necessary for your portfolio. Document your evidence in the Wrap-Up section of the book.

Reflections Log

Fill out the following log to reflect on your learnings. It might be helpful to refer to the Assessment and Reflections Log at the beginning of the challenge to assess your growth.

What did I learn about <u>classroom management and organizational strategies</u>?

Was I able to accomplish my goals?

How did I overcome the challenges in accomplishing my goals?

Congratulations, You Made It!

Identify something you are proud of related to your classroom management or organizational strategies that you can incorporate in your professional portfolio. What evidence do you have to show your success? Use the following chart to record your responses.

Situation:

How I handled it:

Evidence to be included in my portfolio:

📁 **Consider including this in your professional teaching portfolio.**

Instruction

Assessment and Reflections Log

Record your initial beliefs and goals about instruction in this log.

My beliefs about <u>instruction</u>:

My goal(s) for <u>instruction</u>:

How am I going to accomplish my goal(s)?

Who and what can help me?

Challenges to accomplishing my goal(s):

The process or procedure for reaching my goal(s):

CHALLENGE
5

Instruction

"What if they don't listen to my lecture?"

–First-Year Teacher

Instruction has two main components: teaching and learning. Teaching refers to what the teacher does. It includes all the methods and strategies teachers use to set the stage for learning. Good teaching claims to have at least three parts: (1) capturing interest, (2) the actual teaching, and (3) reflection on the experiences for enhanced understanding, reinforcement, and retention. Learning involves all the mental and physical experiences a student has that help him or her understand and retain your instruction.

When you start to deliver the what, when, where, why, and how of a subject to students, the basic question you should ask yourself is, "What should they learn?" By taking time to focus on this question at this point in your planning, you help to ensure that the teaching strategies and activities you select for this group of lessons will be consistent with the learning you hope your students will achieve. Subject matter should be organized logically to make it easy for students to follow. You will have a mix of auditory, visual, and kinetic learners with a wide range of abilities in your classroom. Therefore, you must take into account the students' varied learning styles, preferences, and abilities.

It is important to identify the main concepts of your lesson at the early stages of your instruction to avoid confusion among students about the goal of your lesson. Once you have identified your primary concept, you can focus on other concepts. For example, you can teach thinking skills at the same time you are teaching the content of your subject. Unit purposes, content, and student levels are all important for you to consider when planning instruction.

> *Nine-tenths of education is encouragement.*
>
> —ANATOLE FRANCE

CHALLENGE 5

Practical Problem

What ought to be done to encourage instruction in schools? All teachers are faced with this question as they plan for and teach their classes. The answer to this practical problem will differ for each professional based on his or her philosophy of education. Regardless of how you answer the question, it serves as a framework for this challenge. In the space provided, note what you believe should be done to encourage good instruction in schools.

1. **Reflect on your own experience as a student and the memories you have regarding instruction. Develop a response to each question:**

   ■ **Name a teacher who really got his or her message across to you.**

   _____

   ■ **What instructional strategies worked best for you as a student?**

   _____

   ■ **What did your most favorite teachers do differently from other teachers that made their classes more exciting for you?**

   _____

   ■ **Remember a class that you really enjoyed. What made it so enjoyable?**

   _____

   ■ **Recall a class that you really disliked. What made it so disappointing?**

   _____

   ■ **Who were your most favorite teachers?**

   _____

   ■ **What teacher most influenced you?**

   _____

   ■ **Who was the teacher that most of the students in the school liked?**

   _____

   ■ **Recall your most difficult class. Why was it so difficult?**

   _____

Practical Problem (continued)

My reflections . . .

Practical Problem (continued)

2. After reflecting on the preceding questions, answer the following questions:

- What should be done in regards to instruction in education in general. What are some of the roadblocks and pitfalls of instruction in schools today? (Example: I believe that teachers should have a variety of techniques that meet the unique learning styles of a diverse student population.)

My ideas . . .

- Now that you have thought through each of these questions, what do you now believe about instruction? You may find it useful to discuss your ideas with a mentor, colleague, or peer.

My ideas . . .

CHALLENGE 5

Valued Ends

The following list describes some of the skills, actions, and attitudes associated with teachers who are successful in instruction. In the space provided, identify other qualities that you believe are pertinent to successful instruction. Also include any expectations or goals your administration has identified related to instruction.

Teachers who are successful in instruction:

- Have accurate perceptions about learners
- Effectively use knowledge
- Assist learners to discover personal meaning using the content, their experiences, and prior knowledge
- Accurately discern the purpose and process of learning
- Use appropriate teaching methods and strategies
- Recognize individuality

Qualities I believe are pertinent to successful instruction: _____

_____

_____

Administration's expectations or goals related to instruction: _____

_____

_____

What can I realistically achieve related to instruction to be demonstrated in my teaching portfolio? _____

_____

_____

"I am wondering...?"

Teaching and learning are central to what happens during the school day. Teaching is the cornerstone of your purpose as an educator, and student learning is the end result. Teachers are constantly asking and reflecting on their practice to determine if they are effective. Questions that other beginning teachers have raised about instruction include:

- **How do I know if I am really teaching anything?**
- **What should I do to improve my teaching abilities?**
- **What can I do to vary my instruction?**
- **Might I ever encounter a student who is unable to learn?**
- **Where do I get good ideas about instruction?**
- **How do I determine which textbook is best for my students?**
- **How successful are cooperative learning activities?**
- **How can I motivate the unmotivated student?**
- **What is the importance of critical thinking, and how can I encourage my students to use critical thinking skills?**
- **Where can I find resources to teach students for whom English is a second language?**

In the space that follows, list additional questions you may have about instruction, and determine who can answer each question for your situation.

QUESTION	WHO CAN HELP?

CHALLENGE 5

Focus on the Issue

Instruction

Instruction includes everything that you do as a teacher before, during, and after the students are in your classroom. You are teaching constantly by your example, the lessons you prepare, the way you assess student learning, and the way you analyze what you are doing to become more effective. Most researchers agree that students respond to what they perceive as important (e.g., Fraser & Fisher, 1982; Knight & Waxman, 1990; Winne & Marx, 1977). The task, then, is to find creative ways to determine what is important to students and a means to deliver the knowledge and activities that will result in the desired learning.

In addition, research also indicates that one of the most important factors affecting student learning is the teacher. Wright (1997) notes that students who learn from an ineffective teacher show inadequate progress academically no matter how similar or different they are in terms of their academic ability. Marzano, Pickering, and Pollock (2005) also claim that the overall quality of education can be enhanced with teacher improvement. Your effectiveness is key to the success of your learners. The ability to self-critique and make appropriate change enhances your success in the classroom and increases student achievement.

The chart on the following page shows how to apply instructional strategies to the beginning, middle, and end of a unit.

A practical way to enhance instruction at the beginning of an assignment is to give clear directions. Following are guidelines for giving directions:

METHODS FOR GIVING CLEAR DIRECTIONS

Teachers should:

1. **Give precise directions. Instructions should include statements about**

   (a) **what students will be doing,**

   (b) **why they are doing it,**

   (c) **how they can obtain assistance,**

   (d) **what to do with completed work, and**

   (e) **what to do when they finish.**

   It is also helpful to indicate how much time they will spend on the task. This direction may include a statement about when the work can be completed if it cannot be finished within the designated time limits.

2. **Describe the desired quality of the work. This can increase students' sense of accountability and decrease their anxiety.**

3. **After giving instructions, have students paraphrase the directions, state any problems that might occur to them, and make a commitment.**

4. **Positively accept students' questions about directions.**

5. **Place directions where they can be seen and referred to by students.**

6. **Have students write out instructions before beginning an activity.**

7. **When students seem to be having difficulty following directions, consider breaking tasks into smaller segments.**

Focus on the Issue (continued)

Instruction

STAGE OF UNIT	USING THE NINE CATEGORIES IN INSTRUCTIONAL PLANNING
Instructional Strategies for Use at the Beginning of a Unit	**Setting Learning Goals** 1. Identify clear learning goals. 2. Allow students to identify and record their own learning goals.
Instructional Strategies for Use During a Unit	**Monitoring Learning Goals** 1. Provide students feedback and help them self-assess their progress toward achieving their goals. 2. Ask students to keep track of their achievement of the learning goals and of the effort they are expending to achieve the goals. 3. Periodically celebrate legitimate progress toward learning goals. **Introducing New Knowledge** 1. Guide students in identifying and articulating what they already know about the topics. 2. Provide students with ways of thinking about the topic in advance. 3. Ask students to compare the new knowledge with what is known. 4. Have students keep notes on the knowledge addressed in the unit. 5. Help students represent the knowledge in nonlinguistic ways, periodically sharing these representations with others. 6. Ask students to work sometimes individually, but other times in cooperative groups. **Practicing, Reviewing, and Applying Knowledge** 1. Assign homework that requires students to practice, review, and apply what they have learned; however, be sure to give students explicit feedback on the accuracy of all homework. 2. Engage students in long-term projects that involve generating and testing hypotheses. 3. Ask students to revise the linguistic and nonlinguistic representations of knowledge in their notebooks as they refine their understanding of the knowledge.
Instructional Strategies for Use at the End of a Unit	**Helping Students Determine How Well They Have Achieved Their Goals** 1. Provide students with clear assessments of their progress on each learning goal. 2. Have students assess themselves on each learning goal and compare these assessments with those of the teacher. 3. Ask students to articulate what they have learned about the content and about themselves as learners.

Adapted from Marzano, R. J., Pickering, D. J., & Pollock, J. E., *Classroom Instruction That Works: Research-Based Strategies for Increasing Student Achievement* (pp. 147–154). © 2005 by Merrill Prentice Hall. Reprinted with permission.

Focus on the Issue (continued)
Instruction

   8. **Give directions immediately prior to the activity the directions describe.**

   9. **Model the correct behavior. If students have been asked to raise their hands before answering, raise your hand while answering the question.**

 10. **Hand out worksheets or outlines before taking a field trip.**

Adapted from Jones, V. F., & Jones, L. S., *Comprehensive Classroom Management: Creating Communities of Support and Solving Problems* (7th ed., p. 284). © 2004 by Allyn and Bacon. Reprinted with permission.

Praising students for their efforts and accomplishments is fundamental to good instruction. Following is a list of words or phrases that you might consider including in your repertoire to recognize student achievement:

Wow!	**Good try!**	**You're doing fine!**
Terrific!	**Excellent!**	**Thank you!**
That's great!	**I appreciate . . . !**	**Yes!**
Fantastic!	**Tremendous!**	**Exactly!**
Superb!	**Hurray!**	**Correct!**
Good job!	**Way to go!**	**You did it!**
Nice going!	**Keep it up!**	**Congratulations!**
Awesome!	**Great effort!**	**Perfect!**

Students come to our classrooms with an established set of beliefs about people and events. They bring experiences from a multitude of places that shed light onto the subject matter. According to Eisner (1985, p. 22), students consistently share that they "learn more than they are taught and teachers teach more than they know."

Beginning teachers often become frustrated when they are doing the best possible job they can do and they still don't find the success they expect from their students or from themselves. Taking a look at what you might be doing to hinder your instruction may help you. Several roadblocks to feeling confident about your instruction include:

- Your materials weren't ready.
- You couldn't find something you needed for the lesson.
- Your students finished early and you had nothing else for them to do.
- You didn't have anything planned for the day and were winging it.

These traps will negatively impact and ultimately hurt your effectiveness and your students' success.

CHALLENGE
5

Students Speak Out

High school graduates have experienced 12 years of different instructors. The following sentence stems (highlighted in bold) were completed by students when asked about their instruction:

> **I learned** a lot more when I was allowed to pick the assignment I wanted to do. I don't like to take notes and listen to boring teachers. My science teacher lets us choose our own projects, and we get graded on how we do. I wasn't compared to Hannah, who always gets good grades. I felt like I was graded for my own individual work, by myself, and not compared to her because she did another project by herself. I did a good job. I liked that a lot. (Trevina G., ninth-grade science)

> **I didn't like** it when she just talked and didn't show us on the overhead or the board. I was lost the whole period, so I just sat there and counted the number of times she said, "OK." (Rubin Z., tenth-grade literature)

> **I like it** when we read books that have to do with the things we are talking about in our class. I read this biography of Princess Di, and it helped me to understand England and what we were studying in our book. Everyone in the class got to pick the book they wanted to read, and then we all had to talk on Fridays about what we learned. I think I learned more from everyone else in that class than I did by reading the textbook. (Ean-Chee C., eighth-grade world cultures)

> **I want** to become a teacher. I like learning and all the things that Ms. Weeks teaches us. I like seeing how to apply things to my life. I like actually going into the community and doing the things we talk about in class. I think it helps me to get a better idea of what is going on in the world. (Amber A., twelfth-grade family and consumer sciences)

> **I never want** to bore people the way I get bored in my history class. My teacher keeps talking about things that mean nothing to me. I think he should tell us how all this stuff he is talking about has changed people's lives or made an impact or something I care about. I think I would pay attention more if I saw some connection to my life. I want to know the meaning behind why things happened and how those things affected the people at that time. Drama. I care about drama. I want to understand people. (Natalie S., eleventh-grade history)

The Teachers' Lounge

Instruction is central to the teaching role. When asked about instruction, teachers throughout the country responded to the highlighted sentence stems in the following ways:

<u>No one told me</u> that how students do on tests may have as much to do with my effectiveness as an educator as it does with their ability. I had always blamed students for not doing well but have learned that they may not have understood my teaching. If I see that students are not learning early on, I reteach my lessons in a different way. I took a seminar using Gardner's multiple intelligences and that helped me considerably. (E. Millihan, North Dakota)

<u>I want</u> to get all my lessons on PowerPoint™ so that I can send the lectures to each of my students via e-mail. Then, they can print the lecture before coming to class and fill in the blanks. Those who miss class can have an outline of what we did to keep in their notebooks. (M. Hoover, Idaho)

<u>I wish</u> we had more time to plan and work together as teachers. Everyone seems to come to school and just go into the classroom and do what they have to. My free period is spent grading papers and preparing for class. I would like to find out what other teachers are doing in some of the other courses because I think we could do more collaborative work. (S. Gates, Virginia)

<u>I never want</u> to go back to the time when we didn't have technology in the classroom. I use the television, the computer, the Internet, the Elmo, the stereo—everything to help me to be an effective teacher. I love having the world at my fingertips for the students, and I think they appreciate it. (E. Frederickson, Rhode Island)

<u>Students</u> don't always perform well in small groups. I used to get confused with cooperative learning and group work. I don't anymore because I took a seminar on cooperative learning. The one thing I learned is that you can't give everyone in a group the same grade. You have to find a way to assess each learner. I like cooperative learning. (V. Geraldo, Mississippi)

<u>I like</u> when I order something different for my classroom, and it works. I have been focusing on using games as a way of instruction for some of my learners. I am amazed at how the students seem to like them and they look forward to playing them and learning. It is exciting to see the enthusiasm they generate. (M. Adams, Missouri)

<u>I learned</u> how to have a variety of different things going on in my classroom at the same time so that students have an opportunity to select the way they want to learn. As long as learning is taking place, I feel like I am successful. (J. Neuman, Nebraska)

<u>I don't like</u> that my classes are so large that I can't get to know my students personally and establish any kind of relationship with them. I only see the students for two hours a week, and I have every student in the building. I wish things were different, but this is the way it is at the moment. (H. Donovan, Georgia)

Teacher Tips

Master teachers have established a repertoire of skills that they draw upon when teaching. Some teachers shared these tips related to instruction:

I post the objectives for each of my classes on the Web for students and parents to view. This way everyone knows what I am trying to accomplish in each class that I teach. Having the opportunity to view these objectives ahead of time has encouraged students to be self-directed and bring something to class to contribute to the learning. I have often had parents call to ask if they might provide support or help in an area where they see they can make a contribution. (R. Rohrbaugh, Kentucky)

I find that students learn more when I explain exactly what they are supposed to learn and then demonstrate the steps needed to accomplish a particular task. (J. Ridgely, Idaho)

My students seem to be more motivated if they perceive value in what they are learning. (E. Batt, Georgia)

Use a panel of experts rather than just one guest speaker. Students can see how professionals and adults interact and communicate. (Y. Berkett, Nebraska)

Let students brainstorm ideas for how to present the topics. It seems they show more respect for what they are a part of. (S. Casidy, Iowa)

Use role playing! The more scenarios and activities you can use to break the time into sections, the more likely you are to keep their attention. (D. Dunaway, Virginia)

Move from the simple to the complex, but let the students know what the "big picture" is so they know where you're going. (M. Cooney, Kansas)

I use as many visuals as I can to help students learn. With digital cameras, it's easy to take photographs to show examples. I ask students to share their photos with me too. I have collected a tremendous number of examples to share with my students. (W. Kotzman, Florida)

A Mentor Moment

All teachers find it useful to talk with one another about their roles. It provides an opportunity to vent, see things from different perspectives, and get new ideas. Your mentor will help you as you evaluate yourself in the area of instruction. A mentor teacher offers the following comments in regard to instruction:

> ■ We all know that teachers have a tendency to teach the way they have experienced teaching. What they see modeled is what they think works. In most cases, it worked for them because they selected teaching and are now part of the profession. However, the best advice I have about instruction is that you really have to reach outside your comfort zone and try some things that you have never done before. Don't let other teachers scare you because they tried the same technique and it flopped. It might work beautifully for you and your students. One teacher decided to try five new teaching strategies each semester over the course of a year—not just new ideas, but brand-new strategies. The teacher reported that it was his best year because he was growing and exploring, and the students appreciated his willingness to work with them in trying to make the subject more interesting. (C. Doyle, Montana)

Having another professional help you with your daily questions about teaching can make your experiences as a teacher even more rewarding. Following is a list of questions you might ask your mentor regarding instruction. On the next page is a table you can use to identify those questions you would like to discuss with your mentor. Document your mentor's responses and your thoughts about how to incorporate what you have learned into your practice.

Questions you might ask your mentor to help improve your instruction:

■ How do I successfully use a variety of teaching strategies in my classroom?

■ Where do I find free materials to support my teaching?

■ How do I find out about innovative ideas for incorporating computers into my lesson plans?

■ Where can I find new supplemental materials for my class?

■ Are there policies I need to be aware of when using copyrighted materials in my classroom?

■ What does it mean when they say that everyone's teaching style is different?

> *To teach is to learn twice.*
> —JOSEPH JOUBERT

A Mentor Moment (continued)

Questions for My Mentor	Responses from My Mentor	How to Incorporate Mentor's Ideas into My Practice

A Mentor Moment (continued)

Now that you have had time to focus on your questions about instruction with a mentor, think about what you have learned in relation to being a critical reflective practitioner.

- **Why do you teach the way you do? Develop a rationale for your teaching. If you have completed Challenge 2, refer to the philosophy statement you developed about curriculum. You may go back and change your philosophy statement now that you have considered other possibilities and have had an opportunity to teach. If you have not yet developed a philosophy statement, use these ideas as you develop your philosophy statement at a later point.**

My rationale . . .

- **Identify an incident in which you blamed yourself for your students', their parents', or your administrators' reaction to what you have taught. How might you have turned that incident into a positive experience for them and for you?**

The incident . . .

My response . . .

A Mentor Moment (continued)

■ Is there any way you might communicate to your students the reflection that you have done regarding this particular incident, practice, or policy? Can you share it with your students so that you may model the process of critical reflection? How might you present this to your students?

My reflections . . .

■ Assuming you were able to share your thinking process with the students, what were their responses?

Student responses . . .

CHALLENGE 5

Shared Strategies

Following are some activities and strategies that you might include in your daily practice. You can use these strategies as well as build upon them to create your own.

Self-Analysis

The self-analysis questionnaire below will help you to look at your practice and think about options for creative change.

QUESTIONNAIRE FOR SELF-ANALYSIS OF TEACHING

	Strongly Disagree		Strongly Agree	
	1	2	3	4

1. I know and use a variety of methods to get to know my students.
   Examples:

   | 1 | 2 | 3 | 4 |

2. I have dispositions and skills that allow me to meet individual student needs. Place a star next to areas in which you are skilled and write a checkmark next to areas in which you need to grow.
   ___ Ability ___ Age ___ Interest ___ Language ___ Culture
   ___ Developmental differences ___ Physical differences ___ Gender
   ___ Other differences:

   | 1 | 2 | 3 | 4 |

3. I have goals for each of my students, and those goals reflect students' individual differences.
   Evidence:

   | 1 | 2 | 3 | 4 |

4. Overall, my command of the subject matter is good.
   List areas of special strength and areas for continued growth:

   | 1 | 2 | 3 | 4 |

(continued on next page)

Adapted from Guillaume, A. M., *K–12 Classroom Teaching: A Primer for New Professionals* (2nd ed., p. 10). © 2004 by Merrill Prentice Hall. Reprinted with permission.

Shared Strategies (continued)

QUESTIONNAIRE FOR SELF-ANALYSIS OF TEACHING (continued)

	Strongly Disagree		Strongly Agree	
5. I regularly shape content so that it is accessible to my particular students. Example:	1	2	3	4
6. I know and use a variety of instructional strategies, including direct and discovery methods. List two strategies recently employed:	1	2	3	4
7. The physical and social environment in my classroom is safe and encourages fairness and respect. Evidence:	1	2	3	4
8. My skills as a classroom manager encourage student learning, fairness, and respect. Evidence:	1	2	3	4
9. I know and use a variety of methods to determine whether and what my students are learning. Specific examples:	1	2	3	4
10. I regularly analyze my teaching and modify my actions. I reflect by:	1	2	3	4
11. I talk with professionals about teaching in an effort to learn more. Example:	1	2	3	4

Shared Strategies (continued)

Techniques for Building and Sharing Your Organizational Plan

Being a critical reflective practitioner requires you to reflect on your actions and decisions and develop a rationale for why you do what you do. It also requires that you consider the ideas and expectations of those you are teaching. The following ideas are intended to assist you with instruction, no matter what strategy you select.

- Ask students for their expectations at the beginning of a class (e.g., "What do you hope to learn this year?" or "What do you hope to learn in this unit?").
- Write a daily agenda on the board. To the extent possible, allow learners to provide input about adding, deleting, or rearranging items.
- Provide a graphic organizer—a visual display such as a chart or diagram—on the overhead projector, chalkboard, or chart paper that shows how your instruction will be organized.
- Briefly tell students what will happen during the lesson.
- Preview the lesson's major points.
- If you intend to lecture, provide a note-taking form that helps students organize the information.
- During the lesson, use internal summaries and transition sentences so that students see when you are switching to a different point or activity.
- Refer back to your agenda or chart as the lesson progresses.
- Draw each lesson to closure. Try summarizing by asking students to share in important point or ask for input for the next agenda.

From Guillaume, A. M., *K–12 Classroom Teaching: A Primer for New Professionals* (2nd ed., p. 81). © 2004 by Merrill Prentice Hall.

Learning Activities

Listed below are strategies that have been proven to strengthen student learning. You can adapt them to most lessons.

1. **GRAPHIC ORGANIZERS**
   Use graphic organizers to create mind maps for students, thereby strengthening learning and subsequent recall of material. When the graphic organizers are personalized to match the needs and backgrounds of the students, they become even more powerful. A slightly different twist is to use pictures or drawings instead of words to create a mind map.

2. **CREATIVE RETELLING**
   Weave content information into a story using known genres such as fables, tall tales, songs, and myths. In this manner, the information is transformed into a different setting.

Shared Strategies (continued)

3. **PEER PRESENTING**
   Use an "each one, teach one" model, or in some manner allow students to teach each other. Explaining strengthens understanding.

4. **MODEL MAKING**
   Create models (two- or three-dimensional) to produce a concrete representation of an abstract concept.

5. **PERFORMANCE**
   Transform information or a concept into a performance using drama, music, or dance. Write about the solution to a math problem or create a poem about a science concept.

6. **ROLE PLAYING**
   Provide opportunities for some students to assume the role of historical or fictional characters while other students take on the role of reporter in an interview activity that contributes to whole learning through a simulated experience.

From Skowron, J., *Powerful Lesson Planning Models: The Art of 1000 Decisions* (p. 20). © 2001 by SkyLight Professional Development. Reprinted with permission.

Strategies for Instructing All Learners

Dealing with all the differences one faces in the classroom becomes a tremendous challenge for the beginning teacher. The list that follows provides specific examples of strategies for working with all types of learners:

1. **Present material on tape for students who cannot read successfully. School volunteers, older students, or parents can be asked to make recordings of assigned material.**

2. **Allow students to tape-record answers if writing is difficult or their handwriting is illegible.**

3. **Provide a lot of visual reminders (pictures, maps, charts, graphs) for students who have trouble listening or attending.**

4. **Present handouts that are clear, legible, and uncrowded. Blurred copies [can be] very hard for [students with disabilities] to read.**

5. **Break directions and assignments into small steps. Completion of each step is an accomplishment—reward it.**

6. **Give tests orally if the child has trouble with reading, spelling, or writing. Testing that demonstrates what the student knows rather than language skills gives you a clearer picture of the student's abilities. The student demonstrates abilities, not disabilities.**

7. **Emphasize quality rather than quantity of writing.**

8. **Be consistent with directions, rules, discipline, and organization.**

9. **Arrange the class schedule so that the exceptional student does not miss important activities when he or she goes to the resource room.**

10. **Dispense encouragement freely but fairly. If students make errors, help them find the correct answers, and then reward them.**

Shared Strategies (continued)

11. Discover the exceptional student's strengths and special interests. Capitalize on them in the regular classroom.

12. Carefully establish routines so that the student does not become further handicapped by the confusion of unclear expectations.

13. Arrange desks, tables, and chairs so every person can be easily seen and every word easily heard. Remember, students with hearing impairments need to see your face as you speak.

14. If possible, schedule difficult subjects when there are no outside noises, such as a class at recess.

15. Provide carrels or screens—an "office"—for students who are easily distracted.

16. When checking students' work, check correct answers rather than incorrect answers. The student is still informed of mistakes, but sees his or her successes emphasized.

17. Allow the exceptional student to tape lectures or arrange for a classmate who writes neatly to use carbon paper. Either the carbon copy or a copy of the teacher's notes can be given to the exceptional student.

18. Correct deficient lighting, glare from windows, and light-blocking partitions. Small light problems can be distractions for some exceptional students.

19. Fit the furniture to the child. Discomfort leads to distraction and restlessness.

20. Generally, become sensitive to the obstacles which prevent the exceptional student from exercising his or her abilities.

From Maniet-Bellerman, P. Mainstreaming Children with Learning Disabilities: A Guide to Accompany *L. D. Does Not Mean Learning Dumb!* Pittsburgh: Upward Bound Press. As presented in R. R. McCown and Peter Roop, *Educational Psychological and Classroom Practice: A Partnership.* (pp. 424–425) © 1992 by Allyn and Bacon.

An Amusing Story

I have been teaching history for years and this is the first time this ever happened to me. I handed out the history books at the beginning of the year and found one student completely mesmerized reading the last chapter. I asked her what she was reading, and she claimed she wanted to see if the book was as good as the movie.

Personal Reflection Journal

This challenge encouraged you to reflect critically on instruction. Identify a present situation related to your instruction that needs your attention. Follow the steps below to arrive at a desirable solution. Depending on the nature of your situation, you may use this exercise as a benchmark in your development. If so, include this piece in your professional portfolio.

My thoughts . . .

Identify the situation:

↓

Describe the situation:

↓

Whose advice did you seek in finding a creative solution to the situation?

↓ ↓ ↓

What did this person (or these persons) tell you to do?

Personal Reflection Journal (continued)

How did you deal with the situation?

Would you do the same thing if presented with a similar situation?

If yes, why?	If no, why?

What new knowledge or ideas come to mind as you incorporate what you have learned through this experience?

If you were to establish a goal to enhance your personal professional development in this area, what might that be?

How does what you learned compare to other areas of your teaching?

Personal Reflection Journal (continued)

Instruction is a key to successful teaching and learning. The thinking, discussion, and reading you have done will pay off. Think about other aspects of your role as an educator. In the space provided, outline how you can connect what you have learned about classroom instruction to other areas of your teaching.

Upon reflection, what have you learned that will enhance your development as an educator?

How will you integrate your new knowledge into your practice?

What does it mean to be a critical reflective practitioner in the area of classroom instruction? Develop a clear and concise response that you can include in your professional portfolio.

Consider including this in your professional teaching portfolio.

Standards

Every school differs in its support for teaching standards. However, it is generally agreed that teachers need to possess a level of competence in order to find success. Because of their generic nature, the Interstate New Teacher Assessment and Support Consortium (INTASC) standards have been identified as a framework for you to use to reflect on your practice as an educator. The INTASC standards that address instruction are as follows:

- **PRINCIPLE #1: The teacher understands the central concepts, tools of inquiry, and structures of the discipline(s) he or she teaches and can create learning experiences that make these aspects of subject matter meaningful for students.**

- **PRINCIPLE #2: The teacher understands how children learn and develop, and can provide learning opportunities that support their intellectual, social, and personal development.**

- **PRINCIPLE #3: The teacher understands how students differ in their approaches to learning and creates instructional opportunities that are adapted to diverse learners.**

- **PRINCIPLE #4: The teacher understands and uses a variety of instructional strategies to encourage students' development of critical thinking, problem solving, and performance skills.**

- **PRINCIPLE #5: The teacher uses an understanding of individual and group motivation and behavior to create a learning environment that encourages positive social interaction, active engagement in learning, and self-motivation.**

- **PRINCIPLE #6: The teacher uses knowledge of effective verbal, nonverbal, and media communication techniques to foster active inquiry, collaboration, and supportive interaction in the classroom.**

- **PRINCIPLE #7: The teacher plans instruction based upon knowledge of subject matter, students, the community, and curriculum goals.**

- **PRINCIPLE #8: The teacher understands and uses formal and informal assessment strategies to evaluate and ensure the continuous intellectual, social, and physical development of the learner.**

- **PRINCIPLE #9: The teacher is a reflective practitioner who continually evaluates the effects of his or her choices and actions on others (students, parents, and other professionals in the learning community) and who actively seeks out opportunities to grow professionally.**

- **PRINCIPLE #10: The teacher fosters relationships with school colleagues, parents, and agencies in the larger community to support students' learning and well-being.**

From Interstate New Teacher Assessment and Support Consortium, *Model Standards for Beginning Teacher Licensing, Assessment, and Development: A Resource for State Dialogue.* © 1992 by Council of Chief State School Officers, Washington, DC. Retrieved November 3, 2004, from http://www.ccsso.org/content/pdfs/corestrd.pdf. Used with permission.

Perhaps your school, district, or national organization has established standards pertinent to your professional development in this area. Review them, and the INTASC principles, to determine which one(s) you have met as a result of working through this challenge. It is not necessary to provide evidence for each standard in each challenge. However, by the time you complete this book, you should have evidence of how you can meet each principle or standard necessary for your portfolio. Document your evidence in the Wrap-Up section of the book.

Reflections Log

Fill out the following log to reflect on your learnings. It might be helpful to refer to the Assessment and Reflections Log at the beginning of the challenge to assess your growth.

What did I learn about <u>instruction</u>?

Was I able to accomplish my goals?

How did I overcome the challenges in accomplishing my goals?

CHALLENGE 5

Congratulations, You Made It!

Identify something you are proud of related to instruction that you can incorporate in your professional portfolio. What evidence do you have to show your success? Use the following space to record your responses.

Situation:

How I handled It:

Evidence to be included in my portfolio:

Consider including this in your professional teaching portfolio.

Professional Roles and Responsibilities

Assessment and Reflections Log

Record your initial beliefs and goals about professional roles and responsibilities in this log.

My beliefs about <u>professional roles and responsibilities</u>:

My goal(s) for <u>professional roles and responsibilities</u>:

How am I going to accomplish my goal(s)?

Who and what can help me?

Challenges to accomplishing my goal(s):

The process or procedure for reaching my goal(s):

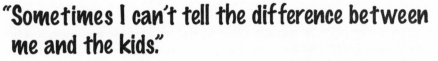

Professional Roles and Responsibilities

CHALLENGE 6

"Sometimes I can't tell the difference between me and the kids."

—First-Year Teacher

Professional roles include those qualities that constitute responsible and ethical conduct. Teachers are trusted with a tremendous power to influence the thinking, motivation, and knowledge of their students. It is incumbent on you to consider how your practice, behavior, and actions will impact the lives of your students.

In this time of transition from being a preservice teacher to being a new professional, it is important that you see yourself as a lifelong learner with greater roles and responsibilities ahead of you. Both your school-based experiences and your university course work are vital and integral components of your professional preparation. How you conduct yourself in these settings reflects on you as a professional teacher.

As a teacher, you decide what is important for your students to learn. Facilitating learning is the fundamental role of the teacher above all other roles in the classroom. You cannot facilitate learning until you are clear about what kind of learning you should facilitate. This decision should be based on a number of different sources, including the needs of the individual learners in the class, the students' past experiences, national and state standards, and more. In order to facilitate learning, you must arrange the students' environment to maximize learning. Through interactions with their environment, students develop new attitudes, skills, and knowledge. The interactions between previously held knowledge and new materials also shape learning experiences. Your success in facilitating learning is dependent on your knowledge of your students and your ability to arrange specific learning environments.

> *A mind is a fire to be kindled, not a vessel to be filled.*
> —PLUTACH

CHALLENGE 6

Practical Problem

What ought to be done about the professional roles and responsibilities of teachers? Teachers are faced with questions and situations regarding professionalism daily as they engage in their practice. The answers to these practical problems will be different for each professional depending on one's ethics and moral reasoning. Regardless of how you might respond to questions about professional roles, it serves as a framework for this challenge.

1. **Think about your own experience as a student, and try to make a connection between what you remember and the professional roles of your teachers. Develop a response to each question:**

   ■ **Do you remember any experiences where you believed your teachers struggled with the dual roles of being an authority figure, mentor, and friend to students?**

   _____

   _____

   ■ **Did you ever have a teacher who never opened up or shared his or her personality to students? How did that make you feel?**

   _____

   _____

   ■ **Do you remember having a teacher who appeared to cross the line with students and perhaps exhibited unethical behavior? What happened? Did you respect him or her?**

   _____

   _____

   ■ **Who do you remember as the most popular teacher among the other teachers at school? What do you think made him or her so well liked?**

   _____

   _____

   ■ **Who would you describe as the most professional teacher you have known?**

   _____

   _____

   ■ **What educator do you remember as encouraging you?**

   _____

   _____

   ■ **Describe a situation where a teacher helped you to do something you wanted to do.**

   _____

   _____

   ■ **Was there a teacher who was your role model in school?**

   _____

   _____

Practical Problem (continued)

■ **Do you remember students taking advantage of a teacher? How did you feel about that situation?**

_____

_____

■ **Who was the most ethical teacher you remember? What made you think he or she was so ethical?**

_____

_____

In the space provided, note what you believe should be done about professional roles and responsibilities of teachers. Also think of the situations that appear in the daily news regarding teacher professional roles and responsibilities. Think of this from a general perspective.

My ideas . . .

_____

_____

_____

_____

_____

_____

_____

_____

_____

_____

_____

_____

_____

_____

Practical Problem (continued)

2. After reflecting on the preceding questions, answer the following question:

 ■ What should be done about this important aspect of your position? Example: Workshops or sessions should be provided for teachers on being a role model.

My ideas . . .

 ■ Now that you have thought through some of the issues surrounding this important dimension of being an educator, what do you believe about professional roles and responsibilities? You may find it useful to discuss your ideas with a mentor, colleague, or peer.

My ideas . . .

CHALLENGE 6

Valued Ends

The following list describes the attitudes and actions associated with teachers who are successful with their professional roles and responsibilities. In the space provided, identify other qualities that you believe are pertinent to responsible conduct in teachers. Also include any expectations or goals your administration has identified related to professional roles and responsibilities of teachers.

Teachers who are successful in their professional roles and responsibilities:

- **Possess adequate perceptions of self**
- **Use an ethical sense of judgment when making decisions**
- **Act with integrity**
- **Are able to think critically**
- **Are altruistic**
- **Are willing to deal with complex concepts as they interface with their subject matter**
- **Can morally defend and cognitively justify their professional practice**

Qualities I believe are pertinent to professional roles and resonsibilities: _____

_____

Administration's expectations or goals related to professional roles and responsibilities: _____

_____

What can I realistically achieve related to professional roles and responsibilities to be demonstrated in my teaching portfolio? _____

_____

CHALLENGE 6

"I am wondering...?"

Questions that other beginning teachers have raised in regard to professional roles and responsibilities include:

- **When will I feel like a professional?**
- **Is there an end to professional development?**
- **Whose interests are being served by the knowledge I want my learners to acquire?**
- **How do I handle it when a student has a crush on me?**
- **What if I really don't like a student?**
- **How much should I let my students know about me?**
- **What is the benefit or advantage of belonging to my professional organization?**
- **Do you think it is appropriate for students to call me by my first name?**
- **Is it okay to wear jeans on dress-down days?**
- **Can I date the single mother or single father of one of my students?**

In the space that follows, list additional questions you may have about professional roles and responsibilities, and determine who can answer each question for your situation.

QUESTION	WHO CAN HELP?

CHALLENGE 6

Focus on the Issue

Professional Roles and Responsibilities

What does it mean to be a professional? Consider the media attention to situations where teachers have engaged in questionable action or behavior. The public grants teachers an incredible amount of authority in the development of children. Your conduct and actions will be critiqued and analyzed by everyone engaged in the learning process. Your role is critical to the development of youth.

According to Schalock (1998), the issue of a teacher's professional role and responsibility for student learning is considered central in various aspects, including student motivation, in teacher unions and between unions and local boards of education, and in teacher preparation and professional development. While the purpose of schooling is learning, the purpose of teaching is to foster the progress of students in their learning. This is best accomplished by a supportive team of responsible professionals focusing on education.

Dewey (1938) believed that learning and experience were interconnected. He claimed that one could not exist without the other. Yet he did not believe all experiences resulted in learning—especially if the learner did not pass through a problematic situation resulting in transformation. He believed that the learner needed to seek interactions and experiences that would help him or her to clarify and expand on new experiences. One of the ways he suggested people could learn was by interacting with others to interpret those experiences. You have a professional responsibility to outline the experiences you need in order to enhance your role as an educator. You also want to identify a person, mentor, or colleague to help you think about the transformation that will take place as you begin teaching.

One of the intangible rewards of being a teacher is the opportunity to work with developing young people full of potential and energy. Although working with the young can be frustrating, exhausting, and personally demanding, it can also be gratifying and rejuvenating (MacDonald, 1999).

> *A teacher affects eternity; he can never tell where his influence stops.*
>
> —HENRY BROOKS ADAM

CHALLENGE 6

Students Speak Out

Students can provide uncanny insight in terms of helping you to determine whether you are an effective educator. Students around the country offered their opinions about professional roles and responsibilities in the following statements, based on the sentence stems highlighted in bold type:

> **I learned** that my family and consumer sciences teacher is on the city council. That impresses me because she helps make important decisions in our community and I see her doing what she tells us to do—get involved. (Karlie C., eleventh-grade family and consumer sciences)

> **I didn't like** it when the coach treated team members and cheerleaders differently than me. I don't think she is a good role model. She shouldn't discriminate against me just because I don't like sports and don't get involved. It's like a clique and I hate it. (Fernando S., twelfth-grade physical education)

> **I like** the way my calc teacher dresses. She's really cool and I like the clothes she picks out. I don't think she tries to dress like us or anything, she just dresses like a woman her age and I like that. I also like the way she wears her hair and her make-up. She's cool. (Amanda M., twelfth-grade calculus)

> **I want** to be a principal. I really like Ms. Knight and the way she gets respect from everyone. She is a role model for me. She cares about everybody in the school. She wants us to do well, and it shows by the way she treats us. Everyone respects her. (Joanna S., twelfth-grade political science)

> **I never want** to act like some of the girls do around Mr. Harcourt. I know he is cute and stuff, but they flirt and act stupid and he plays into it. I don't like it, and I think he should grow up. He is older and should know better. (Leah T., twelfth-grade sociology)

The Teachers' Lounge

Many veteran teachers have experienced how professional roles and responsibilities can influence their teaching, and in turn, their students. When asked about professional roles and responsibilities, teachers throughout the country responded to the highlighted sentence stems in the following ways:

I LEARNED THAT JOINING MY LOCAL PROFESSIONAL ASSOCIATION HELPED ME TO BE CONNECTED TO OTHER TEACHERS AND PROFESSIONALS WHO WERE STRUGGLING WITH SIMILAR SITUATIONS TO THE ONES I FACE. IT GIVES ME A NICE SUPPORT SYSTEM. I THINK I MIGHT RUN FOR AN OFFICE AT THE LOCAL LEVEL.
(B. Emery, Oregon)

I DON'T LIKE MISSING AFTER SCHOOL ACTIVITIES THAT MY STUDENTS ARE INVOLVED IN. I THINK IT HELPS STUDENTS AND PARENTS TO GET TO KNOW ME OUTSIDE THE CLASSROOM. I TRY TO GO TO EVERY GAME AND EVEN CHAPERONE DANCES. I TAKE MY KIDS WITH ME SO THEY CAN GET TO KNOW MY STUDENTS. (D. Kral, Delaware)

I LIKE BEING A TEACHER. I LIKE THAT I HAVE A RESPECTABLE JOB. IT FEELS GOOD TO ME TO KNOW THAT WHAT I DO IS HELPING TO CREATE A BETTER WORLD FOR OTHERS. (Z. Wegman, Iowa)

I WISH WE HAD MORE TIME IN THE DAY TO GET TO KNOW SOME OF THE STUDENTS. I FEEL SO MANY OF THEM DON'T GET GOOD ROLE MODELS AT HOME BECAUSE THEIR PARENTS HAVE TO WORK A COUPLE OF JOBS TO MAKE IT. (E. Weinsetel, Washington, DC)

I WANT TO GET MY NATIONAL BOARD CERTIFICATION. I NEVER REALIZED HOW IMPORTANT IT IS TO HAVE THESE KINDS OF CREDENTIALS UNTIL ONE OF THE TEACHERS IN MY BUILDING GOT CERTIFIED. I AM THINKING ABOUT BEGINNING THE PROCESS NEXT YEAR.
(D. Garrison, Missouri)

I NEVER WANT TO TALK LIKE SOME OF THESE TEACHERS. I THINK TOO MANY OF THE YOUNGER ONES ARE TRYING TO IDENTIFY WITH THE STUDENTS, AND THEY TALK JUST LIKE THEM. WHAT EVER HAPPENED TO GOOD ENGLISH?
(R. Morrison, Alabama)

I REMEMBER A TEACHER WHO WAS ALWAYS SO NEGATIVE AND CONSTANTLY REMINDED ME THAT YOU GET PAID AS MUCH FOR MARCHING AS YOU DO FOR FIGHTING. (M. Budnovitch, Kentucky)

STUDENTS NEED ROLE MODELS, AND I THINK IT IS IMPORTANT FOR THEM TO SEE US AS SUCH. I DON'T THINK WE SHOULD BE THEIR FRIENDS. I THINK WE SHOULD BE FIRM AND FRIENDLY, BUT NOT THEIR FRIENDS. (C. Engleman, Florida)

MY WORST NIGHTMARE IS THAT MY PROFESSIONAL ASSOCIATION WILL ASK ME TO RUN FOR OFFICE AGAIN. I KNOW IT IS A PROFESSIONAL ROLE, BUT I DON'T HAVE TIME.
(S. Gilbertson, Indiana)

NO ONE TOLD ME ABOUT THE TEACHERS' UNION. I ALWAYS THOUGHT THEY WERE BIASED AND WERE INVOLVED IN DISPUTES. I LEARNED THAT I GET LIABILITY INSURANCE AS A MEMBER AND ALSO THEY HAVE GREAT MATERIALS AND RESOURCES FOR MEMBERS. I THINK ALL NEW TEACHERS SHOULD FIND OUT AS MUCH ABOUT THE TEACHERS' UNION AS POSSIBLE.
(C. Curtain, Illinois)

CHALLENGE

6

Teacher Tips

Master teachers have established a repertoire of skills that they draw upon when teaching. Some teachers shared these tips related to professional roles and responsibilities:

Each week find ten to fifteen different books from the library, your resource center, or a bookstore. Display the books in your room in a prominent place, such as the chalk ledge. During the week, depending on what you are teaching, select a book at any time and tell how that book relates to what you are discussing in class. Open the book and read a short section, show an illustration, or mention something captivating about the book. The more enthusiastic you are, the more your students will want to read the books! During the year, you will have promoted reading and shown more than four hundred books to your students. You will also have a broader range of resources to draw upon as you continue teaching. (R. Solomon, North Carolina)

One way to increase your vocabulary and help your students to do the same is to identify a new word each day. Put the word on the board and see how many times you can use it in the course of the class period. Encourage the students to use the word that day. By the end of the year, you and your students will have a considerably larger vocabulary. (L. Doyle, Louisiana)

Model self-confidence—it encourages respect. (K. Duff, New Mexico)

Be careful of teachers or parents who want to share "stories" about others. Ten to one they will share a story about you! (M. Nickels, Montana)

Publicize as many of your student successes as possible. Students love to get the positive exposure and parents enjoy reading positive things about schools. (J. Walsh, Indiana)

If you think that something you want to do is questionable and may be interpreted inappropriately by someone, it is a good idea to discuss it first with your mentor, chair, or supervisor. Don't jeopardize your reputation. (G. Boyer, Iowa)

Students respond to professionals who do what they say. If you say one thing and do another, you lose respect. (D. Lombardo, California)

A Mentor Moment

Becoming a professional is a lifelong experience. Assuming a professional stance is sometimes difficult given all of the decisions you make each day. Your personality is bound to be revealed as you feel more comfortable in your roles as an educator. If you engage in any questionable behaviors such as gossiping or poking fun at others, these behaviors will soon become apparent to your colleagues and students. A mentor can help you tremendously by pointing out the positive and negative characteristics you exhibit. A mentor teacher offers the following to help you grow in understanding your professional roles and responsibilities:

> **Remember that it is important to get involved and ask for help. Don't just stay in your room, and don't be afraid to ask for what you need. (M. Kennedy, Utah)**

Having another professional help you with your daily questions about teaching can make your experiences as a teacher even more rewarding. Following is a list of questions you might ask your mentor regarding professional roles and responsibilities. On the next page is a table you can use to identify those questions you would like to discuss with your mentor. Document your mentor's responses and your thoughts about how to incorporate what you have learned into your practice.

Questions you might ask your mentor to help you improve your skills with professional roles and responsibilities:

- How do I manage all the things I have to do and be involved with the faculty, too?
- I have been told never to be in the classroom alone with a student. Do I need to be careful about this?
- How should I treat students if I am friends with their parents?
- How should I adjust my teaching and classroom if my child or close relative is my student?
- What is a proper way to interact with other faculty?
- What should I do if another faculty member undermines me?
- What if I don't respect my administrator?
- Am I allowed to date a colleague?
- How do I handle student calls at my home?
- How should I respond when students talk about other teachers to me?
- On what grounds can I be fired?

A Mentor Moment (continued)

Questions for My Mentor	Responses from My Mentor	How to Incorporate Mentor's Ideas into My Practice

A Mentor Moment (continued)

Now that you have had the time to focus on your professional roles and responsibilities with a mentor, think about what you have learned in relation to being a critical reflective practitioner.

■ **Why do you believe what you do about professional roles and responsibilities?**

My reflection . . .

■ **Develop a rationale for your practice, actions, and beliefs related to your professional roles and responsibilities.**

My rationale . . .

A Mentor Moment (continued)

- Return to this challenge at a later date and review your rationale (see the preceding item). How has your rationale changed? (You should see growth in your rationale and practice. Include this exercise as part of your yearly personal professional goals. It helps you to see growth and development as you critically reflect on your practice.)

How my rationale had changed . . .

- Identify an incident in which you blamed yourself for a student's, administrator's, fellow teacher's, or parent's reaction to one of your professional ideas or actions. How might you turn that into a positive experience for them and for you?

My ideas . . .

A Mentor Moment (continued)

- Is there any way you might communicate to the person or group you identified in the preceding question the reflection that you have done regarding this particular incident, practice, or policy? Can you share it with them so that you may model the process of critical reflection?

My reflections . . .

- Assuming you were able to share your thinking process with the person or persons, what were their responses?

Their responses . . .

Shared Strategies

CHALLENGE 6

Following are some activities and strategies that you might include in your daily practice. You can use these strategies as well as build upon them to create your own.

Teacher Attributes

The following list helps to connect your behavior to student responsibility. Identifying teacher behaviors also helps us see the importance of our professional role in education.

TEACHER BEHAVIORS TO ENCOURAGE STUDENT RESPONSIBILITY

1. Teachers clearly communicate instructional expectations for students. Students who have high academic expectations usually are responsible and well behaved.

2. Teachers convey a sense of enthusiasm for what they are teaching. A teacher's sense of enthusiasm about learning and student work positively affects student achievement and behavior.

3. Teachers must keep students accountable for their work. Due dates and requirements must be made clear. Students become responsible for the quality and quantity of their work when they are on task and held accountable.

4. Teachers must be aware of what's happening in the classroom. Careful monitoring of student work and behavior helps teachers become aware of what each student is doing.

5. Teachers must teach for success. Students will become more responsible and increase their self-esteem as a result of the teacher employing the first four teacher behaviors.

Adapted from DiGiulio, R., *Positive Classroom Management: A Step-by-Step Guide to Successfully Running the Show Without Destroying Student Dignity* (2nd ed., pp. 45–47). © 2000 by Corwin Press.

An Amusing Story

Students ask me all the time if I will give them the point they need for an A or a B—especially if they are within one point of the higher grade. After arguing with one of our star athletes for several minutes about his being a point away from the grade he thought he deserved, I explained it to him this way: "Suppose you run a football halfway down the field and get tackled one yard from the line. Does the referee give you the touchdown?" No more haggling over grades. (C. Baublitz, Oklahoma)

Personal Reflection Journal

CHALLENGE 6

This challenge encouraged you to examine your professional roles and responsibilities. Identify a situation related to this area of education that needs your attention. Follow the steps below to arrive at a desirable solution. Depending on the nature of your situation, you may use this exercise as a benchmark in your development. If so, include this piece in your professional portfolio.

My thoughts . . .

Identify the situation:

↓

Describe the situation:

↓

Whose advice did you seek in finding a creative solution to the situation?

What did this person (or these persons) tell you to do?

Personal Reflection Journal (continued)

How did you deal with the situation?

Would you do the same thing if presented with a similar situation?

If yes, why?	If no, why?

What new knowledge or ideas come to mind as you incorporate what you have learned through this experience?

If you were to establish a goal to enhance your personal professional development in this area, what might that be?

How does what you learned compare to other areas of your teaching?

Consider including this in your professional teaching portfolio.

Personal Reflection Journal (continued)

Developing professional attributes and qualities is a lifelong process for all professionals. Consider how the situation you have identified as a growth area may be interpreted by other people. Document your ideas.

Upon reflection, what have you learned that will enhance your development as an educator?

How will you integrate your new knowledge into your practice?

What does it mean to be a critical reflective practitioner when determining the curriculum? Develop a clear and concise response that you can include in your professional portfolio.

Consider including this in your professional teaching portfolio.

CHALLENGE 6 Standards

Every school differs in its acceptance of teaching standards. However, it is generally agreed that teachers need to possess a level of competence in order to find success. Because of their generic nature, the Interstate New Teacher Assessment and Support Consortium (INTASC) standards have been identified as a framework for you to use to reflect on your practice as an educator. The INTASC standards that address professional roles and responsibilities are as follows:

> ■ **PRINCIPLE #9: The teacher is a reflective practitioner who continually evaluates the effects of his or her choices and actions on others (students, parents, and other professionals in the learning community) and who actively seeks out opportunities to grow professionally.**

> ■ **PRINCIPLE #10: The teacher fosters relationships with school colleagues, parents, and agencies in the larger community to support students' learning and well-being.**

From Interstate New Teacher Assessment and Support Consortium, *Model Standards for Beginning Teacher Licensing, Assessment, and Development: A Resource for State Dialogue.* © 1992 by Council of Chief State School Officers, Washington, DC. Retrieved November 3, 2004, from http://www.ccsso.org/content/pdfs/corestrd.pdf. Used with permission.

Perhaps your school, district, or national organization has established standards pertinent to your professional development in this area. Review them, and the INTASC principles, to determine which one(s) you have met as a result of working through this chapter. It is not necessary to provide evidence for each standard in each challenge. However, by the time you complete this book, you should have evidence of how you can meet each principle or standard necessary for your portfolio. Document your evidence in the Wrap-Up section of the book.

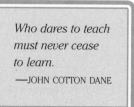

Who dares to teach must never cease to learn.
—JOHN COTTON DANE

Reflections Log

Fill out the following log to reflect on your learnings. It might be helpful to refer to the Assessment and Reflections Log at the beginning of the challenge to assess your growth.

What did I learn about <u>professional roles and responsibilities</u>?

Was I able to accomplish my goals?

How did I overcome the challenges in accomplishing my goals?

Congratulations, You Made It!

Identify something you are proud of related to professional roles and responsibilities that you can incorporate in your professional portfolio. What evidence do you have to show your success? Use the following chart to record your responses.

Situation:

How I handled it:

Evidence to be included in my portfolio:

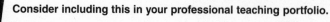 **Consider including this in your professional teaching portfolio.**

Collegiality

Assessment and Reflections Log

Record your initial beliefs and goals about collegiality in this log.

My beliefs about <u>collegiality</u>:

My goal(s) for <u>collegiality</u>:

How am I going to accomplish my goal(s)?

Who and what can help me?

Challenges to accomplishing my goal(s):

The process or procedure for reaching my goal(s):

Collegiality

"I don't know how they have time to go to the faculty room!"

—First-Year Teacher

Having colleagues and working together are essential in finding success as an educator. The process is twofold. First, teachers rely on one another to assist and support student learning. Second, by working together, teachers can create organizational change necessary for educational reform. Collegiality is central to beginning teachers feeling part of an established system.

Collegiality also refers to the existence of high levels of collaboration among teachers and between teachers and school administration. Mutual respect, shared work values, cooperation, and conversations about teaching and learning are all examples of collegiality between professionals.

The theory of individual professional growth has given way to a more contemporary approach toward professional development aimed at collegial teams working and learning together within the school setting. Teachers work together as a team and help one another. Do teachers collaborate well in your school? Are they friendly? Is there a mix of new and seasoned teachers? Do you feel that the administration is on "your team"? As the environment of a school improves, collegial teams of professionals will help to determine the team's staff development needs as well as the degree to which everyone accepts professional development. Working conditions are dependent on the staff. The cohesiveness of the faculty will influence the level of satisfaction in your job.

You, too, have a responsibility to be a colleague to the group of educators who have just included you in their team. Find out how you can contribute to the group. Stay informed on what is happening with your school as well as at the state and national levels. You have much to offer as a new member of an existing structure, and much to learn.

> We must all hang together or assuredly we shall all hang separately.
> —BENJAMIN FRANKLIN

CHALLENGE 7

Practical Problem

What ought to be done about establishing a sense of collegiality in schools? Certainly the thought of teachers relying on one another is paramount to success. No matter how you answer the question, it serves as a framework for this challenge.

1. **Although you may have had little experience with this component of teaching, try to recall the collegiality of your teachers and administrators when you were a student. Develop a response to each question:**

   ■ **Do you remember teachers working together? Was that practice helpful to you as a student?**

   ■ **Do you recall teachers working together for the good of the students or complaining because they were forced to team teach or collaborate?**

   ■ **Could you tell which teachers were friends and which teachers did not get along?**

   ■ **Do you remember the relationships between your teachers and the administrators?**

   ■ **Describe several teachers, or a team of teachers, who seemed to work well together. Why do you think they worked well together?**

   ■ **Do you recall any situations where teachers may not have gotten along?**

   ■ **What was the reputation of the faculty room in your school?**

Practical Problem (continued)

My reflections . . .

Practical Problem (continued)

2. After reflecting on the preceding questions, answer the following questions:

■ What do you believe should be done about establishing a sense of collegiality among educators? (Example: Teachers could be given a school problem to be solved each semester and be supported in finding a creative solution.)

My ideas . . .

■ Now that you have thought through each of these questions, what do you now believe about collegiality? You may find it useful to discuss your ideas with a mentor, colleague, or peer.

My ideas . . .

CHALLENGE 7

Valued Ends

The following list outlines some of the abilities of teachers who are successful in establishing a sense of collegiality in their schools. In the space provided, identify other qualities that you believe are pertinent to successfully establishing collegiality. Also include any expectations or goals your administration has identified related to peer support.

Teachers who are successful in establishing a sense of collegiality in their schools:

- **Are able to deal with their own situations and problems**
- **Possess a positive sense of self in relation to colleagues**
- **Identify with and feel part of a larger system of education**
- **Are involved in the school and community**
- **Perceive themselves as one of a team of persons working together to encourage learning**

Qualities I believe are pertinent to successful collegiality:

Administration's expectations or goals related to the idea of collegiality in schools:

What can I realistically achieve related to establishing a sense of collegiality to be demonstrated in my teaching portfolio?

CHALLENGE 7

"I am wondering...?"

As a teacher, you are part of a team of professionals employed to educate each student in your school. You are not alone. You have as much to offer veteran teachers as they have to offer you. Your contributions are central to the development of each student. Having good colleagues requires you to be a good colleague. Questions that other beginning teachers have raised when faced with fostering collegiality in schools include:

- **How should I seek support within and outside the school?**
- **How can I find a mentor and colleagues to help me?**
- **How do I structure effective ways to collaborate with other colleagues?**
- **How can I begin to feel connected to a new school environment?**
- **What if I am too shy to feel part of the group?**
- **Who are my colleagues?**
- **What should I do to get to know my colleagues in the school?**
- **How do I find time to become involved with other teachers?**
- **Is it appropriate to talk about my social and personal life with other faculty?**
- **How do I meet the school's faculty and staff?**
- **Is it appropriate for me to develop collegial relationships with the support staff?**

In the space that follows, list additional questions you may have about collegiality, and determine who can answer each question for your situation.

QUESTION	WHO CAN HELP?

CHALLENGE 7

Focus on the Issue

Collegiality

Teacher collegiality is an important component to promoting educational change within schools. Although some schools have some kind of training or mentor programs, many beginning teachers become frustrated when dealing with the various responsibilities of a classroom and finding the time needed to socialize with other teachers. Research has supported continuous collegial interaction as a method of teacher development (e.g., Joyce & Showers, 1982; Little, 1982; Ward & Darling, 1996). Successful and adaptable schools are characterized as offering (1) specific support for discussion of classroom practice, (2) mutual observation and critique, (3) shared efforts to design and prepare curriculum, and (4) shared participation in the business of instructional improvement (Little, 1982).

Ward and Darling (1996) suggest that teacher collegiality stimulates educational innovation and professional learning, as well as enhanced levels of student achievement. Creative feedback and alternative directions for teacher practice can be gleaned from effective teacher collegiality. According to Joyce and Showers (1982), peer observations have a profound impact on knowledge and skill transferability from staff development programs to classroom practice. Hargreaves (1988) states that team teaching, exploration of new methods, collaborative approaches to improve teaching, and constructive criticism of classroom performance can better enable teachers to learn from and with one another.

According to Bunting (1999), regularly scheduled interaction with other teachers promotes self-confidence and self-reliance. Ongoing teacher talk sessions can help to inform and encourage teachers to become reflective about what they are doing in the classroom. One idea to encourage collaborative problem solving and interaction is to ask teachers for a single-sentence response to a "problem of the week," which could be posted in a common area, such as the office or a faculty room. Teachers and staff can then generate interesting discussion, new ideas, and a camaraderie around the proposed problem. Implementing ideas such as these helps teachers to gain a sense of community.

Bunting (1999) also suggests that beginning teachers can select a topic that focuses on something they need to know and have a common time to share what they have learned with their colleagues. This way, new teachers can specialize in topics of personal interest, boost their own classroom performance, promote their own personal strengths, and establish a foundation for building collegiality. Teacher book clubs focusing on professional reading are another way to foster self-reliance and a community spirit.

Spreyer (2002) claims that true collegiality is found when teachers seek partnerships with their colleagues. One assumes that like-minded teachers can create opportunities to share teaching ideas and establish opportunities for team teaching. One way to initiate collegiality is to establish an after school get-together for teachers. A new teacher can discuss how things are going for him or her, covering teaching materials as well as games and other activities that are effective in the classroom. In addition, Spreyer suggests that collegiality can be established by joining professional organizations, reading publications, and attending conferences. Personal interaction is essential to communication. One needs to be self-confident in order to communicate authoritatively with colleagues, administrators, and learners.

CHALLENGE
7

Students Speak Out

Students can often provide insightful commentary on issues related to teaching. When asked about the notion of collegiality, students throughout the country had the following to say based on the sentence stems highlighted in bold:

> **I learned** so much more when some of my teachers worked together. It's cool to see them work together to try to teach us something. It makes class more interesting. I get bored always going to the same class listening to the same old lectures. When they work together, it is different and fun. (Harold W., ninth-grade physical science)

> **I didn't like** it when Mr. A., who is so boring, taught with my family and consumer sciences teacher. The whole lesson was boring. We were all passing notes and laughing. I think he just didn't feel like teaching so he brought his class to our room and kept interrupting when Mrs. E. was trying to teach. What a waste. (Tanya S., eleventh-grade family and consumer sciences)

> **I like** it when the student government gives us a problem to solve and the whole school gets to work on finding the answer. We cleaned up our community last year after the hurricane, and it helped everyone feel like we made a difference. I learned a lot from the families we helped and about working together. (Eric N., tenth-grade business education)

> **I want** to see teachers do more things together. I notice that they all seem to stay in their classrooms and come out only to stand in the halls between classes. I wish they would have teacher debates as an assembly or something. It would be cool to see how our teachers interact with each other in the same settings they create for us. (Stephanie S., 12th grade economics)

> **I never want** to see my teachers have to stand outside the school and strike again. It is a shame because they work so hard and they don't seem to be paid enough or get the respect they deserve. I think the thing that hurt me the most is seeing my favorite teacher's picture in the paper holding a picket sign. (Mollie W., 12th grade political science)

The Teachers' Lounge

Veteran teachers have had experiences with collegiality and adapted it into their teaching. In the comments below, teachers throughout the country weighed in on collegiality using the highlighted sentence stems:

I LEARNED SO MUCH FROM BEING PART OF A TEAM. I LEARNED MORE WHEN WORKING WITH TEACHERS OUTSIDE MY CONTENT AREA. IT ALSO HELPED ME UNDERSTAND THEIR SUBJECTS AND SEE THE RELATIONSHIP BETWEEN OUR CURRICULUM AREAS.
(D. Anthony, Indiana)

NO ONE TOLD ME HOW TO USE THE EXPERTISE IN THE SCHOOL. ONCE I FIGURED OUT EVERYONE'S SKILLS AND ABILITIES, I STARTED EMPLOYING MY COLLEAGUES TO COME TO MY CLASSES. I LEARNED A LOT AND IT HAS HELPED US ALL RELY ON ONE ANOTHER A LITTLE MORE RATHER THAN BE ISOLATED (Y. Youngbour, Illinois)

I WANT TO FEEL MORE CONNECTED TO THE OTHER TEACHERS IN MY BUILDING AND DISTRICT. I FEEL SO ISOLATED AT TIMES. I DO A LOT OF PLANNING BY MYSELF AND DON'T HAVE A LOT OF INTERACTION WITH OTHER TEACHERS. I AM THE ONLY MUSIC TEACHER IN THE SCHOOL. (L. Finney, Texas)

I LIKE TEAM TEACHING. I LIKE WORKING WITH OTHER TEACHERS. I SEE WHAT THE STUDENTS LIKE AND DISLIKE ABOUT OTHER TEACHERS BY WORKING WITH THEM. I THINK STUDENTS LIKE THE CHANGE OF PACE.
(H. Tenley, California)

I REMEMBER HOW MUCH SUPPORT MY PRINCIPAL GAVE ME WHEN I FIRST STARTED TEACHING. IF SHE COULDN'T GET WHAT I WANTED, SHE FOUND A WAY FOR ME TO FIND SUCCESS BY GETTING SOMETHING ELSE. I HAVE NEVER HAD THAT KIND OF SUPPORT SINCE SHE LEFT. (P. Wendt, Nevada)

I WISH THERE WOULD BE TIME IN THE DAY TO ENGAGE IN SOME SORT OF DISCUSSION OR INTERACTION WITH OTHER TEACHERS. I FIND THAT MY PREP PERIOD IS USED FOR WORK, AND I NEVER FEEL AS IF I AM CONNECTED TO OTHER TEACHERS.
(B. Bisha, South Carolina)

I NEVER REALLY REALIZED HOW IMPORTANT IT IS TO INTERACT WITH MY FELLOW TEACHERS. ONCE I BECAME FRIENDLY WITH EVERYONE, I FELT AS THOUGH I BELONGED TO THE TEAM. WHEN I FIRST STARTED I WAS SO OVERWHELMED. I TRIED TO DO EVERYTHING AND SELDOM GOT OUTSIDE OF MY ROOM TO TALK TO ANYONE. (V. Gooding, Missouri)

STUDENTS CAN SEE ROLE MODELING OF COOPERATION WHEN THEY SEE US WORKING TOGETHER IN TEAMS.
(L. Mikus, Nebraska)

CHALLENGE 7

Teacher Tips

Master teachers have established a repertoire of skills that they draw upon when teaching. Some teachers shared these tips related to collegiality:

I created a folder for my colleagues who might serve as a substitute for me. The folder has my class lists, fire drill rules, seating charts, alternative schedule information (such as the late day or assembly schedules), and a generic lesson plan with a lot of activities for the students. I also created a form on the computer for my regular class schedule, which includes the location of my teacher's guides, a list of helpful teachers, procedures from the office, special student notes, and my class rules. (M. Browne, Canada)

Develop a Web site for your class. Include highlights of the lessons and the people who you invite to support what you are teaching. Your community colleagues will be happy to have you link to their Web sites. (B. Tragos, New York)

Establish as many colleagues around the world as you can and have your students do interactive activities with your international relationships. (Z. Tucker, Connecticut)

Invite other teachers into your classroom for panel discussions and activities. Students love it when they see teachers interact with one another. (O. Fischer, Maryland)

Volunteer to work with your peers on committees, boards, projects, and school events. It shows you're a team player. (P. Grayson, Vermont)

Organize teacher activities like a basketball game or a rock band. Students will enjoy watching and the teachers will have fun working together. (K. Smith, Washington)

Set up teacher book clubs, bowling, or dinner parties. Do anything to get teachers to know one another so they feel as though they can rely on one another in their jobs. (A. Rogentien, Nevada)

Create an "expertise file" for all teachers in the school to let everyone else know what they feel most comfortable talking about or rely on these experts when planning. (T. Barton, Georgia)

CHALLENGE
7

A Mentor Moment

Mentors are those trusted relationships that help you to grow and mature in your personal and professional roles. Mentors provide a different perspective for you to consider as you look at your practice. Following is a list of statements made by new teachers and mentors about working together as colleagues:

- **Having a colleague helps foster collaboration.**
- **A trusting relationship must be at the heart of working together and being authentic colleagues.**
- **Mentoring relationships allow for sharing experiences and knowledge. Both parties learn.**
- **Questions are sometimes more important than the answers. Working together helps to form a trusting relationship.**
- **Listening to new teachers allows for understanding the problems new teachers face and paves the way for collaborative ways to work together.**
- **My ability to decide what was important came from one of my colleagues. I thought my teaching was good until she helped me see that I could be more effective.**

Having another professional help you with your daily questions about teaching can make your experiences as a teacher even more rewarding. Following is a list of questions you might ask your mentor regarding collegiality. On the next page is a table you can use to identify those questions you would like to discuss with your mentor. Document your mentor's responses and your thoughts about how to incorporate what you have learned into your practice.

Questions you might ask your mentor to help build collegiality:

- **Should I address my colleagues by first name in school? How about outside of school?**
- **How can I improve my communication with other faculty?**
- **Should I use my colleagues as resources? If so, how?**
- **What types of activities should I do with my colleagues?**
- **Can I have other faculty help me if I have a problem I don't think I can handle alone?**
- **How do I make myself a part of my school district?**
- **How can I successfully get involved in the school and the community?**
- **Can you help me set up a new teacher support group?**
- **How do I get other teachers in a group to pull their weight?**

A Mentor Moment (continued)

Questions for My Mentor	Responses from My Mentor	How to Incorporate Mentor's Ideas into My Practice

A Mentor Moment (continued)

Now that you have had time to focus on your questions and concerns about collegiality with a mentor, think about what you have learned in relation to being a critical reflective practitioner.

- **What are your beliefs being a colleague or having colleagues?**

My beliefs . . .

- **Develop a rationale for your thoughts and actions related to being and having colleagues.**

My rationale . . .

A Mentor Moment (continued)

- Return to this challenge at a later date and review your rationale (see the preceding item). How has your rationale changed? (You should see growth in your rationale and practice. Include this exercise as part of your yearly personal professional goals. It helps you to see growth and development as you critically reflect on your practice.)

How my rationale has changed . . .

- Identify an incident in which you blamed yourself for a colleague's reaction to something you did or said. How might you have turned that incident into a positive experience for him or her and for you?

My ideas . . .

A Mentor Moment (continued)

- Is there any way you might communicate to your colleague support group the reflection that you have done regarding this particular incident, practice, or policy? Can you share it with them so that they can see you engage in the process of critical reflection? How might you present this to the faculty at large?

My reflections . . .

- Assuming you were able to share your thinking process with a colleague or the faculty, what was the response?

Their responses . . .

Shared Strategies

Following are some activities and strategies that you might include in your daily practice. You can use these strategies as well as build upon them to create your own.

Who's Who in Your School?

It's important for you to know and recognize names of persons who work in your school. Following is a list of school positions for which you should identify the appropriate person(s). You can add other positions that are specific to your school. Seek out each person on the list to become acquainted. This will help you tremendously as you work together to accomplish the school mission. Make it a point to meet a new person every week.

Principal _____

Assistant principal(s) _____
_____
_____
_____

Librarian(s) _____

Local school board president _____

Local school board members _____
_____
_____
_____

Reading specialist (coordinator) _____

Curriculum coordinator _____

Teachers' union president/delegate _____

Department head(s) _____
_____
_____
_____

Special services _____

Technology coordinator _____

Guidance counselor _____

Speech pathologist _____

(continued on next page)

Shared Strategies (continued)

Psychologist _____

Social worker _____

Case manager _____

School nurse _____

Education support personnel (ESP) _____
_____

Teacher assistants _____
_____
_____
_____

Administrative secretarial staff _____
_____

Clerk(s) _____
_____

Engineer _____

Janitorial staff member(s)
_____

Food service employee(s)
_____

Security personnel
_____

Other
_____
_____
_____

Peer Observation and Coaching Process

One of the primary purposes of peer observation and coaching is to provide an opportunity for teachers to discuss their practice and to reflect on their practice while working to improve student learning.

Peer observation and coaching is a way for teachers to improve student achievement by sharing their classroom practices in a nonthreatening way. This collaboration benefits everyone involved in the process, including the teacher being observed as well as those who observe him or her. Observers are provided with an opportunity to focus on classroom instruction and to engage in collaborative reflection regarding practice. Observed teachers become more comfortable with observers in the classroom, rely on colleagues to address classroom issues, and strengthen instruction through focused observations, discussions, and critical reflection.

Shared Strategies (continued)

The peer observation and coaching process will work only if all involved have established a trusting relationship. The process is not an evaluation. No information should be shared outside of the peer pairing. Discussions between colleagues are to be kept confidential. Both parties recognize that the process is designed to strengthen one another, not to be critical or negative.

Peer observation and coaching generally consists of three steps: (1) a preobservation meeting and discussion generally held in the classroom where the observation will take place, (2) the actual observation, and (3) a postobservation discussion, reflection, and debriefing.

Following are suggested guidelines of the peer observation and coaching process.

Preobservation Meeting

The preobservation meeting sets the stage for the observation, how the observation will be conducted, and what type of information will be collected. The conference should begin with the observed teacher providing a lesson plan for the class and pertinent information regarding the students. The observed teacher may then ask the observing teacher to focus on a particular aspect of practice. Some examples might be:

- **Do I solicit questions from both males and females in the classroom?**
- **How do I respond to student questions?**
- **Are students engaged in my activities?**
- **Do students understand my directions?**
- **Are there any discipline or classroom control issues I am not noticing?**
- **Do I use appropriate pauses to give students time to think?**

The observing teacher should also ask questions to clarify the focus of the observation. These might include questions such as:

- **Do you attempt to ask questions of both the boys and the girls?**
- **What kind of student questions do you anticipate?**
- **If all students were engaged in your activities, what would I see?**
- **How will you know if students understand your directions?**
- **What discipline problems do you know about at present?**
- **How long do you think you should wait for a student response?**

Additionally, the observer might ask logistical questions like:

- **Where shall I sit?**
- **How long do you want me to observe?**
- **Should I be there before you start the class or would you prefer I enter later?**
- **Are there particular students you want me to pay attention to?**
- **Would it help my observation if I completed the assignment before the class?**

Shared Strategies (continued)

Observation

The observer should take notes of as many events as possible that relate to the observed teacher's goals. This note taking should be as objective as possible, with the observer recording what is happening in the classroom. The observer should not formulate opinions or interpretations. The observer should act as a silent participant who notes the classroom activities and interactions while remaining uninvolved in the class. The observer may wish to write questions to be raised during the final meeting, but these questions should be linked directly to observed events. The observer is not to evaluate but rather is to parrot back to the observed teacher what he or she noticed during the observation. It is sometimes useful for the observing teacher to videotape the class and have both teachers watch the tape together.

> *The whole is greater than the sum of the parts.*
> —ANDREW CARNEGIE

The Postobservation Meeting

Ideally, debriefing should occur later that same day. It is inappropriate to wait too long, as important information and memory of what occurred will become distorted. A successful debriefing meeting requires specific details. The debriefing begins with the observer reviewing the preobservation goals. The observer begins the meeting by asking for the teacher's opinion of the class based on their predetermined goals for the observation. The observer listens without comment. The observer then shares details from his or her notes with the teacher who was observed, remembering not to interpret or evaluate. The observed teacher should listen and record relevant information and may want to ask clarifying questions or direct the discussion into other areas if deemed necessary. Together, the teachers can create an action plan or develop an instrument for future observations.

When the conversation around practice is finished, the two teachers should debrief the observation process. Issues to discuss might include:

- What went particularly well in the peer observation and coaching process?
- What did not go as well as desired in the peer observation and coaching process?
- Will the observation and coaching reflection result in change? If not, why not? If so, describe that change.
- If you were to participate in another cycle of peer coaching, what would you do differently?

Because peer observation depends on mutual trust and respect, there is no reason to rush the process. Trust depends on mutually setting and honoring the procedures established by both parties. The preobservation conference and postobservation debriefing and reflection establish boundaries for both teachers. Trust is built over time and with each interaction. A successful peer observation process requires a high level of respect for each individual and contributes to a meaningful collegial relationship.

Personal Reflection Journal

This challenge encouraged you to think about how to be and develop a collegial spirit in your school. Identify a situation related to collegiality that may provide an opportunity for you to grow and develop in this area. Follow the steps below to arrive at a desirable solution. Depending on the nature of your situation, you may use this exercise as a benchmark in your development. If so, include this piece in your professional portfolio.

My thoughts . . .

Identify the situation:

↓

Describe the situation:

↓

Whose advice did you seek in finding a creative solution to the situation?

↓   ↓   ↓

What did this person (or these persons) tell you to do?

Personal Reflection Journal (continued)

How did you deal with the situation?

Would you do the same thing if presented with a similar situation?

If yes, why?

If no, why?

What new knowledge or ideas come to mind as you incorporate what you have learned through this experience?

If you were to establish a goal to enhance your personal professional development in this area, what might that be?

How does what you learned compare to other areas of your teaching?

Consider including this in your professional teaching portfolio.

Personal Reflection Journal (continued)

Establishing a network of collaborations within a desirable climate enhances your ability to do your job. Think about what you have gleaned regarding collegiality and consider ways your ideas could be put into action. Document your ideas and action plan.

Upon reflection, what have you learned that will enhance your development as an educator?

How will you integrate your new knowledge into your practice?

What does it mean to be a critical reflective practitioner related to establishing a sense of collegiality in your school? Develop a clear and concise response that you can include in your professional portfolio.

Consider including this in your professional teaching portfolio.

CHALLENGE 7

Standards

If you are keeping a record of your growth and development as an educator, you may want to link that documentation to a set of teaching standards. Because of their generic nature, the Interstate New Teacher Assessment and Support Consortium (INTASC) standards have been identified as a framework for you to use to reflect on your practice as an educator. The INTASC standards that address collegiality are as follows:

■ **PRINCIPLE #9: The teacher is a reflective practitioner who continually evaluates the effects of his or her choices and actions on others (students, parents, and other professionals in the learning community) and who actively seeks out opportunities to grow professionally.**

■ **PRINCIPLE #10: The teacher fosters relationships with school colleagues, parents, and agencies in the larger community to support students' learning and well-being.**

From Interstate New Teacher Assessment and Support Consortium, *Model Standards for Beginning Teacher Licensing, Assessment, and Development: A Resource for State Dialogue.* © 1992 by Council of Chief State School Officers, Washington, DC. Retrieved November 3, 2004, from http://www.ccsso.org/content/pdfs/corestrd.pdf. Used with permission.

Perhaps your school, district, or national organization has established standards pertinent to your professional development in this area. Review them, and the INTASC principles, to determine which one(s) you have met as a result of working through this challenge. It is not necessary to provide evidence for each standard in each challenge. However, by the time you complete this book, you should have evidence of how you can meet each principle or standard necessary for your portfolio. Document your evidence and include it in the Wrap-Up section of the book.

Reflections Log

Fill out the following log to reflect on your learnings. It might be helpful to refer to the Assessment and Reflections Log at the beginning of the challenge to assess your growth.

What did I learn about <u>collegiality</u>?

Was I able to accomplish my goals?

How did I overcome the challenges in accomplishing my goals?

CHALLENGE 7

Congratulations, You Made It!

Identify something you are proud of related to the notion of collegiality that you can incorporate in your professional portfolio. What evidence do you have to show your success? Use the following chart to record your responses.

Situation:

How I handled it:

Evidence to be included in my portfolio:

Consider including this in your professional teaching portfolio.

Assessment, Evaluation, and Grades

Assessment and Reflections Log

Record your initial beliefs and goals about assessment, evaluation, and grades in this log.

My beliefs about <u>assessment, evaluation, and grades</u>:

My goal(s) for <u>assessment, evaluation, and grades</u>:

How am I going to accomplish my goal(s)?

Who and what can help me?

Challenges to accomplishing my goal(s):

The process or procedure for reaching my goal(s):

Assessment, Evaluation, and Grades

"I don't have time to grade all these projects."

—First-Year Teacher

The words *assessment, evaluation,* and *grades* are often used interchangeably, although they can have very different meanings. The purpose of this challenge is to help you recognize the similarities and differences of these concepts. Assessment is the process you use to determine whether the student is progressing according to your established objectives. Evaluation is the final appraisal of how students accomplish the goals and objectives you established for them to achieve. Grades are the scores (numbers or letters) that you use to identify how you have evaluated student performance.

Reflect upon your experiences in school related to evaluation. Perhaps you were able to accomplish a grade that truly reflected your ability. Perhaps you felt confident with your knowledge and skill but a final exam revealed a less than desirable appraisal of your ability. Most educators admit that assessment and evaluation are central to a positive learning environment. Students want to be challenged but not punished for conscientious effort to be successful.

> Intellectual growth should commence at birth and cease only at death.
>
> —ALBERT EINSTEIN

Think about your prior experiences with evaluation and recall the feelings that were involved as a result of those experiences. What kind of evaluator do you want to be? What is your philosophy of evaluation? This chapter will help you to develop those perspectives.

CHALLENGE

8

Practical Problem

What ought to be done about assessing student progress? What ought to be done about evaluating students and self? What ought to be done about assigning grades for student work and achievement? All teachers deal with these questions. Every teacher establishes different policies based upon his or her philosophy. This challenge is designed to encourage your thinking and reflection about assessment, evaluation, and grades.

1. **Think for a moment about assessment, evaluation, and grades from the perspective of when you were a student. Develop a response to each question:**

   ■ **How did you feel when you got a good grade on a test or a project?**

   ■ **Do you remember the behavior of students who did not do very well on tests?**

   ■ **Do you remember a teacher permitting you to be graded on other projects besides tests alone?**

   ■ **Do you remember a time when you worked as hard as you could and even so received a poor grade on your project or exam?**

   ■ **Discuss a grade you were given that surprised you.**

   ■ **What was the worst grade you ever received?**

   ■ **How did you feel when you earned a good grade?**

   ■ **What do you remember about standardized testing?**

   ■ **Recall an interesting story about report cards.**

Practical Problem (continued)

My reflections . . .

Practical Problem (continued)

2. After reflecting on the preceding questions, answer the following questions:

- What should you do about assessment, evaluation, and grading in your classroom? (Example: Because I believe that grading students has a direct impact on one's self-esteem, I will create ways to help students find success using a variety of assessments.)

My beliefs . . .

- Now that you have thought through each of these questions, what do you currently believe about assessment, evaluation, and grading? You may find it useful to discuss your ideas with a mentor, colleague, or peer.

My beliefs . . .

CHALLENGE
8

Valued Ends

The following list outlines in part some of the skills, behaviors, and attitudes associated with teachers who are successful in assessing, evaluating, and assigning grades. In the space provided, identify other qualities that you believe are pertinent to successful assessment, evaluation, and grades. Also include any expectations or goals your administration has identified related to assessment, evaluation, and grades.

Teachers who are successful in assessing, evaluating, and assigning grades:

- **Are able to assess whether learners have accomplished goals**
- **Are able to determine student capability**
- **See assessment as part of the learning process**
- **Vary assessment to meet individual needs**
- **Use assessment as part of their professional development**
- **Are able to determine the needs of learners and develop appropriate lessons**
- **Revise curriculum based on student performance**
- **Determine if learning objectives have been achieved**

Qualities I believe are pertinent to successful assessment, evaluation, and grading: _____

_____

_____

Administration's expectations or goals related to assessment, evaluation, and grades: _____

_____

_____

What can I realistically achieve related to successful assessment, evaluation, and grading to be demonstrated in my teaching portfolio? _____

_____

CHALLENGE 8

"I am wondering...?"

You might have a lot of questions about assessing learners when you first begin your role as a teacher. This is normal. With focused attention on this area, you will enhance your ability to assess, evaluate, and assign grades. Questions that other beginning teachers have raised when faced with these issues include:

- How do I know if I am an effective educator?
- How do I figure out what assessment to use for different lessons?
- Are there different ways to evaluate students with different needs?
- How do I measure whether or not my goals have been accomplished?
- Do I assume that because a student does well on an exam, he or she has mastered the material?
- What do I do if a student cheats?
- What if I have too many students to evaluate on a regular basis?
- What if a parent gets upset with a grade I give a student?
- What if my administrator changes a grade I assign to a student?
- How do I know if my students have learned what I wanted them to know?

In the space that follows, list additional questions you may have about assessment, evaluation, and grades, and determine who can answer each question for your situation.

QUESTION	WHO CAN HELP?

CHALLENGE 8

Focus on the Issue
Assessment, Evaluation, and Grades

Assessment, evaluation, and the assigning of grades are central to the education process. They are, however, the areas that receive the least attention in terms of research (Stiggins, Conklin, & Bridgeford, 1986). What is the purpose of assessment? We know that assessment is important to the instructional and evaluative components of teaching. Several studies have indicated that well-developed assessment can enhance student learning as well as assist the teacher to improve his or her craft (Halpin & Halpin, 1982; Nungester & Duchastel, 1982; Stiggins, 1985).

The area of concern for most teachers is linking the instructional goals with the assessment. This, according to Bol and Strage (1996), reveals the largest contradiction for teachers—especially beginning teachers. What you establish as a goal must be assessed to determine whether or not your learners have achieved the intended objective. Research results have indicated that while teachers set course objectives such as developing a general interest in and understanding of subject matter, promoting application to real-world situations, and developing higher-order thinking skills, their assessment practices often only reflect basic knowledge. Moreover, teachers are often not even aware of the contradiction between their instructional goals and assessment practices.

According to Hunt et al. (1998), teachers should recognize that assessment is important for them to evaluate whether the curricula and instructional experiences have been effective in educating their students as well as to provide feedback regarding students' growth. In essence, teachers need to develop effective assessment instruments and procedures, to measure their effectiveness, and to provide feedback for their students.

Hobar (1994a) compared traditional assessment models (paper-and-pencil tests) with alternative assessment. Alternative assessment provided a much fairer assessment of the students' actual learning. Traditional assessment was found to generally measure cognitive ability, recognition, or recall of what was learned. There is no question that because students are different from one another in intelligence, interests and motivation, learning styles, and cultural backgrounds, they require different methods of assessment (Gardner, 1993b; Hunt et al., 1998).

According to Hunt et al. (1998), traditional assessment techniques of testing and grading are ineffective for evaluating the multiple intelligences of students, because students are evaluated against the same criteria they each perform on exactly the same evaluative task. Therefore, teachers must use a variety of assessment instruments and procedures to evaluate students' performances for both group and individual performance. In addition, per Hunt et al., assessment should be based not only on the observable student behavior but also on the process and thought patterns students use to arrive at the desired outcomes.

Hunt et al. (1998, p. 191) also differentiated between two concepts regarding student assessment: alternative assessment and authentic assessment. Alternative assessment is a measurement process that is different from traditional testing procedures. Authentic assessment evaluates students while they perform in situations as close to real-life application as possible. On the other hand, alternative assessment measures thought processes that students use to arrive at answers to questions or problems. Students are not just evaluated on what they know or can do; students must be able to explain the processes used to arrive at their responses.

Accordingly, alternative assessment uses different forms compared to traditional testing procedures, including portfolios, performances, exhibits, or other similar techniques, in which assessments are based on critical thinking and problem-solving skills (Hobar, 1994b; Jones, 1994).

Similar to Hunt et al. (1998), McBrien and Brandt (1997) outline the importance of performance assessment. They refer to performance assessment as:

> a measure of assessment based on authentic tasks such as activities, exercises, or problems that require students to show what they can do. Some performance tasks are designed to have students demonstrate their understanding by applying their knowledge to a particular situation. . . . Performance tasks often have more than one acceptable solution; they may call for a student to create a response to a problem and then explain or defend it. The process involves the use of higher-order thinking skills (e.g., cause and effect analysis, deductive or inductive reasoning, experimentation, and problem solving). Performance tasks may be used primarily for assessment at the end of a period of instruction, but are frequently used for learning as well as assessment. (pp. 77–78)

Brualdi (2001) indicates that performance-based assessments, in general, do not have right or wrong answers. Instead, teachers need to assess students on the degrees to which they are successful or unsuccessful. One effective assessment tool is the simple rubric, by which teachers can evaluate at what level of proficiency a student is able to perform a task or display knowledge of a concept.

Hoover (1972) asserts that measurement and evaluation (i.e., tests of all types, rating scales, checklists, anecdotal records, and any other instrument that can be applied effectively to pupil behavior) are continuous processes, which are usually more effective when students understand and become active participants in the experiences.

According to Brualdi (2001), a clearly defined purpose is the first step of good assessment. When defining purpose ask yourself the following questions:

1. **What concept, skill, or knowledge am I trying to assess?**
2. **What should my students know?**
3. **At what level should my students be performing?**
4. **What type of knowledge is being assessed: reasoning, memory, or process? (Stiggins, 1994)**

By answering these questions, you can decide what type of activity best suits your assessment needs.

CHALLENGE

8

Students Speak Out

Ask any person who has ever been in school about assessment, evaluation, and grades and he or she will have much to share. Your students will also be a valuable resource to help you develop your skills in these areas. Using the sentence stems highlighted in bold type, the following statements about evaluation, assessment, and grades were solicited from students throughout the country:

> **I learned** that not every test has to be taken alone. My social studies teacher puts us in pairs and lets us take tests together. We both have our own test and can answer the questions the way we want. We are allowed to talk about the question and our answer before we write down the answer on our own tests. I was really shocked when the teacher did that, but it helps me to see that we are not isolated in the world and that we can always ask for help. Taking the test with my test partner helped me to understand my own responsibility to study. I would be mad if the partner I got didn't study. I think I learn more taking tests in pairs because my partner usually remembers things that I forget and then we can come up with better answers. (AnnaMae S., twelfth-grade government and politics)

> **I like** it when Mr. Alverez gives us an opportunity to develop our own test questions and then reviews them before the test. He doesn't always use the same questions, but it helps us study and I think we all do better. (Marco M., eighth-grade world cultures)

> **I want** to apply what I know to a real-life situation. I like school and I like learning about health, but I would like to take what I am learning and apply it to a situation that makes a difference in someone's life. (Angie D., tenth-grade health and fitness)

> **I didn't like** it when my teacher put all the tests on the desk and told us to pick them up after class. People started running over to the desk, and everyone got to see everyone else's grade. I don't think that is right. (Corly A., seventh-grade math)

> **I never want** to have to memorize a whole term's worth of work again to pass a test. I am sure I will forget most of what I learned, and I know if I ever need to know it I can find it on the Internet. I spent hours memorizing all this information, and I doubt I will ever even use it. I don't even care about this stuff. (John C., seventh-grade world history)

CHALLENGE 8

The Teachers' Lounge

Veteran teachers are often able to shed insight into situations most teachers face. When asked about assessment, evaluation, and grades, teachers throughout the country responded to the highlighted sentence stems in the following ways:

My worst nightmare is when everyone fails the test. I realize that I am partly to blame because it is clear the students didn't get whatever I was trying to teach them. That happened to me once. I was much younger then!
(J. Kipper, Connecticut)

No one told me that I don't have to read every paper and every word of the journals I ask my students to keep.
(G. Kieff, Idaho)

I learned that rubrics are an excellent way to assess student learning. I have found that developing them with the students is even more helpful because then they know exactly what is expected of them.
(M. Stitt, Illinois)

I don't like it when students compare their grades, so I often encourage them to develop individual projects that highlight their personal skills and abilities. That way each student can develop something that he or she likes. I find that they work better and are not so concerned about failing.
(C. Conover, Vermont)

I want to use assessment as part of the learning process. It seems students should be assessing themselves as they progress through their independent work. I am trying to figure out how to create something that students can use to assess themselves as they work and then maybe give to their classmates to assess them, too. I haven't quite figured it out yet, but I will! (J. Duffy, Washington, DC)

Students like to do projects more than studying for a test. I do a lot of problem-based methods and let the students decide for themselves if they met the goal by answering the problem. This way, they assess themselves and have to defend the grade they assign themselves.
(G. Hauck, Utah)

I remember a workshop coordinator who helped me align my assessments with the national standards. I thought that was the most valuable in-service we ever had around here.
(T. Enloe, Wyoming)

I like to post my notes on the Internet for everyone to review. This helps students be organized and study for my exams. (J. Sutton, New Mexico)

I never want to be one of those teachers who use the same test year after year. I have seen some teachers still use the same notes they used ten years ago. I can't believe that. (E. Everhardt, Delaware)

I wish we didn't have to give students grades. I see how they respond when they don't do as well as expected. I see the competition. I see the dismay when they fail. I wish there were a better way to assess student success.
(B. Zollinger, California)

Teacher Tips

Master teachers have established a repertoire of skills that they draw upon when teaching. Some teachers shared these tips related to assessment, evaluation, and grades:

Sometimes students have a difficult time thinking quickly and get intimidated when their classmates respond instantaneously to questions. Therefore, each time I ask a question in class, I make the entire class wait for fifteen seconds before raising their hands to answer the question. This gives those students a few moments to formulate their responses. (A. Senft, New York)

I find that student understanding increases and they get better grades when I ask questions that require them to apply, analyze, synthesize, and evaluate what I am teaching in addition to simply recalling facts. (J. Dean, Kansas)

Use other methods to assess student learning besides paper-and-pencil tests. (G. Samuelson, Idaho)

Make sure to test what you've taught. Don't expect students to know something you haven't covered in class. Be fair and consistent. (T. Gregoire, Colorado)

I often use group exams. I don't think students are ever in a situation where they are isolated from information. I let them take exams in groups to see how they interact and respect one another. I always give individual grades, however, because students need to be able to turn in their own exam even though they can discuss the answers before responding. (L. Pineda-Romero, Louisiana)

I post every exam I give in my class on the Internet on my class Web page. I also post the answers. This helps students to prepare for my exams. Recently, I started posting examples of responses that were close to correct but not correct. Students seemed to like that. I have also posted examples of excellent, fair, and poor essay questions. I include my responses in a different color ink. Students and/or parents can see very clearly how I assess and evaluate. I have never had anyone challenge my grades since I started this. It takes a little effort, but I have become the assessment guru in our school. P. S. Be sure NOT to post student names or grades. (E. Hardy, Arkansas)

A Mentor Moment

A mentor will be able to help you considerably as you begin teaching and face issues of evaluation and assessment. Much will depend upon your philosophy of these important components of your practice.

Having another professional help you with your daily questions about teaching can make your experiences as a teacher even more rewarding. Following is a list of questions you might ask your mentor regarding assessment, evaluation, and grades. On the next page is a table you can use to identify those questions you would like to discuss with your mentor. Document your mentor's responses and your thoughts about how to incorporate what you have learned into your practice.

Questions you might ask your mentor:

- **What are rubrics and how can I use them effectively?**
- **How can I be fair when my students have so many different needs and learning styles?**
- **How does standardized testing affect my teaching in the classroom?**
- **Can cooperative learning be evaluated effectively? How?**
- **Which is better, using a standardized grading scale or a curved grading scale?**
- **How should group work be evaluated, one group grade or individual grades?**
- **Should test questions be directly related to school, state, or national curriculum standards?**
- **Do students perform better under a timed test or when given all the time they need?**
- **How will I know if students have achieved desired course outcomes?**

A Mentor Moment (continued)

Questions for My Mentor	Responses from My Mentor	How to Incorporate Mentor's Ideas into My Practice

A Mentor Moment (continued)

Now that you have had time to focus on your questions about assessment, evaluation, and grading with a mentor, think about what you have learned in relation to being a critical reflective practitioner.

■ **What do you presently believe about assessment, evaluation, and grading?**

My beliefs . . .

■ **Why do you assess and grade the way you do? Develop a rationale for your beliefs.**

My rationale . . .

A Mentor Moment (continued)

- Return to this challenge at a later date and review your rationale (see the preceding item). How has your rationale changed? (You should see growth in your rationale and practice. Include this exercise as part of your yearly personal professional goals. It should help you to see your development as you critically reflect upon your practice.)

How my new rationale has changed . . .

- Identify an incident in which you blamed yourself for your students', their parents', or your administrators' reaction regarding assessment, evaluation, or grading. How might you have turned that into a positive experience for them and for you?

My ideas . . .

A Mentor Moment (continued)

- Is there any way you might communicate to your students, their parents, or your administrators the reflection that you have done regarding this particular incident, practice, or policy? Can you share it with them so that you may model the process of critical reflection? How might you present this to those who were involved in the incident?

My reflections . . .

A Mentor Moment (continued)

■ Assuming you were able to share your thinking process with the group that was impacted, what was their response?

The response . . .

CHALLENGE 8

Shared Strategies

Following are some activities and strategies that can assist you in justifying your rationale for evaluating. Use them to inform your practice. See others to continue your development.

Standardized vs. Classroom Assessment

The following Venn diagram illustrates the differences between standardized tests and classroom assessments.

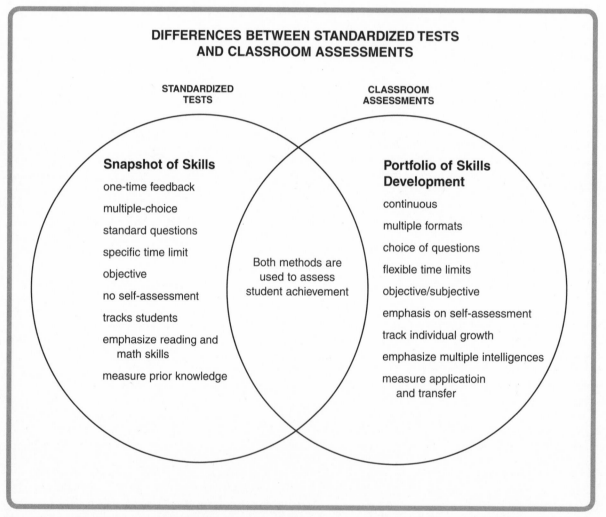

DIFFERENCES BETWEEN STANDARDIZED TESTS AND CLASSROOM ASSESSMENTS

STANDARDIZED TESTS

CLASSROOM ASSESSMENTS

Snapshot of Skills

one-time feedback

multiple-choice

standard questions

specific time limit

objective

no self-assessment

tracks students

emphasize reading and math skills

measure prior knowledge

Both methods are used to assess student achievement

Portfolio of Skills Development

continuous

multiple formats

choice of questions

flexible time limits

objective/subjective

emphasis on self-assessment

track individual growth

emphasize multiple intelligences

measure applicatioin and transfer

From Burke, K., *How to Assess Authentic Learning* (3rd ed., p. 34). © 1999 by SkyLight Training and Publishing, Inc. Reprinted with permission.

Shared Strategies (continued)

This table shows the components of balanced assessment: traditional, portfolio, and performance assessments. It is best to include all three types of assessment in your evaluation plan.

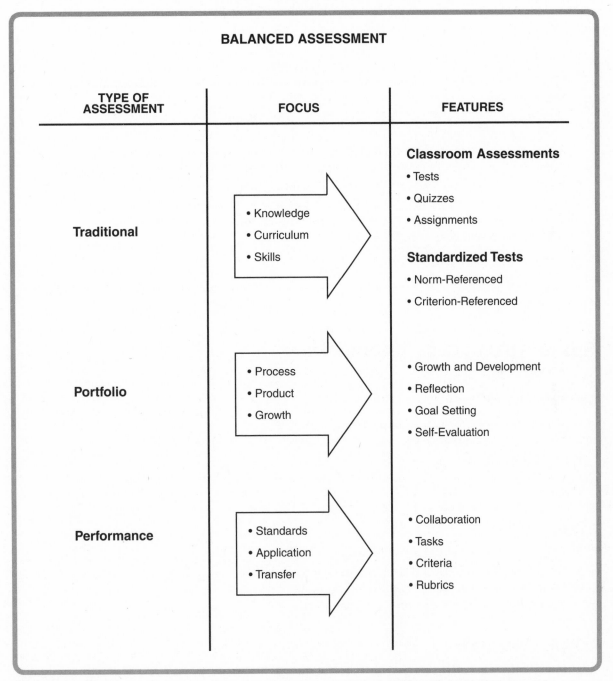

From Burke, K., *How to Assess Authentic Learning* (3rd ed., p. xxiv). © 1999 by SkyLight Training and Publishing, Inc. Reprinted with permission.

Shared Strategies (continued)

Portfolios

Portfolios are a popular and effective way to evaluate student learning. Portfolios may focus on different topics and different types of work. Following is a list of portfolio types you might like in your assessment process:

- *Writing* — dated writing samples to show process and product
- *Process folios* — first and second drafts of assignments, along with final product, to show growth
- *Literacy* — combination of reading, writing, speaking, and listening pieces
- *Best-work* — student and teacher selections of the student's best work
- *Unit* — one unit of study (Egypt, angles, frogs, elections)
- *Integrated* — a thematic study that brings in different disciplines (e.g., "Health and Wellness"—language arts, science, math, health, and physical education)
- *Year-long* — key artifacts from entire year to show growth and development
- *Career* — important artifacts (resumes, recommendations, commendations) collected for showcase employability
- *Standards* — evidence to document meeting standards

From Burke, K., *How to Assess Authentic Learning* (3rd ed.). © 1999 by SkyLight Training and Publishing, Inc. Reprinted with permission.

Tips for Constructing Test Questions

Consider the following tips when you are constructing test questions:

True-False Items

- Avoid absolute words like *all, never,* and *always.*
- Make sure items are clearly true or false, rather than ambiguous.
- Limit true-false questions to 10.
- Consider asking students to make false questions true to encourage higher-order thinking.

Matching Items

- Limit list to between 5 and 10 items.
- Use homogeneous lists. (Don't mix names with dates.)
- Give clear instructions. (Write letter, number, etc.)
- Give more choices than there are questions.

Multiple-Choice Items

- State main idea in the core or stem of the question.
- Use reasonable incorrect choices. (Avoid ridiculous choices.)
- Make options the same length (nothing very long or very short).
- Include multiple correct answers (a and b, all of the above).

Shared Strategies (continued)

Completion Items

- Structure for a brief, specific answer for each item.
- Avoid passages lifted directly from text (emphasis on memorization).
- Use blanks of equal length.
- Avoid multiple blanks that sometimes make a sentence too confusing.

Essay Items

- Avoid all-encompassing. ("Discuss" is ambiguous . . . tell all you know about a subject.)
- Define criteria for evaluation.
- Give point value.
- Use some higher-order thinking verbs like *predict* or *compare and contrast* rather than all recall verbs like *list* and *name*.

Adapted from Board of Education for the City of Etobicoke, *Making the Grade: Evaluating Student Progress* (pp. 112–187). © 1987 by Prentice-Hall Canada.

An Amusing Story

I had a student who took off his watch every time he took a test and laid it on the corner of his desk. I watched him closely as he took the exam and noticed that he rubbed it when he seemed to be pondering a question that stumped him. I was curious—thinking that perhaps he might be cheating in some way. I invited him to stay after class and related what I noticed. He told me it was his lucky charm and that by rubbing the watch it would help him with that particular question. I didn't understand until I looked at the face of his watch. It was a Guess watch. (D. Baublitz, North Dakota)

CHALLENGE 8

Personal Reflection Journal

This challenge encouraged you to critically reflect on assessment, evaluation, and grades. Identify a situation related to one of these issues that you can use as an example to encourage your development. Follow the steps below to arrive at a desirable solution. Depending on the nature of your situation, you may consider using this exercise as a benchmark. If so, include this piece in your professional portfolio.

My thoughts . . .

Identify the situation:

Describe the situation:

Whose advice did you seek in finding a creative solution to the situation?

What did this person (or these persons) tell you to do?

Personal Reflection Journal (continued)

How did you deal with the situation?

Would you do the same thing if presented with a similar situation?

If yes, why?

If no, why?

What new knowledge or ideas come to mind as you incorporate what you have learned through this experience?

If you were to establish a goal to enhance your personal professional development in this area, what might that be?

How does what you learned compare to other areas of your teaching?

Personal Reflection Journal (continued)

Assessing student progress and evaluating achievement of your desired goals is central to effective teaching and learning. Think about how this aspect of your teaching repertoire impacts other areas of your teaching. Document your thoughts and the relationships you perceive based on what you have learned in this challenge.

Upon reflection, what have you learned that will enhance your development as an educator?

How will you integrate your new knowledge into your practice?

What does it mean to be a critical reflective practitioner in the area of assessment, evaluation, and grades? Develop a clear and concise response that you can include in your professional portfolio.

Consider including this in your professional teaching portfolio.

CHALLENGE

8

Standards

Different schools adapt and use different teaching standards. Yet all agree that teachers need to possess a level of competence in order to find success. Because of their generic nature, the Interstate New Teacher Assessment and Support Consortium (INTASC) standards have been identified as a framework for you to use to reflect on your practice as an educator. The INTASC standards that address evaluation, assessment, and grades are as follows:

■ **PRINCIPLE #8: The teacher understands and uses formal and informal assessment strategies to evaluate and ensure the continuous intellectual, social, and physical development of the learner.**

■ **PRINCIPLE #9: The teacher is a reflective practitioner who continually evaluates the effects of his or her choices and actions on others (students, parents, and other professionals in the learning community) and who actively seeks out opportunities to grow professionally.**

From Interstate New Teacher Assessment and Support Consortium, *Model Standards for Beginning Teacher Licensing, Assessment, and Development: A Resource for State Dialogue.* © 1992 by Council of Chief State School Officers, Washington, DC. Retrieved November 3, 2004, from http://www.ccsso.org/content/pdfs/corestrd.pdf. Used with permission.

Perhaps your school, district, or national organization has established standards pertinent to your professional development in this area. Review them, and the INTASC principles, to determine which one(s) you have met as a result of working through this challenge. It is not necessary to provide evidence for each standard in each challenge. However, by the time you complete this book, you should have evidence of how you can meet each principle or standard necessary for your portfolio. Document your evidence and include it in the Wrap-Up section of the book.

Reflections Log

Fill out the following log to reflect on your learnings. It might be helpful to refer to the Assessment and Reflections Log at the beginning of the challenge to assess your growth.

What did I learn about <u>assessment, evaluation, and grades?</u>

Was I able to accomplish my goals?

How did I overcome the challenges in accomplishing my goals?

CHALLENGE 8

Congratulations, You Made It!

Identify something you are proud of related to the topic of this challenge that you can incorporate in your professional portfolio. What evidence do you have to show your success? Use the following chart to record your responses.

Situation:

How I handled it:

Evidence to be included in my portfolio:

Consider including this in your professional teaching portfolio.

Professional Development

CHALLENGE 9

Assessment and Reflections Log

Record your initial beliefs and goals about professional development in this log.

My beliefs about <u>professional development</u>:

My goal(s) for <u>professional development</u>:

How am I going to accomplish my goal(s)?

Who and what can help me?

Challenges to accomplishing my goal(s):

The process or procedure for reaching my goal(s):

CHALLENGE

9

Professional Development

"I didn't realize there were so many professional opportunities for teachers."–First-Year Teacher

Professional development is generally considered to be a person's activities and projects that promote his or her continual professional growth. You have much to consider when you first assume your role as an educator. However, you also have an obligation to begin charting the course for your own professional development based on your perceived needs and those identified by your mentors and administrators.

Just as you expect your students to continue to learn and explore, your professional development should be ongoing. Your growth—within and outside of your classroom—is a product of your ability to reflect on your experiences and your participation in educational opportunities to enhance and extend your professional objectives. As a professional, you are now responsible for establishing your own goals based on your aspirations and identified areas of weakness. Taking part in professional development programs, such as exploring new approaches to engage students with new ideas, possible strategies for assessment, and different ways of organization, not only advance you professionally but also benefit your students and school. Beyond the classroom, you will evolve as a participant in a wider educational community. Through reading, talking with colleagues, taking the initiative to press for changes, and speaking out on current issues, you will face new challenges and advance yourself professionally.

> *Not to know is bad; not to wish to know is worse.*
> —NIGERIAN PROVERB

Equally important is your desire and commitment to keep up to date on new instructional methods and educational strategies by determining how well they facilitate student learning. Incorporate these new strategies into your ever-growing and complex professional repertoire. As a professional educator, your teaching methods will constantly grow and change.

CHALLENGE 9

Practical Problem

What ought to be done about your professional development? Everyone who teaches is faced with this question, and the answer is different for each professional. Determining a professional development plan serves as a framework for this challenge. The questions below are designed to encourage you to think about your own professional development.

1. **Reflect on your own experience as a student, and try to recall examples of teachers involved in professional development activities. Develop a response to each question.**

   ■ **Did a teacher ever share what he or she was doing to enhance his or her development? What did he or she share?**

   _____
   _____
   _____
   _____

   ■ **What did you think teachers were doing during their in-service days?**

   _____
   _____
   _____
   _____

   ■ **Did you ever say that a teacher was acting professionally or unprofessionally? What did you mean?**

   _____
   _____
   _____
   _____

   ■ **What teacher or administrator do you recall as being very professional? What characteristics did that person exhibit that made you think of him or her in that way?**

   _____
   _____
   _____
   _____

Practical Problem (continued)

My reflections . . .

Practical Problem (continued)

2. After reflecting on the preceding questions, think about professional development from a broader perspective:

■ What should be done about professional development in teaching? (Example: Teachers should be grouped into teams to work on similar aspects of professional development and to encourage collegiality and peer support.)

My ideas . . .

■ Now that you have thought through each of these questions, what ideas do you have that might enhance professional development for you and other teachers in your school? You may find it useful to discuss your ideas with a mentor, colleague, or peer.

My ideas . . .

CHALLENGE 9

Valued Ends

The following list describes some of the personal characteristics associated with teachers who are successful in professional development. In the space provided, identify other qualities that you believe are pertinent to successful professional development. Also include any expectations or goals your administration has identified related to your growth and development as a professional.

Teachers who are successful in professional development:

- **Are able and willing to self-diagnose and change according to that diagnosis**
- **Are committed to lifelong learning**
- **Assume responsibility for their own professional development**
- **Are willing to fail and make alterations based on their mistakes and failures**
- **Are able to make judgments based on ethical orientation**
- **Are intelligent professionals with the ability to use self, knowledge, and resources to solve problems for which they are responsible**

Qualities I believe are pertinent to successful professional development: _____

_____

_____

Administration's expectations or goals related to professional development: _____

_____

_____

What can I realistically achieve related to successful professional development to be demonstrated in my teaching portfolio? _____

_____

_____

_____

CHALLENGE 9

"I am wondering...?"

All teachers assume responsibility for establishing their own goals and means for accomplishing them. As a result, most teachers have questions about how best to approach professional development. Questions that other beginning teachers have raised about the topic include:

- **What ought to be done to determine whether my goals are met?**
- **How do I choose from all the things that interest me?**
- **How do I determine what I need to do for my own professional development?**
- **How should I continue my professional development?**
- **Does the school district pay for any of my professional development?**
- **Are there books I should be reading that might help me with my teaching?**
- **What professional associations are the best for me to join?**
- **How will professional associations help my professional development?**
- **Is there anything local or statewide that is good for my professional development?**

In the space that follows, list additional questions you may have about professional development, and determine who can answer each question for your situation.

QUESTION	WHO CAN HELP?

Focus on the Issue

Professional Development

Just as you would not expect a surgeon to operate on you solely armed with the advanced education and preparation gleaned from his or her days in medical school, you can't expect a teacher to possess the knowledge and skills necessary to be an effective educator without additional professional development opportunities. Current literature promotes an array of experiences that teachers can engage in to support their personal professional development. What characteristics and qualities ought professional educators seek to acquire? Gentzler (1987, p. 41) proposes a list of competencies for professional development, which have been altered to meet the needs of all educators. This list, in part, includes:

- *A commitment to the mission of education:* **How do you fit into the larger educational profession? Are you committed to that mission, or are you just affiliating with education for the time being until you decide on another career option? If you are committed, you will identify with your peers who are also committed to this noble profession. Think about the difference between someone who is committed to a goal and focuses energy and passion toward that goal as opposed to one who simply accepts the goals of education.**

- *A willingness to deal with the complex concepts relevant to the practice of education:* **Because you deal with people as an educator, you will not always get the same response given the same stimuli. As such, you will want to cultivate the ability to explore and become familiar with the many complex issues that surround education. It's easy to go into the classroom and focus solely on the students. However, your obligation as an educator demands that you be part of a team of educated professionals who are working together to enhance learning not only for your school's students but for the public at large.**

- *A sense of purpose that transcends self-interest:* **Most teachers will tell you they are not in the education profession for the salary. Most would say they are cultivating an altruistic stance, which includes characteristics such as being honest, helpful, and compassionate. Altruism is juxtaposed to the egocentric, where the person is more focused on self and motivated by what he or she can get out of teaching rather than what he or she can give.**

- *The ability to identify with a community of peers:* **Certainly, this is a characteristic worth cultivating as one develops within the profession. Education is a dynamic process including every aspect of our lives. It makes sense to cultivate relationships that will help establish a feeling of belonging so that you can be effective in your role and feel connected to the larger profession committed to the same goals as you have identified for yourself.**

- *Participation in dialogue within the professional community through examined critique and reflection:* **Professional educators must find time to work together to explore and discuss the questions within education. If they do not, the general public and legislators may make decisions that could potentially be difficult to handle. Joining and actively participating in a professional association is one way to be involved in that dialogue.**

Focus on the Issue (continued)

Professional Development

■ *Self-direction in selection of experiences, opportunities, and relationships that encourage professional growth:* **Self-directed professionals recognize that they are responsible for satisfying their own needs for ongoing growth and learning. Although a principal, an administrator, a curriculum specialist, or a mentor can assist you in identifying that which is necessary for your growth, the decision is ultimately yours. Cultivating a self-directed stance toward your growth is a significant quality worthy of development for professionals.**

■ *An ability to justify one's professional practice as it interfaces with the larger society and profession:* **Professional educators need to be able to make reasoned judgments based on experiences and knowledge that can be gleaned from a variety of sources. It is inappropriate for an educator to act impulsively or strictly as he or she pleases. Instead, to be autonomous suggests that you behave in a knowledgeable, ethical, and responsible way in the situations that you face.**

Educators have a unique opportunity to select those experiences that best fit their professional agendas. Think about some specific skills or abilities that you would like to develop that may enhance your growth. These experiences do not necessarily need to be classroom skills. They may take the form of more personal characteristics that can help you develop a professional position. Maybe you want to focus on your ability to accept constructive criticism. Think about how this ability will help you to grow. What might you do to encourage this ability? Suppose you want to overcome self-doubt. Set an agenda for yourself that documents those feelings or expressions of self-doubt and what you might do to overcome them. Reflect back to a time in your professional career when you were less confident. Compare that to where you are now. What did you do that encouraged your professional self-esteem? Many beginning teachers deal with stress—the stress of understanding their role in an entirely new situation. Maybe you want to learn to manage stress. If so, what are some strategies you might employ? Another area that some beginning teachers identify that needs attention is enhancing their understanding of ethics in education. How do you cope with ethical issues? Are you willing to compromise? Should you compromise? What designates right and wrong for you? The National Education Association has identified a code of ethics that might help you to begin your focus on ethical concerns (see http://www.nea.org/aboutnea/code.html or the appendix). Another interesting concern that beginning teachers often wrestle with is their devotion to students. What does this mean? What is the difference between being devoted and caring or being intrusive and crossing the professional line? Becoming socialized into an existing structure is not easy. However, it can be easier if you identify an area of concern and focus your energy on understanding it.

Your life in the classroom will at times be predictable and at other times unpredictable. Your expectations may be self-defeating prophecies. Think carefully when identifying those areas that you want to focus on that will enhance your professional agenda. When you work with your mentor and your supervisor, be sure to share what you believe your weaknesses are and how you intend to modify them to become stronger.

Focus on the Issue (continued)
Professional Development

DEVELOPING A TEACHING PHILOSOPHY: BELIEFS ABOUT TEACHING AND LEARNING

Three words that describe me as a teacher are:

1.

2.

3.

Three beliefs I have about teaching are:

1.

2.

3.

In *Seven Habits of Highly Effective People* (1989), Covey says that being proactive "means that as human beings, we are responsible for our own lives" (p. 71). "It is inspiring," says Covey, "to realize that in choosing our response to circumstance, we powerfully affect our circumstance" (p. 86). Covey is discussing the basic principle that when life does not go the way that it should, truly effective people do not throw their hands up in the air, cry "victim," and give up or move on. People who apply Covey's idea of being proactive to their teaching careers become educational leaders.

Professional development should be self-directed. It is your responsibility to set goals for yourself and take steps to accomplish those goals. Consider the following:

- **What obligations do you have as a professional?**
- **If you have not been assigned a mentor, find one.**
- **Join your professional association and become active.**
- **Read the faculty handbook and make sure you understand it.**
- **Seek information and knowledge about teaching and your content area. Do not expect that it is the school's responsibility to continue to educate you. It is now your responsibility.**
- **Take classes that can assist you in becoming a better educator. (Rogers, Ludington, & Graham, 1997)**

CHALLENGE

9

Students Speak Out

Students provide valuable insight into educational issues. Listening to their perspectives often sparks ideas that might prove fruitful in your professional growth. Using the sentence stems highlighted in bold, the following statements about professional development were solicited from students throughout the country:

"**I learned** a new leadership activity that I can use in my 4-H group from Ms. Roderick's class. She goes to these workshops all the time that give her ideas to use with her students. She comes back and tries them with us, and it makes class more fun. I plan to use this at our next retreat. (Allyson W., twelfth-grade family and consumer sciences)"

"**I didn't like** it when teachers complained about going to in-service meetings. Two of my teachers spent five minutes in the hall talking about how bored they were at the meetings they went to yesterday. Now they know what we go through when we sit every day and listen to them. They should let the kids plan an in-service for the teachers. I think it would be hilarious. (Dustin B., eleventh-grade speech and communica-"

"**I liked** it when my music teacher included us in developing a presentation for the state meeting. A group of us helped her to come up with this workshop, and we all got to go and present it. Everyone liked it, and we got a lot of good contacts from people who were there. (Cybil S., twelfth-grade music/chorus)"

"**I want** to become a professional speaker. I went to a national meeting with the science department teachers in my school, and I really liked the keynote speakers. I had a great time. I didn't know that teachers have these kinds of things to go to to learn. I want to do this when I graduate. (Mac D., twelfth-grade biology)"

"**I never want** to be as random and outdated as my health teacher. My dad had him in school, and Dad said he teaches the same stuff now that he taught back then. He needs to quit or get some new material. (Jackson R., twelfth-grade physical education)"

CHALLENGE 9

The Teachers' Lounge

Once a person is involved in a role long enough, he or she often has some advice for those just beginning. Using the highlighted sentence stems, teachers throughout the country had the following to say about professional development:

I LEARNED TO ASK COLLEAGUES TO COME AND OBSERVE ME ON A REGULAR BASIS. AT FIRST IT WAS DISCONCERTING BECAUSE I DIDN'T FEEL ALL THAT COMFORTABLE HAVING OTHER TEACHERS IN MY CLASSROOM. AS THEY HELPED ME, IT MADE ME FEEL MORE CONFIDENT AND GAVE ME A LOT OF SKILLS THAT I WOULDN'T HAVE HAD IF I DID NOT ASKED FOR HELP. IT ALSO HELPED US TO SEE HOW TO DO MORE INTEGRATED TEACHING BECAUSE WE WERE ABLE TO MAKE CONNECTIONS WITH SOME OF THE CONTENT. (R. Rogers, Tennessee)

I DON'T LIKE TEACHERS WHO COMPLAIN ABOUT EVERYTHING AND EVERYONE. CHOOSE YOUR FRIENDS WISELY. IF THE GROUP IN THE LOUNGE WHINES, COMPLAINS, AND GOSSIPS, EAT ELSEWHERE. SEEK COLLEAGUES WHO SEEM HAPPY, ENTHUSIASTIC, AND PROFESSIONAL.
(K. Amereilo, New York)

I LIKE GETTING OFF SCHOOL TO GO TO A WORKSHOP OR A CONFERENCE. IT HELPS TO REJUVENATE ME, AND I ALWAYS COME BACK WITH MORE IDEAS AND CONTACTS. I THINK EVERY FIRST-YEAR TEACHER SHOULD GO TO AT LEAST ONE WORKSHOP A YEAR. (K. Bell, Illinois)

I WISH I HAD TIME TO TAKE A CLASS OR SEMINAR TO LEARN SOMETHING NEW. I WENT TO A WORKSHOP LAST SUMMER, AND I LEARNED SO MUCH. I GUESS I JUST NEED TO MAKE THE TIME TO DO IT.
(P. Burgess, Alaska)

I WANT TO TRY ONE NEW METHOD OR STRATEGY EACH MONTH. I ALSO LIKE OBSERVING OTHER TEACHERS IN OUR PEER-TEACHING PROGRAM BECAUSE I GET A LOT OF IDEAS.
(M. Crozier, Virginia)

I NEVER WANT TO MISS ANOTHER NATIONAL ASCD MEETING IN MY LIFE. THIS IS THE FIFTH YEAR I HAVE GONE, AND IT IS BETTER THAN A VACATION. I HAVE MET OTHER TEACHERS FROM ALL OVER THE COUNTRY, AND WE HAVE A WONDERFUL TIME. WE STAY CONNECTED ALL YEAR ON E-MAIL.
(N. Sanchez, Massachusetts)

I REMEMBER NOT HAVING THE RESOURCES THAT ARE AVAILABLE TO TEACHERS NOW. WHO WOULD HAVE EVER THOUGHT OF A COMPUTER SITTING ON OUR DESKS, GIVING US ACCESS TO KNOWLEDGE FROM ALL OVER THE WORLD?
(E. Ireland, Pennsylvania)

STUDENTS KNOW IF YOU ARE CONSCIENTIOUS ABOUT YOUR OWN WORK. I THINK THE SERIOUS STUDENTS RESPOND FAVORABLY TO TEACHERS WHO THEY SEE ARE TRYING AS HARD AS THEY ARE TO MAKE THEIR LEARNING EXPERIENCE A GOOD ONE. (M. Linnnenbrink, Hawaii)

MY WORST NIGHTMARE WAS WHEN A PARENT OF ONE OF MY STUDENTS CAME AND TOLD ME THAT WHEN HE WAS IN SCHOOL HE REMEMBERS DOING THE SAME ACTIVITY THAT I HAVE HIS SON DOING. I ALMOST DIED. I REALIZED IT WAS TIME FOR ME TO GET SOME NEW ACTIVITIES!
(S. Gilbert, New Hampshire)

NO ONE TOLD ME THAT THE SCHOOL DISTRICT MIGHT PAY FOR CLASSES AND SEMINARS AND THAT ALL I HAD TO DO IS ASK.
(T. Neidiger, Missouri)

CHALLENGE 9

Teacher Tips

Master teachers have established a repertoire of skills that they draw upon when teaching. Some teachers shared these tips related to professional development:

Every year I ask my principal to help support me to do to a professional development conference. She has always found the money and I have come back to school with a host of new ideas. (N. Boschert, Washington)

The library in our district buys professional development tapes and CDs. I usually check one out at the beginning of the year and try to incorporate it into my yearly professional goals. I include evidence in my portfolio of what I have learned. (O. Wilmarth, California)

I try to take an online course each year to help me stay fresh and updated. I have met a lot of people online who have formed a new professional network for me. (D. Anderson, Delaware)

CHALLENGE 9

A Mentor Moment

The following is provided by a mentor teacher to help you in the area of professional development:

> Teaching is incredibly demanding. You have to learn to replenish all of the energy that will be taken from you by students, parents, and administrators. Do something good for yourself periodically. Otherwise you could get burned out. (R. Burdette, Ohio)

Having another professional help you with your daily questions about teaching can make your experiences as a teacher even more rewarding. Following is a list of questions you might ask your mentor regarding professional development. On the next page is a table you can use to identify those questions you would like to discuss with your mentor. Document your mentor's responses and your thoughts about how to incorporate what you have learned into your practice.

Questions you might ask your mentor:

- **What about finding activities on a regional or the national level for my professional development?**
- **What professional publications are going to be beneficial for me?**
- **How can I stay committed to lifelong learning?**
- **How can I encourage professional goals in my students?**

A Mentor Moment (continued)

Questions for My Mentor	Responses from My Mentor	How to Incorporate Mentor's Ideas into My Practice

A Mentor Moment (continued)

Now that you have had the time to focus on your questions about professional development with a mentor, think about what you have learned in relation to being a critical reflective practitioner.

■ **What do you presently believe about professional development? Why do you do the professional development activities that you do?**

My beliefs . . .

_____

_____

_____

_____

_____

_____

_____

_____

■ **Develop a rationale for your actions.**

My rationale . . .

_____

_____

_____

_____

_____

_____

_____

_____

A Mentor Moment (continued)

■ Return to this challenge at a later date and review your rationale (see the preceding item). How has your rationale changed? (You should see growth in your rationale and practice. Include this exercise as part of your yearly personal professional goals. It helps you to see growth and development as you critically reflect upon your practice.)

How my rationale has changed . . .

■ Identify an incident in which you blamed yourself for your students', their parents', or your administrators' reaction to something related to your professional development. How might you have turned that into a positive experience for them and for you?

My ideas . . .

A Mentor Moment (continued)

■ Is there any way you might communicate to your students, their parents, or your administrators the reflection that you have done regarding this particular incident? Can you share it with them so that you may model the process of critical reflection? How might you present this to those who were involved in the incident?

My reflections . . .
_____
_____
_____
_____
_____
_____
_____
_____

■ Assuming you were able to share your thinking process with those involved in the incident, what were their responses?

Their responses . . .
_____
_____
_____
_____
_____
_____
_____
_____

CHALLENGE 9

Shared Strategies

Professional development is a personal process. It can be self- or other-directed, meaning you can select the activities, challenges, and resources that best meet your desired goals, or you can rely on your administration or a mentor to outline them for you. The following strategies can help you reflect on your growth, consider what to include in your professional portfolio, and choose learning experiences to enhance your professional development.

Reflection

Reflecting upon your teaching practice is essential to your professional development. Use the following worksheet to reflect upon your actions in the classroom.

REFLECTIONS BASICS

What Do You Do? Why Do You Do It? Should You Do It Again?

ON ACTION What *has* happened?	IN ACTION What *is* happening?
What did I do?	What am I doing?
Why did I do it?	Why am I doing it?
What happened as a result of what I did?	What is happening as a result of what I am doing?
What will I do next time?	What should I do next?
Why?	Why?

THINK!

What have I just experienced?

How does that compare with what I know and believe?

So what does that mean?

McCormick, J. H., *The Professional Growth Plan: A School Leader's Guide to the Process* (p. 117). © 2002 by SkyLight Professional Development. Reprinted with permission.

Shared Strategies (continued)

Professional Teaching Portfolio

Maintaining an up-to-date portfolio will be a great tool for you to examine your own growth and to share with your supervisors. The following is a list of evidence you might consider including in your portfolio.

DOCUMENTATION ARTIFACTS

Activity Plans

Activity Reflections

Anecdotal Records

Assessments

Awards

CD-ROMs

Checklists

Classroom Observations

Conference Summaries

Curriculum Materials

Grade Sheets/Evaluation Reports

Homework Assignments

Instructional Materials

Instructional Planning Calendars

Learning Logs

Lesson Plans

Likert Scales

Management Plans

Mentoring Activities

New Certification/Degree

Newsletters

Newspaper Articles

Observation Reflections

Observational Instruments

Parent Contact Data

Parent Contact Log

Parent Correspondence

Peer Reviews

Performance Assessments

Photographs

Pre/Post Self-Assessments

Professional Presentations

Rating Scales

Reading Logs

Revised Professional Growth Plans

Reading Reflections

Standardized Test Scores

Student Projects

Student Work Samples

Surveys
- Student
- Parent
- Colleague

Tally Sheets

Teacher Journal

Transcripts

Unit Plans

Video/Audio Tapes

Visual Maps

Work Logs

McCormick, J. H., *The Professional Growth Plan: A School Leader's Guide to the Process* (p. 108). © 2002 by SkyLight Professional Development. Reprinted with permission.

Shared Strategies (continued)

Professional Development Activites

You are now in charge of your own development. Just as you plan for your students, you should plan for yourself. The following shows a variety of experiences that you can select to encourage your own growth.

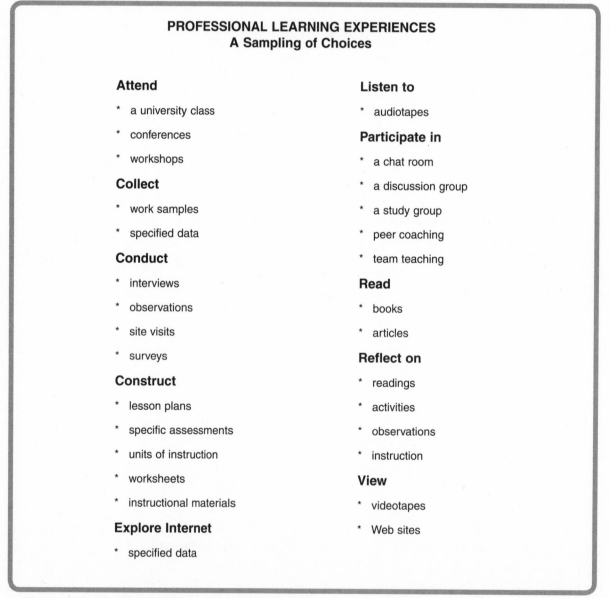

PROFESSIONAL LEARNING EXPERIENCES
A Sampling of Choices

Attend

* a university class

* conferences

* workshops

Collect

* work samples

* specified data

Conduct

* interviews

* observations

* site visits

* surveys

Construct

* lesson plans

* specific assessments

* units of instruction

* worksheets

* instructional materials

Explore Internet

* specified data

Listen to

* audiotapes

Participate in

* a chat room

* a discussion group

* a study group

* peer coaching

* team teaching

Read

* books

* articles

Reflect on

* readings

* activities

* observations

* instruction

View

* videotapes

* Web sites

McCormick, J. H., *The Professional Growth Plan: A School Leader's Guide to the Process* (p. 104). © 2002 by SkyLight Professional Development. Reprinted with permission.

Personal Reflection Journal

This challenge encouraged you to explore your own professional development. Identify a situation related to this topic that needs your attention. Follow the steps below to arrive at a desirable solution. Depending on the nature of your situation, you may use this exercise as a benchmark in your development. If so, include this piece in your professional portfolio.

My thoughts . . .

Identify the situation:

↓

Describe the situation:

↓

Whose advice did you seek in finding a creative solution to the situation?

↓

What did this person (or these persons) tell you to do?

Personal Reflection Journal (continued)

How did you deal with the situation?

Would you do the same thing if presented with a similar situation?

If yes, why?	If no, why?

What new knowledge or ideas come to mind as you incorporate what you have learned through this experience?

If you were to establish a goal to enhance your personal professional development in this area, what might that be?

How does what you learned compare to other areas of your teaching?

Personal Reflection Journal (continued)

Consider what you have learned in this situation, how might you use this to influence your teaching?

Upon reflection, what have you learned that will enhance your development as an educator?

How will you integrate your new knowledge into your practice?

What does it mean to be a critical reflective practitioner when determining your own professional development plan? Develop a clear and concise response that you can include in your professional portfolio.

Consider including this in your professional teaching portfolio.

CHALLENGE

9 Standards

Professional development is central to your success as an educator. The ability to identify your strengths and weaknesses and find appropriate means to enhance your strengths is one of the characteristics of a professional. The Interstate New Teacher Assessment and Support Consortium (INTASC) standards have been identified as a framework for you to use to reflect on your notions of professional development. The INTASC standards that address professional development are as follows:

- **PRINCIPLE #9: The teacher is a reflective practitioner who continually evaluates the effects of his or her choices and actions on others (students, parents, and other professionals in the learning community) and who actively seeks out opportunities to grow professionally.**

- **PRINCIPLE #10: The teacher fosters relationships with school colleagues, parents, and agencies in the larger community to support students' learning and well-being.**

From Interstate New Teacher Assessment and Support Consortium, *Model Standards for Beginning Teacher Licensing, Assessment, and Development: A Resource for State Dialogue.* © 1992 by Council of Chief State School Officers, Washington, DC. Retrieved November 3, 2004, from http://www.ccsso.org/content/pdfs/corestrd.pdf. Used with permission.

Perhaps your school, district, or national organization has established standards pertinent to your professional development in this area. Review them, and the INTASC principles, to determine which one(s) you have met as a result of working through this challenge. It is not necessary to provide evidence for each standard in each challenge. However, by the time you complete this book, you should have evidence of how you can meet each principle or standard necessary for your portfolio. Document your evidence and include it in the Wrap-Up section of the book.

An Amusing Story

As a teacher, I have often been called upon to give presentations for local community groups. I generally don't ask for an honorarium as I see this as a contribution to the professional development of the group that calls me. One evening, I was given a check in the amount of $100. I suggested that the group keep it and put it toward something they felt was worthwhile—perhaps a scholarship for a student, etc. The president was very pleased and exclaimed, "Oh, no, we have plenty of money for scholarships. What we really need to do is start a fund so that we can get some decent speakers." (C. Holloway, Oklahoma)

Reflections Log

Fill out the following log to reflect on your learnings. It might be helpful to refer to the Assessment and Reflections Log at the beginning of the challenge to assess your growth.

What did I learn about <u>professional development</u>?

Was I able to accomplish my goals?

How did I overcome the challenges in accomplishing my goals?

Congratulations, You Made It!

Identify something you are proud of related to this challenge that you can incorporate in your professional portfolio. What evidence do you have to show your success? Use the following chart to record your responses.

Situation:

How I handled it:

Evidence to be included in my Portfolio:

 **Consider including this in your professional teaching portfolio.**

Administrators, Parents, and the Community

Assessment and Reflections Log

Record your initial beliefs and goals about administrators, parents, and the community in this log.

My beliefs about <u>administrators, parents, and the community</u>:

My goal(s) for <u>administrators, parents, and the community</u>:

How am I going to accomplish my goal(s)?

Who and what can help me?

Challenges to accomplishing my goal(s):

The process or procedure for reaching my goal(s):

CHALLENGE

10

Administrators, Parents, and the Community

"I have the school board president's daughter in my class!"

—First-Year Teacher

Administrators, parents, and the public are essential to your success as a teacher. Each will work with you if you maintain a professional posture, exhibit ethical behaviors, make sound and rational decisions, and remain fair and consistent. Administrators are hired to provide the vision, resources, and counsel necessary for an effective school. Parents want what is best for their children and will work with you in helping their children find success. The public is also concerned about the well-being and education of the children in their community. You have an important role in the development of future generations. Getting these people on board with you can enhance your effectiveness and make your role enjoyable.

What does it mean to be a professional educator? What do others, such as colleagues, parents, and community members, expect of educators? This challenge focuses on developing relationships and honing survival skills necessary to negotiate the politics of the workplace. Dealing with the principal, other administrative staff, as well as the janitors is important because they are significant figures in schools. Giving staff members the respect they deserve will work to your advantage. Many people are watching you as a new teacher. How do you want to appear to others? If you are humble and approachable, others will be more willing to share advice and help you when you need it. Take advantage of opportunities to build relationships and connections within your school.

Schools that promote community and parental involvement experience noticeably different accomplishments than schools that do not. In these schools, teachers and parents share joint expectations for student development and

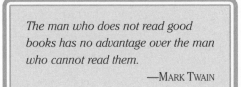

The man who does not read good books has no advantage over the man who cannot read them.

—MARK TWAIN

success. How are these common expectations transmitted inside and outside the classroom? What are the distinct roles of the teacher, administrator, parent, and public in this collection of efforts? Communities, parents, and teachers all want students to learn and experience success. Build a coalition on this common goal. How can new teachers develop their proficiency about issues facing the school and community? How can an insightful teacher take hold of the history and culture of a school and its community and assimilate this knowledge in daily lessons? Build a network of support in your community. Create a file of professional resources and related organizations and social agencies whose interests complement your efforts as a teacher. Take advantage of parent-teacher conferences to connect and build relationships with parents. Prepare for a productive session of conferences with students' parents by confronting possible issues in the community before they become a problem. Accountability is also a powerful issue in these considerations; always be accountable to parents, students, and the community for your actions.

Teachers are critical to students' academic success. But influences beyond the classroom are just as important or even more so—especially the impression parents have of you. Working with parents requires knowledge and skills. Parents have many reasons for their involvement or lack of involvement in schools. Putting forth effort to increase parents' involvement in their children's education will increase your students' success.

Practical Problem

What ought to be done about satisfying the needs of the various persons and groups I serve? All teachers are faced with this situation daily. Your answer to this practical problem will be different from your colleagues' answers. Regardless of how you respond to this question, it serves as a framework for this challenge. In the space provided, note what you believe should be done about working with administrators, parents, and the community.

1. Reflect on your own experience as a student, and think about the working relationships between administrators, parents, and the community. Develop a response to the following questions:

   ■ How did you feel about the school administration as a student?

   ■ Was the principal's office only a place for students who were misbehaving?

   ■ Did you feel that the teachers and administration were working together for you or against you as a student?

   ■ What did you think about the relationships between administrators and teachers as a student?

   ■ Do you remember parents being encouraged to be part of your education?

   ■ Did parents volunteer at the school? In what roles?

   ■ How did the public view education in your community?

   ■ Did your administrators have public support?

Practical Problem (continued)

■ Describe your favorite principal.

_____

_____

■ What was your recollection of the superintendent of your school district?

_____

_____

■ What was your biggest fear when your parents went to see your teachers on parent-teacher night?

_____

_____

■ Do you recall anything your teacher may have told your parents about you?

_____

_____

2. After reflecting on the preceding questions, think about the following question from a broad perspective:

■ What should be done about working with administrators, parents, and the community? (Example: Administrators should support faculty.)

My ideas . . .

_____

_____

_____

_____

_____

_____

_____

Practical Problem (continued)

■ **What do you presently believe about administrators, parents, and the community?**

My beliefs . . .

CHALLENGE 10

Valued Ends

The following list describes several of the skills, behaviors, and attitudes associated with teachers who have found success in satisfying the needs of various groups. In the space provided, identify other qualities that you have that are pertinent to successfully satisfying the needs of those you serve. Include any expectations or goals your administration has identified related to this topic and how you might achieve these goals.

Teachers who are successful in satisfying the needs of administrators, parents, and the community:

■ **Can effectively communicate**

■ **Are well informed**

■ **View people as well intentioned**

■ **Possess an adequate self-image**

■ **Are concerned with larger educational goals**

■ **Are fair and honest in interactions**

Qualities I believe are pertinent to successfully satisfying the needs of administrators, parents, and the community: _____

_____

_____

Administration's expectations or goals related to administrators, parents, and the community: _____

_____

_____

What can I realistically achieve related to success with administrators, parents, and the community to be demonstrated in my teaching portfolio? _____

_____

_____

_____

"I am wondering...?"

Even though you might feel alone when you first begin your role as a teacher, all teachers have had similar experiences when they started teaching. Questions that other beginning teachers have raised in regard to working with administrators, parents, and the community include:

- **What is the purpose of the school board?**
- **What strategies could I use to include parents in my classroom?**
- **What if I don't respect my principal?**
- **What do I do with an irate parent?**
- **How do I interact with parents?**
- **Is it appropriate for me to accept a date with a parent of a student? Am I permitted to ask a single parent out on a date?**
- **How can I gain support for my program from my administrators and the community?**
- **What should I do if I suspect child abuse?**
- **What are the laws dealing with sexual harassment in this state?**
- **What am I allowed to tell a parent?**

In the space that follows, list additional questions you may have about working with administrators, parents, and the community, and determine who can answer each question for your situation.

QUESTION	WHO CAN HELP?

Focus on the Issue

Administrators, Parents, and the Community

Parents, guardians, and adults are the primary teachers of students. However, it is a well-known fact that children and adolescents learn constantly. They mimic actions, words, values, attitudes, ideas, preferences, and dislikes from peers, adults, and what they see and hear in the media. Students do not come to the classroom without a lot of prior knowledge. As a teacher, you will see quickly that everyone is involved in the education process. Your administrators have believed in you and your capabilities and have hired you to succeed in the classroom, school, and community. Count on them as your allies. The parents and guardians of your students are trusting you to guide their children in ethical and honest ways to prepare them for the world in which they live. The public trusts that the job you do is worthy of their support. They expect you to make sound and rational decisions. Soliciting support and advice when needed from any or all of those sources will assist you as you carry out your role as a new educator.

A professional educator must do more than just ask questions, however. To find success he or she must foster relationships with school colleagues, parents, and agencies in the larger community to support students' learning and well-being. A teacher's role includes being knowledgeable of the community in which he or she teaches and of the learners' diverse backgrounds, traditions, beliefs, and values.

Prior research related to the socialization of teachers and administrators in schools has stressed the importance of shared values and beliefs related to the school's goals for students. These studies reveal the vital collaborative role that teachers and school administrators play in student achievement (e.g., Elmore, 1995; Rosenholtz, 1989). Wiley (2001) also indicates that school leadership and the professional community have contextual effects on student achievement. Results show that the social organization of teachers and administrators within schools affects student achievement.

Recent research has also revealed that parents' interpersonal activities, including both home and school involvement with students, will enhance positive educational outcomes, such as promoting high school graduation, academic performance, and college attendance. At-home academic involvement includes such things as talking with students about their activities at school, providing assistance with homework assignments, and making the home environment conducive to the learning process. At-school involvement includes attending school-related activities, conferences, events, and meetings, participating in parent-teacher organizations, and serving in decision-making roles, such as on the school board (Adams & Christenson, 2000; Catsambis, 2001; Hickman, Bartholomae, & McKenry, 2000; Keith et al., 1998; Kung & Farrell, 2000; Okagaki & Frensch, 1998; Powell & Steelman, 1993; Shumow & Miller, 2001). You might find ways to include parents or guardians in your classroom activities by inviting them to speak, assist in field trips, or serve on panels. You might also be creative in assigning dual homework projects in which the students' parents or guardians complete an assignment and the students grade them. Be sure to have the parents or guardians submit their assignments without names so that no one is offended or embarrassed!

Focus on the Issue (continued)
Administrators, Parents, and the Community

Encouraging relationships with parents, other teachers, and your administrators can improve student motivation. Therefore, it behooves you to make a commitment to establishing positive relationships with the various groups who are involved in the education process. Wentzel (1998) examines adolescents' supportive relationships with parents, teachers, and peers in relation to student motivation toward school and class-related interests, academic goal orientations, and social goal pursuit. Wentzel's study also reveals that peer support was a positive predictor of prosocial goal pursuit, and parent support was a positive predictor of school-related interest and goal orientations.

Not all students have resident parents. According to Menning (2002), understanding the effects of nonresident parents on the long-term well-being of their children is also important (Amato, 1993; McLanahan & Booth, 1989; Seltzer, 1994; Seltzer & Bianchi, 1988). Research indicates that three out of five children are estimated to be born to a single parent or will lose a parent to divorce (Bumpass, 1984). Menning (2002) reports that while absent parents' activities did not significantly affect students' educational outcomes (i.e., youths will finish high school or go on to postsecondary schooling), the joint effects of activities and financial support on youths' educational attainment were significant. Being mindful to invite and include all those in your students' education can only serve to help you become a successful educator.

Throughout your career, you will be asked to meet with parents regarding mutual concerns about a student's work or actions. According to MacDonald (1999), communication skills in these personal encounters, involving the ability to relate sensitively and authentically on a nonacademic level, are important to your success as an educator. They list some underlying principles of human interaction related to communication:

- **People tend to withdraw from close interaction when fear, uncertainty, or suspicion is present.**
- **People are much more likely to share their true selves when they feel they are being understood and accepted.**
- **Feelings and emotions are generally more powerful than facts and reason in human interaction.**
- **Your body language communicates a great deal more than what you say.**
- **Words do not carry meanings, people do.**
- **Telling someone something does not ensure they hear what you actually say. (pp. 250–251)**

Paying attention to these principles should assist you when you meet with parents.

Focus on the Issue (continued)
Administrators, Parents, and the Community

Based on these principles, MacDonald provides some suggestions in conducting productive parent meetings:

- **Set the stage and arrange the meeting at a mutually convenient time and place.**

- **Overcome any psychological barriers in meeting with students' parents. Parents may have anxiety, stereotypes, and preconceived notions or adversarial feelings toward the meeting or you. It is your job to help them feel comfortable.**

- **Provide direction and focus to the meeting. It is equally important to properly conclude and follow up the meeting.**

Often beginning teachers ask a lot of questions about their relationships with parents. Spreyer (2002, p. 112) provides the following suggestions:

- **Keep your relationships with parents professional, polite, and friendly.**

- **Never talk about students in the staff room or where the conversation may be overheard.**

- **Be encouraging, but don't be solicitous.**

- **Be aware of parent volunteers at school and tell them that you appreciate their efforts to help.**

Establishing positive relationships with those who are also involved in the educational process will help you to be an effective educator. Remember that your job revolves around the success of your students. Focus on what you can do to enhance their learning.

An Amusing Story

I decided to invite one of the administrators to my computer class so he could see my need for new equipment. The superintendent suggested that the students were very fortunate because when he learned to type, the typewriter was not even electric. One of my students raised her hand and said, "Wow, did they have battery-operated typewriters back then?" (D. Mobley, Indiana)

Students Speak Out

Students are often willing to share stories about their relationships with teachers. Using the sentence stems highlighted in bold type, the following statements about how teachers relate to administrators, parents, and the community were solicited from students throughout the country:

> **I learned** to behave when the principal walks into our class. I saw how Ms. Joseph acted when Dr. Davidson came into our room. She got real nervous and started treating us real nice. Then I found out that if we misbehave, she might get into trouble. (Vernon L., eighth-grade computer science)

> **I didn't like** it when my teacher told my parents the truth about what happened in class. I told them a lie, and when they found out I lied, I got into so much trouble. I was afraid to go to school and face Mr. Owen. My parents made me say something to him, so I wrote a note and left it on his desk. If he wouldn't have told them, none of this would have happened. (Jill C., ninth-grade physical science)

> **I like** it when our principal talks to us in the halls. He walks out of his office and calls us by name. I remember when he first learned who I was. I really feel special when he says hi to me. (Madeline D., tenth-grade business writing)

> **I want** to run for school board. My friend was elected to the board last year, and she got a lot of experience. I think it will help me when I get to college. Our school puts a student on the board each year. I think it would be cool to represent the student body like that. (Breon G., eleventh-grade civics)

> **I never realized** how difficult it is to be a new teacher. Ms. Goodling is only a couple of years older than we are and it is hard for us to see her as a teacher. I think kids try to get away with stuff because she is young. She handles herself really good, but it sure would be hard. Michael is only 2 years younger than she is because he was held back in grade school. (Veronica, E. twelfth-grade family and consumer sciences)

CHALLENGE 10

The Teachers' Lounge

Every veteran teacher in your school will be able to shed insight into most any situation you present to them. When asked about administrators, parents, and the community, teachers throughout the country responded to the highlighted sentence stems in the following ways:

I LEARNED WHY THE STUDENTS ARE THE WAY THEY ARE AFTER I MET THEIR PARENTS! (D. Dietz, Missouri)

I DON'T LIKE IT WHEN PEOPLE JUDGE ALL TEACHERS BASED ON A FEW BAD SITUATIONS REPORTED ON THE NEWS FROM TIME TO TIME. FOR THE MOST PART, EVERYONE I KNOW IN EDUCATION IS DOING A TREMENDOUS JOB. (P. Wallace, Tennessee)

I LIKE IT WHEN STUDENTS ARE ENCOURAGED TO MAKE A PRESENTATION TO THE ADMINISTRATORS AND THE SCHOOL BOARD ABOUT WHAT THEY HAVE LEARNED. (M. Revkin, West Virginia)

I WISH MY SCHOOL HAD A PARENT VISITATION DAY. IT WOULD BE PERFECT IF THE PARENTS COULD ACTUALLY SEE WHAT GOES ON IN A CLASS. I THINK THEY WOULD BE HAPPY TO KNOW HOW WELL MOST OF THE KIDS DO. (L. Pineda, Maine)

I WANT TO TAKE A SEMINAR ON HOW TO DIFFUSE PARENT ANGER. I AM AFRAID TO CONFRONT PARENTS. WHEN THEY DISAGREE WITH ME, I DON'T KNOW WHAT TO DO. (M. Phan, Maryland)

I NEVER WANT TO HAVE TO WORK IN A SCHOOL WHERE THE ADMINISTRATOR DOESN'T SUPPORT THE TEACHER. (B. McGuire, Georgia)

I REMEMBER WHEN I HAD A PARENT COME IN AND CHALLENGE ME ON MY CURRICULUM DECISIONS. THANK GOODNESS THE PRINCIPAL STOOD UP FOR ME. I HAD NO IDEA WHAT WAS GOING ON. THAT IS WHY IT PAYS TO HAVE A SUPPORTIVE ADMINISTRATOR. (R. Martinez, Louisiana)

NO ONE TOLD ME THAT BEING A TEACHER IS SUCH A NOBLE PROFESSION. ALL YOU EVER HEAR IS HOW TEACHERS ARE NOT RESPECTED AND UNDERPAID. ON THE CONTRARY, I LOVE MY JOB AND SEE HOW MY INFLUENCE IS SHAPING CITIZENS IN OUR COMMUNITY. (A. Germano, Texas)

MY WORST NIGHTMARE IS BEING SEEN IN PUBLIC BY A STUDENT IN MY BATHING SUIT. (R. Mundis, Alabama)

STUDENTS OFTEN OVERCOME BAD PARENTING. IT'S AMAZING HOW KIDS REACT TO GOOD ROLE MODELS. I LOVE TEACHING, AND MY STUDENTS ARE SO RECEPTIVE TO LEARNING. (C. Kagima, South Carolina)

CHALLENGE 10

Teacher Tips

Master teachers have established a repertoire of skills that they draw upon when teaching. Some teachers shared these tips related to administrators, parents, and the community:

I mail a biweekly newsletter so that parents have an idea of what I am doing in the classroom. With computer technology, this is very easy. I also make the newsletter available on my Web page so that parents can see what we are doing in class. For those who do not have access to a computer, I make a paper copy of the newsletter available. I give examples of student work and highlight some of the projects from my class in the newsletter. I also name a student of the week and show the criteria for that honor. Parents help me by encouraging their child to get assignments done. I also post a calendar telling all the due dates for all my assignments. Using the computer has helped me interact with parents and has boosted their support for my class. (R. Mosley, Virginia)

I invite all the parents of my students to take an active part in the class. Anyone who is interested meets with me once a month at a designated time in the evening. We brainstorm ideas. Much has come from the parents. I now have parents do such things as construct elaborate bulletin boards, design posters, mentor students who are interested in certain careers, tutor students, and serve as guest speakers. Having the parents be part of the learning environment has boosted student participation and the learning that takes place in my class. (C. Hegg, Michigan)

Every time my students complete a major project, I find a way to get them recognized in the local paper or on television. They love the exposure and it supports my classes. (M. Scheffer, Alabama)

I have a small class, so every semester I invite a parent to come to school and talk for 20 minutes about anything they think is important—some parents bring some fascinating discussions to my class. The parents feel good too because they can share their ideas and be challenged by my students. (R. Russell, Virginia)

I ask my principal and vice principal to come to my class and form a point/counterpoint dialogue with one another about important issues facing the school. Sometimes they share perspectives that help the students to see their rationale for their policies. (A Leahy, New York)

I ask my students to create a lesson each semester sharing all that they learned in my class. They develop skits, panels, scenarios, all kinds of things. Then I invite the parents and my administrators. It's a great time. Last year I had two calls from community members asking if they could attend! (J. Zillessen, New Mexico)

A Mentor Moment

The following is provided by a mentor teacher to help you in the area of administrators, parents, and the community:

> **Introduce yourself to your administrators, the librarian, the custodian, the secretaries, and the support staff. Many times you think they will know you are new, but they don't. It shows self-confidence to introduce yourself and let school staff know who you are and what you do. (S. Ciardiello, Wisconsin)**

Having another professional help you with your daily questions about teaching can make your experiences as a teacher even more rewarding. Following is a list of questions you might ask your mentor regarding administrators, parents, and the community. On the next page is a table you can use to identify those questions you would like to discuss with your mentor. Document your mentor's responses and your thoughts about how to incorporate what you have learned into your practice.

Questions you might ask your mentor:

- **What is the role of the guidance counselor?**
- **What if my principal doesn't support me?**
- **Am I legally responsible for anything that happens in my class?**
- **What should I do if I suspect abuse from a school employee?**
- **What should I do if inappropriate comments are made toward me by a student or faculty member?**
- **How can parents' help be used as an asset in the classroom?**

A Mentor Moment (continued)

Questions for My Mentor	Responses from My Mentor	How to Incorporate Mentor's Ideas into My Practice

Think about a situation or circumstance regarding an administrator, a parent, and the community that will help you to develop as a teacher. Reflect on that event and how you responded to it. Instead of blaming yourself or the parent, administrator, or community, identify how you could use that situation or circumstance to improve your effectiveness and/or student learning.

My ideas . . .

A Mentor Moment (continued)

- Reflect now on how you might use this example with your administrator, colleagues, or class to engage others in the critical reflective process. It may be as simple as sharing why you have selected to do something differently than the way you have done it in the past. Regardless, the process should help your learners to see you as a critical reflective practitioner.

My reflections . . .

- What does it mean to be a critical reflective practitioner when interacting with administrators, parents, and the community?

My rationale . . .

Shared Strategies

CHALLENGE 10

Following are some activities and strategies that you might include in your daily practice. You can use these strategies as well as build upon them to create your own.

Communication Skills

The following chart offers some tips for collaborative communication that you can use with administrators, parents, and the community.

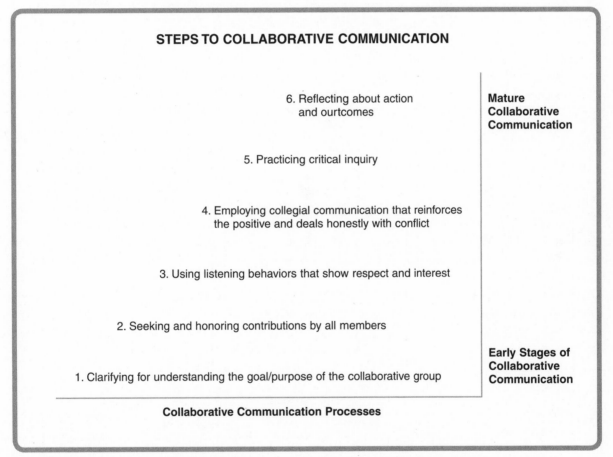

STEPS TO COLLABORATIVE COMMUNICATION

6. Reflecting about action and ourtcomes — **Mature Collaborative Communication**

5. Practicing critical inquiry

4. Employing collegial communication that reinforces the positive and deals honestly with conflict

3. Using listening behaviors that show respect and interest

2. Seeking and honoring contributions by all members

1. Clarifying for understanding the goal/purpose of the collaborative group — **Early Stages of Collaborative Communication**

Collaborative Communication Processes

From Merideth, E. M., *Leadership Strategies for Teachers* (p. 95). © 2000 by SkyLight Professional Development. Reprinted with permission.

Shared Strategies (continued)

Decision-Making Model

You can use the following figure as a guide to help make decisions in your interactions with parents, administrators, and the community.

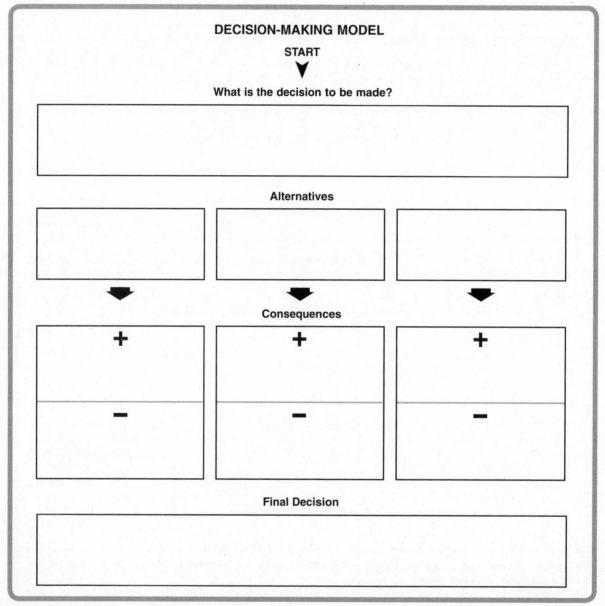

From Burke, K., *What to Do with the Kid Who . . .: Developing Cooperation, Self-Discipline, and Responsibility in the Classroom* (2nd, p. 163). © 2000 by SkyLight Professional Development. Reprinted with permission.

Personal Reflection Journal

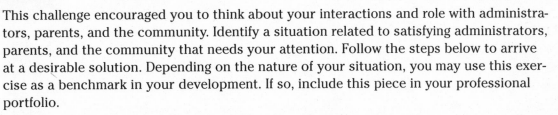

This challenge encouraged you to think about your interactions and role with administrators, parents, and the community. Identify a situation related to satisfying administrators, parents, and the community that needs your attention. Follow the steps below to arrive at a desirable solution. Depending on the nature of your situation, you may use this exercise as a benchmark in your development. If so, include this piece in your professional portfolio.

My thoughts . . .

Identify the situation:

↓

Describe the situation:

↓

Whose advice did you seek in finding a creative solution to the situation?

↓   ↓   ↓

What did this person (or these persons) tell you to do?

Personal Reflection Journal (continued)

How did you deal with the situation?

Would you do the same thing if presented with a similar situation?

If yes, why?	If no, why?

What new knowledge or ideas come to mind as you incorporate what you have learned through this experience?

If you were to establish a goal to enhance your personal professional development in this area, what might that be?

How does what you learned compare to other areas of your teaching?

Personal Reflection Journal (continued)

Being able to communicate and network with parents, administrators, and the community will help you become a better educator. Outline how you can connect what you have learned in this challenge with other areas of your teaching.

Upon reflection, what have you learned that will enhance your development as an educator?

How will you integrate your new knowledge into your practice?

What does it mean to be a critical reflective practitioner when interacting with the various publics you serve? Develop a clear and concise response that you can include in your professional portfolio.

Consider including this in your professional teaching portfolio.

Standards

Schools accept teaching standards as a way to guide teachers to possess a level of competence in order to find success. Because of their generic nature, the Interstate New Teacher Assessment and Support Consortium (INTASC) standards have been identified as a framework for you to use to reflect on your practice as an educator. The INTASC standards that address dealing with administrators, parents, and the public are as follows:

- **PRINCIPLE #6:** The teacher uses knowledge of effective verbal, nonverbal, and media communication techniques to foster active inquiry, collaboration, and supportive interaction in the classroom.

- **PRINCIPLE #7:** The teacher plans instruction based upon knowledge of subject matter, students, the community, and curriculum goals.

- **PRINCIPLE #9:** The teacher is a reflective practitioner who continually evaluates the effects of his or her choices and actions on others (students, parents, and other professionals in the learning community) and who actively seeks out opportunities to grow professionally.

- **PRINCIPLE #10:** The teacher fosters relationships with school colleagues, parents, and agencies in the larger community to support students' learning and well-being.

From Interstate New Teacher Assessment and Support Consortium, *Model Standards for Beginning Teacher Licensing, Assessment, and Development: A Resource for State Dialogue.* © 1992 by Council of Chief State School Officers, Washington, DC. Retrieved November 3, 2004, from http://www.ccsso.org/content/pdfs/corestrd.pdf. Used with permission.

Perhaps your school, district, or national organization has established standards pertinent to your professional development in this area. Review them, and the INTASC principles, to determine which one(s) you have met as a result of working through this challenge. It is not necessary to provide evidence for each standard in each challenge. However, by the time you complete this book, you should have evidence of how you can meet each principle or standard necessary for your portfolio. Document your evidence and include it in the Wrap-Up section of the book.

Reflections Log

Fill out the following log to reflect on your learnings. It might be helpful to refer to the Assessment and Reflections Log at the beginning of the challenge to assess your growth.

What did I learn about administrators, parents, and the community?

Was I able to accomplish my goals?

How did I overcome the challenges in accomplishing my goals?

CHALLENGE 10

Congratulations, You Made It!

Identify something you are proud of related to this challenge that you can incorporate in your professional portfolio. What evidence do you have to show your success? Use the following chart to record your responses.

Situation:

How I handled it:

Evidence to be included in my portfolio:

Consider including this in your professional teaching portfolio.

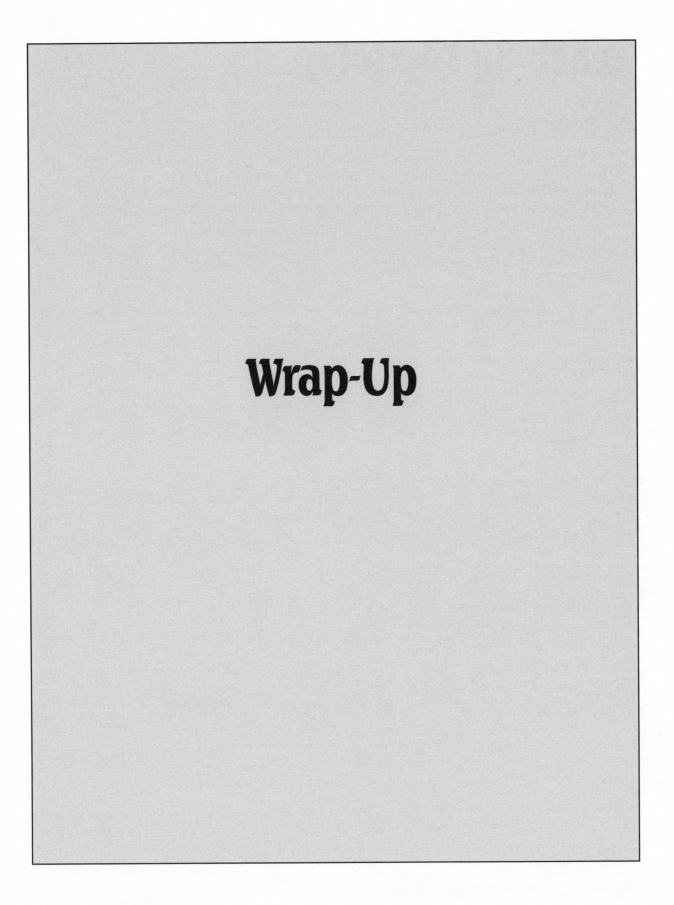

Wrap-Up

Teaching Portfolio

List the standards you are required to use for your teaching portfolio in the space provided. If you do not have standards, use the INTASC standards outlined in the appendix. For each standard, identify the evidence you have that supports your attainment of the standard. Upon reflection decide which materials you want to include in your teaching portfolio that best exemplify your success in meeting the standard.

Standard

1. _____

   Evidence:

2. _____

   Evidence:

3. _____

   Evidence:

4. _____

   Evidence:

5. _____

    Evidence:

6. _____

    Evidence:

7. _____

    Evidence:

8. _____

    Evidence:

9. _____

    Evidence:

10. _____

    Evidence:

INTASC Standards

PRINCIPLE 1: MAKING CONTENT MEANINGFUL
The teacher understands the central concepts, tools of inquiry, and structures of the discipline(s) he or she teaches and can create learning experiences that make these aspects of subject matter meaningful for students.

EVIDENCE:

PRINCIPLE 2: CHILD DEVELOPMENT AND LEARNING THEORY
The teacher understands how children learn and develop and can provide learning opportunities that support their intellectual, social, and personal development.

EVIDENCE:

PRINCIPLE 3: LEARNING STYLES/DIVERSITY
The teacher understands how students differ in their approaches to learning and creates instructional opportunities that are adapted to diverse learners.
EVIDENCE:

PRINCIPLE 4: INSTRUCTIONAL STRATEGIES/PROBLEM SOLVING
The teacher understands and uses a variety of instructional strategies to encourage students' development of critical thinking, problem solving, and performance skills.
EVIDENCE:

PRINCIPLE 5: MOTIVATION AND BEHAVIOR
The teacher uses an understanding of individual and group motivation and behavior to create a learning environment that encourages positive social interaction, active engagement in learning, and self-motivation.
EVIDENCE:

PRINCIPLE 6: COMMUNICATION/KNOWLEDGE
The teacher uses knowledge of effective verbal, nonverbal, and media communication techniques to foster active inquiry, collaboration, and supportive interaction in the classroom.
EVIDENCE:

PRINCIPLE 7: PLANNING FOR INSTRUCTION
The teacher plans instruction based upon knowledge of subject matter, students, the community, and curriculum goals.
EVIDENCE:

PRINCIPLE 8: ASSESSMENT
The teacher understands and uses formal and informal assessment strategies to evaluate and ensure the continuous intellectual, social, and physical development of the learner.
EVIDENCE:

PRINCIPLE 9: PROFESSIONAL GROWTH/REFLECTION

The teacher is a reflective practitioner who continually evaluates the effects of his or her choices and actions on others (students, parents, and other professionals in the learning community) and who actively seeks out opportunities to grow professionally.

EVIDENCE:

PRINCIPLE 10: INTERPERSONAL RELATIONSHIPS

The teacher fosters relationships with school colleagues, parents, and agencies in the larger community to support students' learning and well-being.

EVIDENCE:

From Interstate New Teacher Assessment and Support Consortium, *Model Standards for Beginning Teacher Licensing, Assessment, and Development: A Resource for State Dialogue.* © 1992 by Council of Chief State School Officers, Washington, DC. Retrieved November 3, 2004, from http://www.ccsso.org/content/pdfs/corestrd.pdf. Used with permission.

Matrix: Evidence of Standards

Using the matrix below, identify the kind of evidence you have for each standard you intend to include in your portfolio. Supply a variety of examples and with each example write a brief reflection and explain what changes you have or will make as a result of your reflection. This is a good matrix to include at the beginning of your teaching portfolio.

	Word Documents	PowerPoint Slides	Images	Web Sites	Active Teacher Research	PDF Files	
1.							
2.							
3.							
4.							
5.							
6.							
7.							
8.							
9.							
10.							

STANDARDS

	Observations	Student Work	Peer Reviews	Mentor Reviews	Self Assessments	Other

Appendix

INTASC Standards

The five major propositions that undergird INTASC's standards are:
- Teachers are committed to students and their learning.
- Teachers know the subjects they teach and how to teach those subjects to diverse learners.
- Teachers are responsible for managing and monitoring student learning.
- Teachers think systematically about their practice and learn from experience.
- Teachers are members of learning communities.

The INTASC standards are:
- Principle #1: The teacher understands the central concepts, tools of inquiry, and structures of the discipline(s) he or she teaches and can create learning experiences that make these aspects of subject matter meaningful for students.
- Principle #2: The teacher understands how children learn and develop, and can provide learning opportunities that support their intellectual, social, and personal development.
- Principle #3: The teacher understands how students differ in their approaches to learning and creates instructional opportunities that are adapted to diverse learners.
- Principle #4: The teacher understands and uses a variety of instructional strategies to encourage students' development of critical thinking, problem solving, and performance skills.
- Principle #5: The teacher uses an understanding of individual and group motivation and behavior to create a learning environment that encourages positive social interaction, active engagement in learning, and self-motivation.
- Principle #6: The teacher uses knowledge of effective verbal, nonverbal, and media communication techniques to foster active inquiry, collaboration, and supportive interaction in the classroom.
- Principle #7: The teacher plans instruction based upon knowledge of subject matter, students, the community, and curriculum goals.
- Principle #8: The teacher understands and uses formal and informal assessment strategies to evaluate and ensure the continuous intellectual, social, and physical development of the learner.
- Principle #9: The teacher is a reflective practitioner who continually evaluates the effects of his or her choices and actions on others (students, parents, and other professionals in the learning community) and who actively seeks out opportunities to grow professionally.
- Principle #10: The teacher fosters relationships with school colleagues, parents, and agencies in the larger community to support students' learning and well-being.

The five major propositions and the standards are from pages 7–8, 14, 16, 18, 20, 22, 25, 27, 29, 31, and 33 of Interstate New Teacher Assessment and Support Consortium, *Model Standards for Beginning Teacher Licensing, Assessment, and Development: A Resource for State Dialogue.* © 1992 by Council of Chief State School Officers, Washington, DC. Retrieved November 3, 2004, from http://www.ccsso.org/content/pdfs/corestrd.pdf. Used with permission.

NEA Code of Ethics

One of the central characteristics of all professions is that its members adhere to an agreed upon code of ethics. Whether or not you are a member of the National Education Association (NEA), this organization has identified an ethical code that provides an overview and philosophical framework from which to view ethical action as a professional. The NEA Code of Ethics follows. Your school may also have a code of ethics that you will be able to use as you develop your personal philosophy about teaching and to substantiate your professional actions. Refer to this code frequently as you ponder your daily actions and decisions as an educator.

Code of Ethics of the Education Profession

Preamble

The educator, believing in the worth and dignity of each human being, recognizes the supreme importance of the pursuit of truth, devotion to excellence, and the nurture of democratic principles. Essential to these goals is the protection of freedom to learn and to teach and the guarantee of equal educational opportunity for all. The educator accepts the responsibility to adhere to the highest ethical standards.

The educator recognizes the magnitude of the responsibility inherent in the teaching process. The desire for the respect and confidence of one's colleagues, of students, of parents, and of the members of the community provides the incentive to attain and maintain the highest possible degree of ethical conduct. The Code of Ethics of the Education Profession indicates the aspiration of all educators and provides standards by which to judge conduct.

The remedies specified by the NEA and/or its affiliates for the violation of any provision of the Code shall be exclusive and no such provision shall be enforceable in any form other than one specifically designated by the NEA or its affiliates.

PRINCIPLE 1

Commitment to the Student
The educator strives to help each student realize his or her potential as a worthy and effective member of society. The educator therefore works to stimulate the spirit of inquiry, the acquisition of knowledge and understanding, and the thoughtful formulation of worthy goals.

In fulfillment of the obligation to the student, the educator—

1. Shall not unreasonably restrain the student from independent action in the pursuit of learning.
2. Shall not unreasonably deny the student access to varying points of view.
3. Shall not deliberately suppress or distort subject matter relevant to the student's progress.
4. Shall make reasonable effort to protect the student from conditions harmful to learning or to health and safety.
5. Shall not intentionally expose the student to embarrassment or disparagement.
6. Shall not on the basis of race, color, creed, sex, national origin, marital status, political or religious beliefs, family, social or cultural background or sexual orientation, unfairly—
    a) Exclude any student from participation in any program.
    b) Deny benefits to any student.
    c) Grant any advantage to any student.
7. Shall not use professional relationships with students for private advantage.
8. Shall not disclose information about students obtained in the course of professional service unless disclosure serves a compelling professional purpose or is required by law.

PRINCIPLE II

Commitment to the Profession

The education profession is vested by the public with a trust and responsibility requiring the highest ideals of professional service. In the belief that the quality of the services of the education profession directly influences the nation and its citizens, the educator shall exert every effort to raise professional standards, to promote a climate that encourages the exercise of professional judgment, to achieve conditions that attract persons worthy of the trust to careers in education, and to assist in preventing the practice of the profession by unqualified persons.

In fulfillment of the obligation to the profession, the educator—

1. Shall not in an application for a professional position deliberately make a false statement or fail to disclose a material fact related to competency and qualifications.
2. Shall not misrepresent his or her professional qualifications.
3. Shall not assist any entry into the profession of a person known to be unqualified in respect to character, education, or other relevant attribute.
4. Shall not knowingly make a false statement concerning the qualifications of a candidate for a professional position.
5. Shall not assist a noneducator in the unauthorized practice of teaching.
6. Shall not disclose information about colleagues obtained in the course of professional service unless disclosure serves a compelling professional purpose or is required by law.
7. Shall not knowingly make false or malicious statements about a colleague.
8. Shall not accept a gratuity, gift, or favor that might impair or appear to influence professional decisions or action.

–Adopted by the 1975 NEA Representative Assembly

References

Adams, K. S., & Christenson, S. L. (2000). Trust and the family-school relationship examination of parent-teacher differences in elementary and secondary grades. *Journal of School Psychology, 38*(5), 477–497.

Airasian, P. W. (1991). *Classroom assessment.* New York: McGraw-Hill.

Allen, D. (Ed.). (1998). *Assessing student learning: From grading to understanding.* New York: Teachers College Press.

Amato, P. (1993). Children's adjustment to divorce: Theories, hypotheses, and empirical support. *Journal of Marriage and Family, 55*(1), 23–38.

Applegate, J. H., et al. (1977). *The first year teacher study.* Paper presented at the annual meeting of the American Educational Research Association, New York. (ERIC Document Reproduction Service No. ED135766).

Armstrong, D. G. (1997). Rating curriculum documents. *The High School Journal, 81*(1), 1–7.

Arredondo, D. E., & Rucinski, T. T. (1998). Principal perceptions and beliefs about integrated curriculum use. *Journal of Educational Administration, 36*(3), 286–298.

Baker, J., & Zigmond, N. (1990). Are regular education classes equipped to accommodate students with learning disabilities? *Exceptional Children, 5*(6), 515–526.

Banks, J. A., & Banks, C. A. (Eds.). (1997). *Multicultural education: Issues and perspectives.* Boston: Allyn and Bacon.

Barclay, K., & Boone, E. (1996). *The parent difference: Uniting school, family, and community.* Arlington Heights, IL: IRI/SkyLight Training and Publishing.

Barth, R. S. (1990). *Improving schools from within: Teachers, parents, and principals can make the difference.* San Francisco: Jossey-Bass

Beamon, G. W. (2001). *Teaching with adolescent learning in mind.* Arlington Heights, IL: SkyLight Professional Development.

Beane, J. A. (1991). The middle school: The natural home of integrated curriculum. *Educational Leadership, 49*(2), 9–13.

Beane, J. A. (1992). Turning the floor over: Reflections on a middle school curriculum. *Middle School Journal, 23*(3), 33–40.

Beane, J. A. (1993a). Problems and possibilities for an integrative curriculum. In R. Fogarty (Ed.), *Integrating the curricula: A collection* (pp. 69–83). Palatine, IL: IRI/Skylight Publishing.

Beane, J. A. (1993b). Problems and possibilities for an integrative curriculum. *Middle School Journal, 25*(1), 18–23.

Beane, J. A. (Ed.). (1995). *Toward a coherent curriculum: 1995 yearbook of the ASCD.* Alexandria, VA: Association for Supervision and Curriculum Development.

Behar, L. S., & Ornstein, A. (1994). Domains of curriculum knowledge: An empirical analysis. *The High School Journal, 77*(4), 322–329.

Bellanca, J., & Fogarty, R. (2003). *Blueprints for achievement in the cooperative classroom.* Glenview, IL: SkyLight Professional Development.

Bellon, J. J., Bellon, E. C., & Blank, M. A. (1992). *Teaching from a research knowledge base: A development and renewal process.* New York: Macmillan.

Bernhardt, V. L. (1994). *The school portfolio: A comprehensive framework for school improvement.* Princeton Junction, NJ: Eye on Education.

Blythe, T., Allen, D., & Powell, B. (1999). *Looking together at student work: A companion guide to assessing student learning.* New York: Teachers College Press.

Board of Education for the City of Etobicoke. (1987). *Making the grade: Evaluating student progress.* Scarborough, Ontario, Canada: Prentice-Hall Canada.

Bol, L., & Strage, A. (1996). The contradiction between teachers' instructional goals and their assessment practices in high school biology courses. *Science Education, 80*(2), 145–163.

Bolotin-Joseph, P., & Burnaford, G. E. (Eds.). (1994). *Images of schoolteachers in twentieth-century America: Paragons, polarities, complexities.* New York: St. Martin's Press.

Bradley, D. F., King-Sears, M. E., & Tessier-Switlick, D. E. (1997). *Teaching students in inclusive settings: From theory to practice.* Needham Heights, MA: Allyn and Bacon.

Brandt, R. (1988). On teaching thinking: A conversation with Arthur Costa. *Educational Leadership, 45*(7), 10–13.

Brandt, R. (1991). On interdisciplinary curriculum: A conversation with Heidi Hayes Jacobs. *Educational Leadership, 49*(2), 24–26.

Brause, R. S. (1998). First day fears: Anxiety can be a good thing. *English Journal, 88*(1), 27–28.

Brookfield, S. (1995). *Becoming a critical reflective teacher.* San Francisco: Jossey-Bass.

Brookhart, S. M., & Durkin, D. T. (2003). Classroom assessment, student motivation, and achievement in high school social studies classes. *Applied Measurement in Education, 16*(1), 27–54.

Brooks, J. G., & Brooks, M. G. (1993). *In search of understanding: The case for the constructivist classroom.* Alexandria, VA: Association for Supervision and Curriculum Development.

Brophy, J., & Alleman, J. (1991). A caveat: Curriculum integration isn't always a good idea. *Educational Leadership, 49*(2), 66–70.

Brown, D. S. (1988). Twelve middle-school teachers' planning. *Elementary School Journal, 89*(1), 69–87.

Brown, D. S. (1993). Description of two novice secondary teachers' planning. *Curriculum Inquiry, 23*(1), 63–84.

Brown, M. (1979). *A conceptual scheme and decision-rules for the selection and organization of home economics curriculum content.* Madison: Wisconsin Department of Public Instruction.

Brown, M., & Paolucci, B. (1979). *Home economics: A definition.* Washington, DC: American Home Economics Association.

Brown, R. (1989). Testing and thoughtfulness. *Educational Leadership, 46*(7), 113–115.

Brualdi, A. C. (2001). Implementing performance assessment. *Ed at a Distance Journal, 15*(4).

Bullough, R. V. (1989). *First-year teacher: A case study.* New York: Teachers College Press.

Bumpass, L. (1984). Children and marital disruption: A replication and an update. *Demography, 21,* 71–82.

Bunting, C. (1999). Teacher, improve thyself: A call for self-reliant, reflective, practitioners. *Classroom Leadership, 2*(9).

Burke, K. (1999). *The mindful school: How to assess authentic learning* (3rd ed.). Arlington Heights, IL: SkyLight Training and Publishing.

Burke, K. (2000). *What to do with the kid who . . .: Developing cooperation, self-discipline, and responsibility in the classroom* (2nd ed.). Arlington Heights, IL: SkyLight Professional Development.

Burke, K. (Ed.). (2002). Mentoring guidebook level 1: Starting the journey. Arlington Heights, IL: SkyLight Professional Development.

Burke, K. (2005). *How to assess authentic learning* (4th ed.). Glenview, IL: LessonLab.

Burke, K., Fogarty, R., & Belgrad, S. (2002a). *The portfolio connection* (2nd ed.). Arlington Heights, IL: SkyLight Professional Development.

Burke, K., Fogarty, R., & Belgrad, S. (2002b). *The portfolio connection training manual.* Arlington Heights, IL: SkyLight Professional Development.

Caine, R. N. (1993). *Making connections: Teaching and the human brain* (2nd ed.). New York: Innovative Learning Publications, Addison-Wesley Publications.

Caine, R. N., & Caine, G. (1991). *Making connections: Teaching and the human brain.* New York: Innovative Learning Publications, Addison-Wesley Publications.

Canady, R., & Rettig, M. (1996). The power of innovative scheduling. In R. Fogarty (Ed.), *Block scheduling: A collection of articles* (pp. 31–44). Palatine, IL: IRI/SkyLight Training and Publishing.

Carbone, N. (1993). Trying to create a community: A first-day lesson plan. *Computers and Composition, 10*(4), 81–88.

Carnegie Council on Adolescent Development. (1989). *Great transition: Preparing adolescents from a new century.* New York: Carnegie Corporation of New York.

Carroll, D. (2001). Considering paraeducator training, roles, and responsibilities. *Council for Exceptional Children, 34*(2), 60–64.

Catsambis, S. (2001). Expanding knowledge of parental involvement in children's secondary education: Connections with high school seniors' academic success. *Social Psychology of Education, 5*(2), 149–177.

Chavez, R. C. (1984). The use of high inference measures to study classroom climates: A review. *Review of Educational Research, 54*(2), 237–261.

Cochran-Smith, M. L., & Lytle, S. L. (2001). Beyond certainty: Taking an inquiry stance on practice. In A. M. Lieberman & L. Miller (Eds.), *Teachers caught in the action: Professional development that matters* (pp. 44–55). New York: Teachers College Press.

Coles, R. (1997). *The moral intelligence of children: How to raise a moral child.* New York: Random House.

Conzemius, A., & O'Neill, J. (2001). *Building shared responsibility for student learning.* Alexandria, VA: Association for Supervision and Curriculum Development.

Costa, A., & Garmston, R. (1994). *Cognitive coaching: A foundation for renaissance schools.* Norwood, MA: Christopher-Gordon.

Covey, S. R. (1989). *Seven habits of highly effective people: Restoring the character ethic.* New York: Simon & Schuster.

Covington, M. V., & Teel, K. M. (1996). *Overcoming student failure: Changing motives and incentives for learning.* Washington, DC: American Psychological Association.

Cruickshank, D., & Applegate, J. (1981). Reflective teaching as a strategy for teacher growth. *Educational Leadership, 38*(7), 553–554.

Csikszentmihalyi, M. (1990). *Flow: The psychology of optimal experience.* New York: Harper Perennial.

Darder, A. (1991). *Culture and power in the classroom: A critical foundation for bicultural education.* Westport: Bergin & Garvey.

Darling-Hammond, L. (1994). What matters most: A competent teacher for every child. *Phi Delta Kappan, 78*(3), 193–200.

Darling-Hammond, L., & McLaughlin, M. (1995). Policies that support professional development in an era of reform. *Phi Delta Kappan, 76*(8), 597–604.

Darling-Hammond, L., & Sclan, E. M. (1996). Who teaches and why: Dilemmas of building a profession for twenty-first century schools. In J. Sikula, T. Buttery, & E. Guyton (Eds.), *Handbook of research on teacher education* (pp. 67–101). New York: Macmillan.

Dewey, J. (1913). *Interest and effort in education.* Boston: Houghton Mifflin.

Dewey, J. (1933). The process and product of reflective activity: Psychological process and logical form. In R. D. Archambault (Ed.), *John Dewey on education: Selected writings* (pp. 242–249). Chicago: University of Chicago Press.

Dewey, J. (1938). *Experience and education.* New York: Collier.

Dietz, M. (1995). Using portfolios as a framework for professional development. *Journal of Staff Development, 16*(2), 40–43.

Diez, M. (1994, October). *The portfolio: Sonnet, mirror, and map.* Keynote presented at Linking Liberal Arts and Teacher Education: Encouraging Reflection Through Portfolios, San Diego, CA.

DiGiulio, R. (2000). *Positive classroom management: A step-by-step guide to successfully running the show without destroying student dignity* (2nd ed.). Thousand Oaks, CA: Corwin Press.

Doyle, M. B. (1998). My child has a new shadow . . . and it doesn't resemble her! *Disability Solutions, 3*(1), 5–9.

Drake, S. M. (1993). *Planning integrated curriculum.* Alexandria, VA: Association for Supervision and Curriculum Development.

DuFour, R. (2000). Clear connections: Everyone benefits when schools work to involve parents. *Journal of Staff Development, 21*(2), 59–60.

Eisner, E. W. (1985). *The educational imagination: On the design and evaluation of school programs* (2nd ed.). New York: Macmillan.

Eisner, E. W. (1991). *The enlightened eye: Qualitative inquiry and the enhancement of educational practice.* New York: Macmillan.

Elmore, R. F. (1995). Structural reform and educational practice. *Educational Researcher, 24*(9), 23–26.

English, F. W. (2000). *Deciding what to teach and test: Developing, aligning, and auditing the curriculum.* Thousand Oaks, CA: Corwin Press.

Falvey, M. (1995). *Inclusive and heterogeneous schooling: Assessment, curriculum, and instruction.* Baltimore, MD: Paul H. Brookes.

Fogarty, R. (2002). *How to integrate the curricula* (2nd ed.). Glenview, IL: SkyLight Professional Development.

Fogarty, R., & Bellanca, J. (1993). *Patterns for thinking, patterns for transfer.* Palatine, IL: IRI/Skylight Publishing.

Fogarty, R., Perkins, D., & Barell, J. (1992). *The mindful school: How to teach for transfer.* Palatine, IL: IRI/Skylight Training and Publishing.

Fraser, B. J., & Fisher, D. L. (1982). Predicting students' outcomes from their perceptions of classroom psychological environment. *American Educational Research Journal, 19*(4), 498–518.

Frender, G. (1990). *Learning to learn: Strengthening study skills and brain power.* Nashville, TN: Incentive Publications.

Friend, M., & Bursuck, W. D. (Ed.). (1999). *Including students with special needs: A practical guide for classroom teachers* (2nd ed.). Boston: Allyn and Bacon.

Fullan, M., & Hargreaves, A. (1991). What's worth fighting for: Working together for your school, Toronto, Ontario, Public School Teachers Federation. In David Tuohy (Ed.), *The inner world of teaching: Exploring assumptions which promote change and development.* Philadelphia, PA: Falmer Press.

Fullan, M. G., & Stiegelbauer, S. (1991). *The new meaning of educational change.* New York: Teachers College Press.

Fuller, M. L., & Olsen, G. (1998). *Home-school relations: Working successfully with parents and families.* Needham Heights, MA: Allyn and Bacon.

Gardner, H. (1983). *Frames of mind: The theory of multiple intelligences.* New York: Basic Books.

Gardner, H. (1993a). *Frames of mind: The theory of multiple intelligences* (10th anniversary ed.). New York: Basic Books.

Gardner, H. (1993b). *Multiple intelligences: The theory in practice.* New York: HarperCollins.

Gehrke, N. J. (1993). Explorations of teachers' development of integrative curriculums. In R. Fogarty (Ed.), *Integrating the curricula: A collection* (pp. 167–180). Palatine, IL: IRI/Skylight Publishing.

Gentzler, Y. S. (1987). A conceptualization of competence: Constructs for professional development. *Journal of Home Economics, 79*(4), 39–42.

Gersten, R. (1999). The changing face of bilingual education. *Educational Leadership, 56*(7), 41–45.

Giangreco, M. F., Edelman, S. W., Broer, S. M., & Doyle, M. B. (2001). Paraprofessional support of students with disabilities: Literature from the past decade. *Council for Exceptional Children, 68*(1), 45–63.

Glasser, W. (1998). *The quality school teacher: A companion volume to the quality school.* New York: HarperCollins.

Glatthorn, A. (1996). *The teacher's portfolio: Fostering and documenting professional development.* Rockport, MA: Proactive Publications.

Glazer, S. M., & Brown, C. S. (1993). *Portfolios and beyond: Collaborative assessment in reading and writing.* Norwood, MA: Christopher-Gordon.

Glickman, C. D. (1993). *Renewing America's schools: A guide for school-based action.* San Francisco: Jossey-Bass.

Glickman, C. D. (2002). *Leadership for learning: How to help teachers succeed.* Alexandria, VA: Association for Supervision and Curriculum Development.

Gordon, S. P., & Maxey, S. (2000). *How to help beginning teachers succeed* (2nd ed.). Alexandria, VA: Association for Curriculum and Supervision.

Gronlund, N. E. (1998). *Assessment of student achievement* (6th ed.). Boston: Allyn and Bacon.

Guillaume, A. M. (2004). *K–12 classroom teaching: A primer for new professionals.* (2nd ed.). Upper Saddle River, NJ: Merill Prentice Hall.

Guthrie, J., & McCann, A. (1997). Characteristics of classrooms that promote motivations and strategies for learning. In J. Guthrie and A. Wigfield (Eds.), *Reading engagement: Motivating readers through integrated instruction* (pp. 128–148). Newark, DE: International Reading Association.

Halpin, G., & Halpin, G. (1982). Experimental investigations of the effects of study and testing on student learning, retention, and ratings of instruction. *Journal of Educational Research, 74*(1), 32–38.

Hansen, J. (1992). Literacy portfolios: Helping students know themselves. *Educational Leadership, 49*(8), 66–68.

Hargreaves, A. (1988). Teaching quality: A sociological analysis. *Journal of Curriculum Studies, 20*(3), 211–231.

Harmin, M. (1994). *Inspiring active learning: A handbook for teachers.* Alexandria, VA: Association for Supervision and Curriculum Development.

Harp, B. (1994). *Assessment and evaluation for student centered learning* (2nd ed.). Norwood, MA: Christopher-Gordon.

Henson, K. T. (1988). *Methods and strategies for teaching in secondary and middle schools.* New York: Longman.

Herman, J. A., Aschbacher, P. R., & Winters, R. (1992). *A practical guide to alternative assessment.* Alexandria, VA: Association for Supervision and Curriculum Development.

Hickman, G., Bartholomae, S., & McKenry, P. (2000). Influence of parenting styles on the adjustment and academic achievement of traditional college freshmen. *Journal of College Student Development, 41*(1), 41–54.

Higgins, P. (1999). Unconventional first days: Encouraging students to wonder about social life and learning. *Teaching Sociology, 27*(3), 258–263.

Hills, J. R. (1991). Apathy concerning grading and testing. *Phi Delta Kappan, 72*(7), 540–545.

Hobar, N. (1994a). *Alternative assessment: Mirroring quality instruction. A workshop for Horry County Schools.* Cockesville, MD: Workforce 2000 Inc.

Hobar, N. (1994b). *Alternative assessment: Performance assessment task development. A workshop for Horry County Schools.* Cockesville, MD: Workforce 2000 Inc.

Hoerr, T. (1996). Collegiality: A new way to define instructional leadership. *Phi Delta Kappan, 77*(5), 380–381.

Hollingsworth, S. (1989). Prior beliefs and cognitive change in learning to teach. *American Educational Research Journal, 26*(2), 160–189.

Hoover, K. H. (1972). *Learning and teaching in the secondary school* (3rd ed.). Boston: Allyn and Bacon.

Hough, D. L., & St. Clair, B. (1995). The effects of integrated curricula on young adolescent problem-solving. *Research in Middle Level Education Quarterly, 19*(1), 1–25.

Hunt, G., Wiseman, D., & Bowden, S. (1998). *The middle level teachers' handbook.* Springfield, IL: Charles C. Thomas Publisher, Ltd.

Interstate New Teacher Assessment and Support Consortium. (1992). *Model standards for beginning teacher licensing, assessment, and development: A resource for state dialogue.* Washington, DC: Council of Chief State School Officers. Retrieved November 3, 2004, from http://www.ccsso.org/content/pdfs/corestrd.pdf

Jacobs, H. H. (Ed.). (1990). *Interdisciplinary curriculum: Design and implementation.* Alexandria, VA: Association for Supervision and Curriculum Development.

Jacobs, H. H. (1991). Planning for curriculum integration. *Educational Leadership, 49*(2), 27–28.

Jacobs, H. H. (1997). *Mapping the big picture: Integrating curriculum and assessment K–12.* Alexandria, VA: Association for Supervision and Curriculum Development.

Jersild, A. (1955). *When teachers face themselves.* New York: Teachers College Press.

Johnson, D. W., & Johnson, R. (1974). Instructional goal structure: Cooperative, competitive, or individualistic. *Review of Educational Research, 44*(2), 213–240.

Johnson, D. W., & Johnson, R. R. (1995). *Reducing violence through conflict resolution.* Alexandria, VA: Association for Supervision and Curriculum Development.

Johnson, N. J., & Rose, L. M. (1997). *Portfolios: Clarifying, constructing, and enhancing.* Lancaster, PA: Basil Technomic Publishing Company.

Johnson, R., & Johnson, D. (1982, October). Cooperation in learning: Ignored but powerful. *Lyceum.*

Jones, F. H. (1987). *Positive classroom discipline.* New York: McGraw-Hill.

Jones, M. G. (1994). Performance-based assessment in middle school science. *Middle School Journal, 25*(4), 35–38.

Jones, V. F., & Jones, L. S. (2004). *Comprehensive classroom management: Creating communities of support and solving problems* (7th ed.). Boston: Allyn and Bacon.

Joram, E., & Gabriele, A. J. (1998). Preservice teachers' prior beliefs: Transforming obstacles into opportunities. *Teaching and Teacher Education, 14*(2), 175–191.

Joyce, B., & Showers, B. (1982). The coaching of teaching. *Educational Leadership, 6*(3), 227–241.

Joyce, B. R., Weil, M., & Calhoun, E. (2001). *Models of teaching* (6th ed.). Boston: Allyn and Bacon.

Kagan, D. M. (1992). Professional growth among preservice and beginning teachers. *Review of Educational Research, 62*(2), 129–169.

Kaywell, J. F., & Feyton, C. M. (1992, February/March). Practical advice for student teachers. *The High School Journal,* 156–161.

Keith, T. Z., Keith, P. B., Quirk, K. J., Sperduto, J., Santillo, S., & Killings, S. (1998). Longitudinal effects of parent involvement on high school grades: Similarities and differences across gender and ethnic groups. *Journal of School Psychology, 36*(3), 335–363.

Kindsvatter, R., Wilen, W., & Ishler, M. (1988). *Dynamics of effective teaching.* New York: Longman.

Knight, S. L., & Waxman, H. C. (1990). Investigating the effects of the classroom learning environment on students: Motivation in social studies. *Journal of Social Studies Research, 14,* 1–12.

Kovalik, S. (1993). *ITI: The model: Integrated thematic instruction.* Oak Creek, AZ: Books for Educators.

Kung, E. M., & Farrell, A. D. (2000). The role of parents and peers in early adolescent substance use: An examination of mediating and moderating effects. *Journal of Child and Family Studies, 9*(4), 509–528.

LaBrecque, R. J. (1998). *Effective department and team leaders: A practical guide.* Norwood, MA: Christopher-Gordon.

Lazear, D. (2003). *Eight ways of teaching: The artistry of teaching with multiple intelligences.* Glenview, IL: SkyLight Professional Development.

Leinhardt, G. (1992). What research on learning tells us about teaching. *Educational Leadership, 49*(7), 20–25.

LeRiche, L. W. (1993). Social theory and the curriculum. *The High School Journal, 76*(2), 145–159.

Leu, D. J., Diadiun, D., Jr., & Leu, K. R. (1999). *Teaching with the Internet: Lessons from the classroom.* Norwood, MA: Christopher-Gordon.

Lewin, L., & Shoemaker, B. J. (1998). *Great performances; Creating classroom-based assessment tasks.* Alexandria, VA: Association for Supervision and Curriculum Development.

Lewis, A. (1993). Getting unstuck: Curriculum as a tool of reform. In R. Fogarty (Ed.), *Integrating the curricula: A collection* (pp. 49–60). Palatine, IL: IRI/Skylight Publishing.

Lieberman, A. (Ed.). (1988). *Building a professional culture in school.* New York: Teachers College Press.

Lindeman, B. (2001). Reaching out to immigrant parents. *Educational Leadership, 58*(6), 62–66.

Lipsky, D. K., & Gartner, A. (1997). *Inclusion and school reform: Transforming America's classrooms.* Baltimore, MD: Paul H. Brookes Publishing.

Little, J. W. (1982). Norms of collegiality and experimentation: Workplace conditions of school success. *American Educational Research Journal, 19*(3), 325–340.

Lounsbury, J. H. (Ed.). (1992). *Connecting curriculum through interdisciplinary instruction.* Columbus, OH: National Middle School Association.

MacDonald, R. E. (1999). *A handbook for beginning teachers* (2nd ed.). New York: Longman.

Maehr, M. L., & Meyer, H. A. (1997). Understanding motivation and schooling: Where we've been, where we are, and where we need to go. *Educational Psychology, 9,* 371–409.

Manderville, G. K., & Rivers, J. L. (1991). The South Carolina PET study. *Elementary School Journal, 91*(4), 377–407.

Maniet-Bellerman, P. (1992). Mainstreaming children with learning disabilities: A guide to accompany *L. D. does not mean learning dumb!* Pittsburgh: Upward Bound Press. As presented in R. R. McCown and P. Rop (1992), Educational psychological and classroom practice: A partnership (pp. 424-425). Boston: Allyn and Bacon.

Marcus, S. A., & McDonald, P. (1990). *Tools for the cooperative classroom.* Palatine, IL: IRI/Skylight.

Marzano, R. J., Pickering, D. J., & Pollock, J. E. (2005). *Classroom instruction that works: Research-based strategies for increasing student achievement.* Upper Saddle River, NJ: Merill Prentice Hall.

Masterpoli, M. A., & Scruggs, T. E. (2000). *The inclusive classroom: Strategies for effective instruction.* Upper Saddle River, NJ: Merrill.

Mayer, J. D., & Salovey, P. (1993). The intelligence of emotional intelligence. *Intelligence, 17*(4), 422–433.

McBrien, J. L., & Brandt, R. S. (1997). *The language of learning: A guide to education terms.* Alexandria, VA: Association for Supervision and Curriculum Development.

McCormick, J. H. (2002). *The professional growth plan: A school leader's guide to the process.* Arlington Heights, IL: SkyLight Professional Development.

McDaniel, T. R. (1986). A primer on classroom discipline: Principles old and new. *Phi Delta Kappan, 68*(1), 63–67.

McLanahan, S. S., & Booth, K. (1989). Mother-only families: Problems, prospects, and politics. *Journal of Marriage and Family, 51*(3), 557–580.

McVay, P. (1998). Paraprofessionals in the classroom: What role do they play? *Disability Solutions, 3*(1), 1–4.

Meek, A. (1999). *Communicating with the public: A guide for school leaders.* Alexandria VA: Association for Supervision and Curriculum Development.

Mehrens, W. A. (1992). Using performance assessment for accountability purposes. *Educational Measurement: Issues and Practices, 11*(1), 3–9.

Menning, C. L. (2002). Absent parents are more than money: The joint effect of activities and financial support on youths' educational attainment. *Journal of Family Issues, 23*(5), 648–671.

Merideth, E. M. (2000). *Leadership strategies for teachers.* Arlington Heights, IL: SkyLight Professional Development.

Midwood, D., O'Connor, K., & Simpson, M. (1993). *Assess for success: Assessment, evaluation, and reporting for successful learning.* Toronto, Ontario, Canada: Ontario Secondary School Teachers' Federation.

Mills-Courts, K., & Amiran, M. R. (1991). Metacognition and the use of portfolios. In P. Belanoff & M. Dickson (Eds.), *Portfolios: Process and product* (pp. 101–111). Portsmouth, NH: Boynton and Cook.

Moore, T. (Ed.). (1997). *The education of the heart.* New York: Harper Perennial.

Morgan, J., & Ashbaker, B. Y. (2001). *A teacher's guide to working with paraeducators and other classroom aides.* Alexandria, VA: Association for Supervision and Curriculum Development.

Moye, V. (1997). *Conditions that support transfer for change.* Arlington Heights, IL: IRI/SkyLight Training and Publishing.

National Association of Secondary School Principals' on Middle Level Education. (1985). *An agenda for excellence at the middle level.* Reston, VA: National Association of Secondary School Principals.

National Middle School Association. (1982). *This we believe.* Columbus, OH: Author.

National Research Council. (1996). *National science education standards.* Washington, DC: National Academy Press.

Nungester, R. J., & Duchastel, P. C. (1982). Testing versus review: Effects on retention. *Journal of Educational Research, 74*(1), 18–22.

Okagaki, L., & Frensch, P. (1998). Parenting and children's school achievement: A multiethnic perspective. *American Educational Research Journal, 35*(1), 123–144.

Orelove, F., & Sobsey, D. (1996). *Educating children with multiple disabilities.* Baltimore, MD: Paul H. Brookes Publishing.

Orlich, D. C., Harder, R. J., Callahan, R. C., Kravas, C. H., Kauchak, D. P., Pendergrass, R. A., Keogh, A. J., & Hellene, D. I. (1980). *Teaching strategies: A guide to better instruction.* Lexington, MA: D. C. Heath and Company.

Ornstein, A. C. (1991). Philosophical as a basis for curriculum decisions. *The High School Journal, 74*(2), 102–109.

Ornstein, A. C. (1997, April/May). How teachers plan lessons. *The High School Journal,* 227–237.

Ornstein, A. C., & Hunkins, F. P. (2004). *Curriculum: Foundations, principles, and issues.* Boston: Allyn and Bacon.

Paulson, F. L., Paulson, P. R., & Meyer, C. A. (1991). What makes a portfolio a portfolio? *Educational Leadership, 48*(5), 60–63.

Pino, E. C. (1997). Empowerment not just lip service: A framework for special needs classroom implementation. *To Catch a Falling Star,* 55–63.

Popham, W. J. (1999). *Classroom assessment: What teachers need to know* (2nd ed.). Boston: Allyn and Bacon

Portner, H. (2001). *Training mentors is not enough: Everything else schools and districts need to do.* Thousand Oaks, CA: Corwin Press.

Powell, B., & Steelman, L. C. (1993). The educational benefits of being spaced out: Sibship density and educational progress. *American Sociological Review, 58*(3), 367–381.

Pultorak, E. G. (1993). Facilitating reflective thought in novice teachers. *Journal of Teacher Education, 44*(3), 288–295.

Reiser, R. A., & Dick, W. (1996). *Instructional planning: A guide for teachers* (2nd ed.). Boston: Allyn and Bacon.

Relan, A., & Kimpston, R. (1993). Curriculum integration: A critical analysis of practical and conceptual issues. In R. Fogarty (Ed.), *Integrating the curricula: A collection* (pp. 31–47). Palatine, IL: IRI/Skylight Publishing.

Renck-Jalongo, M. (1991). *Creating learning communities: The role of the teacher in the 21st century.* Bloomington, IN: National Educational Service.

Rennie, L. J. (1991). The relationship between affect and achievement in science. *Journal of Research in Science Teaching, 28*(2), 193–209.

Resnick, L. (1992). *Learning about learning.* Alexandria, VA: Association for Supervision and Curriculum Development.

Richardson, J. (1996, October). School culture: A key to improved student learning. *School Team Innovator.* Retrieved July 11, 2004, from http://www.nsdc.org/library/publications/innovator/inn10-96rich.cfm

Riveria-Pedrotty, D., & Smith-Deutsch, D. (1997). *Teaching students with learning and behavior problems* (3rd ed.). Needham Heights, MA: Allyn and Bacon.

Roberts-Presson, M. (2001). *Your mentor: A practical guide for first-year teachers in grades 1–3.* Thousand Oaks, CA: Corwin Press.

Rodriguez, E. R. & Bellanca, J. (1996). *What is it about me you can't teach? An instructional guide for the urban educator.* Arlington Heights, IL: IRI/SkyLight Training and Publishing.

Rogers, S., Ludington, J., & Graham, S. (1997). *Motivation and learning: A teacher's guide to building excitement for learning and igniting the drive for quality.* Golden, CO: Peak Learning Systems.

Rolheiser, C., Bower, B., & Stevahn, L. (2000). *The portfolio organizer: Succeeding with portfolios in your classroom.* Alexandria, VA: Association for Supervision and Curriculum Development.

Rosenblum-Lowden, R. (2000). *You have to go to school—You're the teacher!* (2nd ed.). Thousand Oaks, CA: Corwin Press.

Rosenholtz, S. J. (1989). *Teachers' workplace: The social organization of schools.* New York: Teachers College Press.

Sapon-Shevin, M. (1991). Cooperative learning in inclusive classrooms: Learning to become a community. *Cooperative Learning, 12*(1), 8–9.

Scardamalia, M., & Bereiter, C. (1991). Higher levels of agency for children in knowledge building: A challenge for the design of new knowledge media. *The Journal of the Learning Sciences, 7*(1), 37–68.

Schalock, H. D. (1998). Student progress in learning: Teacher responsibility, accountability, and reality. *Journal of Personnel Evaluation in Education, 12*(3), 237–246.

Schön, D. (1983). *The reflective practitioner.* San Francisco: Jossey-Bass.

Schön, D. (1987). *Educating the reflective practitioner.* San Francisco: Jossey-Bass.

Schoonmaker, F. (2001). Curriculum making, models, practices, and issues: A knowledge fetish? In L. Corno (Ed.), *Education across a century: The centennial volume: One hundredth yearbook of the National Society for the Study of Education,* Part I (pp. 1–33). Chicago: University of Chicago Press.

Seltzer, J. A. (1994). Consequences of marital dissolution for children. *Annual Review of Sociology, 20,* 235–266.

Seltzer, J. A., & Bianchi, S. M. (1988). Children's contact with absent parents. *Journal of Marriage and Family, 50*(3), 663–667.

Shaklee, B. D., Barbour, N. E., Ambrose, R., & Hansford, S. J. (1997). *Designing and using portfolios.* Boston: Allyn and Bacon.

Shelton, C. F., & Pollingue, A. B. (2000). *The exceptional teacher's handbook: The first-year special education teacher's guide for success.* Thousand Oaks, CA: Corwin Press.

Shumow, L., & Miller, J. D. (2001). Parents' at-home and at-school involvement with young adolescents. *Journal of Early Adolescence, 21*(1), 68–91.

Skowron, J. (2001). *Powerful lesson planning models: The art of 1000 decisions.* Arlington Heights, IL: SkyLight Professional Development.

Smith, D. D., & Luckasson, R. (1995). *Introduction to special education—Teaching in an age of challenge* (2nd ed.). Boston: Allyn and Bacon.

Smyth, J. (1989). Developing and sustaining critical reflection in teacher education. *Journal of Teacher Education, 40*(2), 2–9.

Smyth, W. J. (1992). Teachers' work and the politics of reflection. *American Educational Research Journal, 29*(2), 267–300.

Solomon, P. G. (1998). *The curriculum bridge: From standards to actual classroom practice.* Thousand Oaks, CA: Corwin Press.

Sousa, D. (1995). *How the brain learns: A classroom teacher's guide.* Reston, VA: National Association of Secondary Schools.

Sparks-Langer, G. M., & Colton, A. B. (1991). Synthesis of research on teachers' reflective thinking. *Educational Leadership, 48*(6), 37–44.

Sparks-Langer, G. M., & Simmons, J. M. (1990). Reflective pedagogical thinking: How can we promote it and measure it? *Journal of Teacher Education, 41*(4), 23–32.

Spear-Swerling, L., & Sternberg, R. J. (1998). Curing our "epidemic" of learning disabilities. *Phi Delta Kappan, 81*(5), 397–401.

Spreyer, L. (2002). *Teaching is an art: An A–Z handbook for successful teaching in middle schools and high schools.* Thousand Oaks, CA: Sage.

Stiggins, R. J. (1985). Improving assessment where it means the most: In the classroom. *Educational Leadership, 43*(2), 69–74.

Stiggins, R. J. (1994). *Student-centered classroom assessment.* New York: Merrill Macmillan Publishing.

Stiggins, R. J. (2001). *Student-involved classroom assessment* (3rd ed.) Upper Saddle River, NJ: Merrill Prentice Hall.

Stiggins, R. J., Conklin, N. F., & Bridgeford, N. J. (1986). Classroom assessment: A key to effective education. *Educational Management: Issues and Practice, 5*(2), 5–17.

Stone, R. (2002). *Best practices for high school classrooms: What award-wining secondary teachers do.* Thousand Oaks, CA: Corwin Press.

Stronge, J. (2002). *Qualities of effective teachers.* Alexandria, VA: Association for Supervision and Curriculum Development.

Tateyama-Sniezek, K. (1990). Cooperative learning: Does it improve the academic achievement of students with handicaps? *Exceptional Children, 56*(5), 426–437.

Thornburg, H. (1980). Early adolescents: Their developmental characteristics. *The High School Journal, 65*(6), 272–278.

Tomlinson, C. (1999). *The differentiated classroom.* Alexandria, VA: Association for Supervision and Curriculum Development.

Traub, J. (1999). The bilingual barrier. *The New York Times, 31,* 32–35.

Tripp, D. (1993). *Critical incidents in teaching: Developing professional judgment.* New York: Routledge.

Van Manen, M. (1997). Linking ways of knowing with ways of being practical. *Curriculum Inquiry, 6*(3), 205–228.

Vaughn, S., Bos, C. S., & Schumm, J. S. (2000). *Teaching exceptional, diverse, and at-risk students in the general education classroom* (2nd ed.). Boston: Allyn and Bacon.

Vavrus, L. (1990). Put portfolios to the test. *Instructor, 100*(1), 48–53.

Von Secker, C. E., & Lissitz, R. W. (1999). Estimating the impact of instructional practices on student achievement in science. *Journal of Research in Science Teaching, 36*(10), 1110–1126.

Ward, A., & Darling, L. (1996). Learning through conversation: A reflection on collaboration. *Action in Teacher Education, 18*(3), 80–86.

Wentzel, K. R. (1998). Social relationships and motivation in middle school: The role of parents, teachers, and peers. *Journal of Educational Psychology, 90*(2), 202–209.

Wiggins, G. (1989). Teaching to the (authentic) test. *Educational Leadership, 46*(7), 121–127.

Wildman, T. M., & Niles, J. A. (1987). Reflective teachers: Tensions between abstractions and realities. *Journal of Teacher Education, 38*(4), 25–31.

Wiley, S. D. (2001). Contextual effects on student achievement: School leadership and professional community. *Journal of Educational Change, 2*(1), 1–33.

Winne, P. H., & Marx, R. W. (1977). Reconceptualizing research on teaching. *Journal of Educational Psychology, 69*(6), 668–678.

Withrow, F., Long, H., & Marx, G. (1999). *Preparing schools and school systems for the 21st century.* Arlington, VA: American Association of School Administrators.

Wolf, D. (1989). Portfolio assessment: Sampling student work. *Educational Leadership, 46*(7), 35–39.

Wolf, K. (1996). Developing an effective teaching portfolio. *Educational Leadership, 53*(6), 34.

Wolfgang, C. (1999). *Solving discipline problems.* Needham Heights, MA: Allyn and Bacon.

Wortham, S. C. (2001). *Assessment in early childhood education* (3rd ed.). Upper Saddle River, NJ: Merrill Prentice Hall.

Wright, S. P. (1997). Teacher and classroom context effects on student achievement: Implications for teacher evaluation. *Journal of Personnel Evaluation in Education, 11*(1), 57–67.

Yinger, R. J. (1980). A study of teacher planning. *Elementary School Journal, 80*(3), 107–127.

Yinger, R. J., & Clark, C. (1981). *Reflective journal writing: Theory and practice.* East Lansing: Michigan State University Institute for Research on Teaching.

Zeichner, K. M. (1994). Research on teacher thinking and different views of reflective practice in teaching and teacher education. In I. Carlgren, G. Handal, and S. Vaage (Eds.), *Teachers' minds and actions: Research on teachers' thinking and practice.* Bristol, PA: Falmer Press.

Zemelman, S., Daniels, H., & Hyde, A. (1993). *Best practice: New standards for teaching and learning in America's schools.* Portsmouth, NH: Heinemann.

Zionts, P. (Ed.). (1997). *Inclusion strategies for students with learning and behavior problems: Perspectives, experiences, and best practices.* Austin, TX: Pro-Ed.

Zubrowski, B. (2002). A curriculum framework based on archetypical phenomena and technologies. *Science Education, 86*(4), 481–501.

Zumwalt, K. K. (1988). Are we improving or undermining teaching? In L. N. Tanner (Ed.), *Critical issues in curriculum: Eighty-seventh yearbook of the National Society for the Study of Education, Part I.* Chicago: University of Chicago Press.

Index